REVISE
AS LEVEL
PSYCHOLOGY

ROZ BRODY

For my dad for always giving me the courage to be myself, John for his wit and wisdom, Tommy for his unconditional love, and of course my mother for making me the person I am.

DIANA DWYER

For my partner, Len Jackson, who has enriched my life beyond measure.

REVISE
AS LEVEL
PSYCHOLOGY

ROZ BRODY

**Senior Tutor, Brighton, Hove, and Sussex
Sixth Form College, UK**

DIANA DWYER

**Head of Psychology, The West Bridgford
School, Nottingham, UK**

Psychology Press
Taylor & Francis Group

an informa business

Published 2008 by Psychology Press
27 Church Road, Hove, East Sussex, BN3 2FA

www.psypress.com
www.a-levelpsychology.co.uk

Simultaneously published in the USA and Canada
by Psychology Press
270 Madison Avenue, New York, NY 10016

Psychology Press is part of the Taylor & Francis Group, an Informa business

© 2008 by Psychology Press

British Library Cataloguing in Publication Data
A catalogue record for this book is available from the British Library

ISBN 978-1-84169-731-4

Cartoons drawn by Sean Longcroft, Beehive, Brighton, East Sussex
Cover design by Richard Massing
Typeset in the UK by RefineCatch Limited, Bungay, Suffolk
Printed and bound in Great Britain by Ashford Colour Press Ltd.

CONTENTS

PREPARING FOR THE EXAM

1

Okay, so you have the date of the exam and you are sitting or lying down thinking about revising. This is the hardest part—starting revision.

It's no good putting it off any longer. The exam date is looming and you want to feel confident that you will perform well. This revision guide will help you to do so, without overwhelming you with unnecessary information. Although this guide has been written for use alongside Michael Eysenck's *AS Level Psychology, Fourth Edition* (**ASP4**), if you have been using another AS psychology textbook in class, then this book should still help you to revise effectively.

Time is of the essence, and you need to focus your energy so that you gain the most amount of knowledge in the least amount of time.

No more excuses and no more delays—now you HAVE to start revising!

REVISION TECHNIQUES

Remember that you need time to revise thoroughly. Even if you don't feel in the mood to revise, you know you need to, so just begin. Stick with it for 30 minutes. Go somewhere that you can't be distracted and do these two things:

■ **First, think about how you learn information. Use the diagram below to work out the strategies that will suit you:**

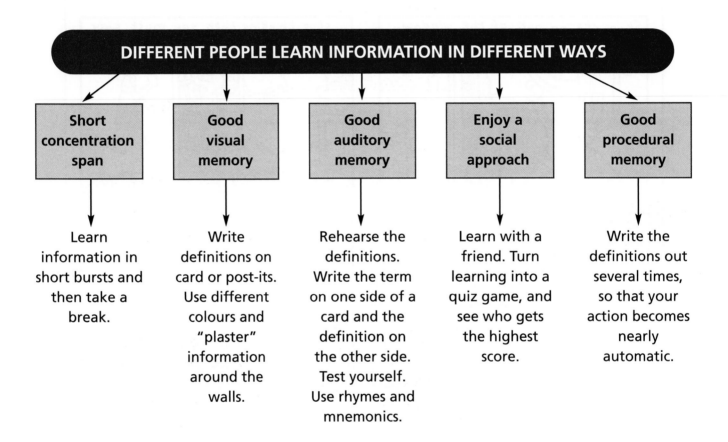

DIFFERENT PEOPLE LEARN INFORMATION IN DIFFERENT WAYS

Short concentration span	Good visual memory	Good auditory memory	Enjoy a social approach	Good procedural memory
Learn information in short bursts and then take a break.	Write definitions on card or post-its. Use different colours and "plaster" information around the walls.	Rehearse the definitions. Write the term on one side of a card and the definition on the other side. Test yourself. Use rhymes and mnemonics.	Learn with a friend. Turn learning into a quiz game, and see who gets the highest score.	Write the definitions out several times, so that your action becomes nearly automatic.

■ **Second, list what you need to know for the exam:**

The AS psychology exam is divided into two units:

- **UNIT 1 PSYA 1**
  Cognitive Psychology, Developmental Psychology, and Research Methods
- **UNIT 2 PSYA2**
  Biological Psychology, Social Psychology, and Individual Differences

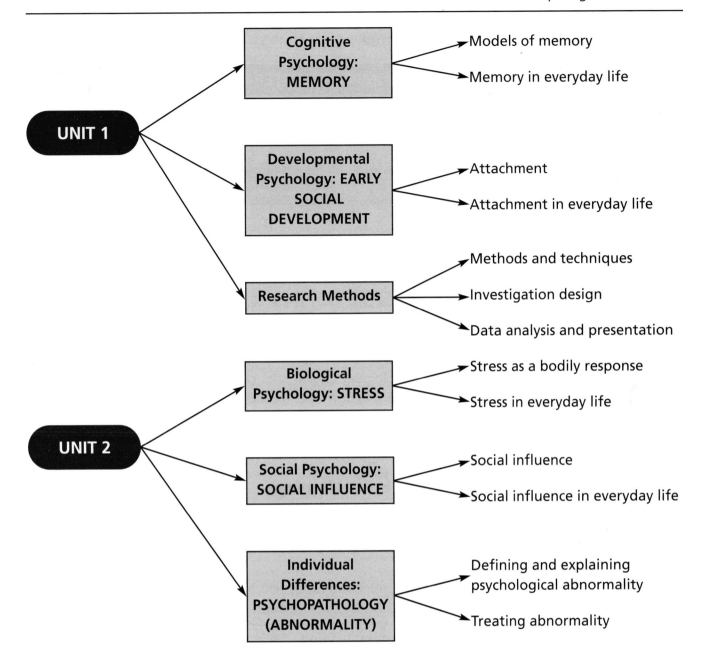

It might look like a lot to learn, but remember that there are only six major areas (memory, early social development, research methods, stress, social influence, and psychopathology). Each of the topics is covered in a chapter in this book, which include guidelines on the research you will need to know for the exam along with the important terms and concepts that will aid your understanding. The chapters also give you an overview of each of the subsections (in the main textbook they are called sections) together with evaluations (strengths and weaknesses) of both theories and research. So DON'T PANIC.

As you go through each chapter make sure that you do the following:

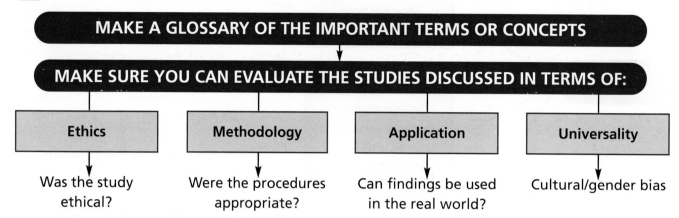

MAKE A GLOSSARY OF THE IMPORTANT TERMS OR CONCEPTS

MAKE SURE YOU CAN EVALUATE THE STUDIES DISCUSSED IN TERMS OF:

Ethics	Methodology	Application	Universality
Was the study ethical?	Were the procedures appropriate?	Can findings be used in the real world?	Cultural/gender bias

HOW YOU WILL BE ASSESSED

Psychology is classified as a science and the exams assess you in terms of three Assessment Objectives known as **AO1, AO2,** and **AO3.** These assessment objectives correspond to the following skills:

- **AO1** is concerned with knowledge and understanding of science and of *How Science Works*.
- **AO2** is concerned with application of knowledge and understanding of science and of *How Science Works*.
- **AO3** is concerned with *How Science Works* in relation to Psychology and involves understanding how psychological research is designed, conducted, and reported.

Let's look at these in more detail by looking at the exact wording of The AQA–A Specification for Psychology:

AO1	**Knowledge and understanding of science and of *How Science Works*** Candidates should be able to: • Recognise, recall, and show understanding of scientific knowledge • Select, organise, and communicate relevant information in a variety of forms
AO2	**Application of knowledge and understanding of science and of *How Science Works*** Candidates should be able to: • Analyse and evaluate scientific knowledge and processes • Apply scientific knowledge and processes to unfamiliar situations including those related to issues • Assess the validity, reliability, and credibility of scientific information
AO3	**Design, conduct, report, and interpret *How Science Works*** Candidates should be able to: • Describe ethical, safe, and skilful practical techniques and processes, selecting appropriate qualitative and quantitative methods • Know how to make, record, and communicate reliable and valid observations and measurements with appropriate precision and accuracy, through using primary and secondary sources • Analyse, interpret, explain, and evaluate the methodology, results, and impact of their own and others' experimental and investigative activities in a variety of ways

EVALUATING PSYCHOLOGICAL STUDIES

It is not unusual for exam questions to ask you to evaluate or criticise a study. You may be surprised to learn that, with a bit of thought, you can do this for yourself. Honestly, you do not need to learn an evaluation of every study from a textbook, but you can learn to write your own evaluations. Just follow these guidelines:

1. What method was used?

Whatever the method, there will be at least one (usually two) positive points about it, and at least one (usually two) limitations. What is more, the advantages of one method tend to be the disadvantages or limitations of another method. Chapter 4 (Research Methods) covers the advantages and disadvantages of each method. Let's take an example and see how it works. If the study was an experiment, it will have the advantage of the careful control of all the variables, enabling conclusions about cause and effect to be made. The study will be replicable (able to be repeated in exactly the same way), so its reliability (the consistency of the results) can be tested. However, as experiments are usually conducted in very controlled and artificial conditions (not corresponding to real life), the study in question is likely to lack ecological validity, and therefore the findings do not necessarily tell us much about everyday behaviour.

2. What about the number and type of participants?

You can usually make at least one evaluative point—either positive or negative—concerning the participants. For example, if a large number of participants was used, and as long as the sample was not too biased (so participants did not all come from one particular group), then the results can be broadly generalised. However, the sample of the participants is often biased. In many studies, only students were used. Although there's nothing wrong with students—they are a wonderful bunch of people—they are not *representative* of the general population. They tend to be young, middle-class, and well educated. Think about other possible biases, such as whether the participants were all male. This was the case in Friedman and Rosenman's study of heart disease (1974; see ASP4 p.148), where using only males enabled them to gain a valuable insight into the relationship between personality type and coronary heart disease. Nevertheless, their findings do not tell us much about heart disease amongst women. Another bias can be race, so consider whether the participants were all from one ethnic group. If a study used animals (such as Brady's "executive monkey" study; 1958; see ASP4 p.225), then we must be cautious about using the findings to formulate theories that apply to humans. That is not to say that the findings are not useful as they provide information that can provide the basis for further research, but we need to be cautious in their application.

3. How important are the findings in terms of their application?

Some studies only really provide fairly trivial and/or obvious information, whereas others involve important findings that can be of considerable use. If we return to Friedman and Rosenman's research study, this has provided important testable hypotheses about the causes and prevention of coronary heart disease. Likewise, Loftus and Palmer's research on leading questions (1974; see ASP4 p.69) has provided essential information about interviewing eyewitnesses of crime.

4. Was the study ethical?

There are some studies in which there is unacceptable cruelty, especially to animals, but try to give a balanced view when writing about such research. In fact, always introduce an ethical point by saying that all research is a balance between costs (such as embarrassment, deception, distress in humans, pain and suffering in animals) and the benefits gained. Then go on to outline these costs and benefits in a reasoned way. Remember that the specification asks that you "communicate your knowledge in a *clear and effective* manner".

Experimental research can be both pointless and unethical.

WHAT NOT TO SAY IN EXAMS

There are certain inappropriate comments that any experienced teacher comes across time and again. They are inappropriate because they are either inaccurate, ill-informed, sweeping, or judgemental in an uninformed way. Let's consider a few of these.

Don't say this!	Why not?
"I don't think this was a very good study because . . ."	Don't express personal opinions. If the study wasn't a good one, give a clear explanation as to why not. It would be better to say "This study can be criticised on the grounds that . . ."
"This proves that . . ."	Psychology is not an exact science in which theories can be proved, as they can in physics or maths. Be cautious and say things like "This indicates that . . ."

"This explanation is a load of rubbish . . ."	Does this one need to be spelt out? Every point should be well argued.
"This research was dead unethical. They shouldn't have done it."	Well, maybe "they" shouldn't have, but the language is colloquial, there's no balance, and there's no explanation.
"Freud was wrong because he was obsessed with sex."	Well, maybe he was, but this is not a balanced or reasonable comment. You should be discussing Freud's theory, not him. By all means mention the considerable emphasis on sex in his theory, but give an informed commentary with appropriate support.
"This study was definitely unethical."	Okay, there are a few studies that could reasonably be said to be unethical, but for the vast majority it is better to say that they were "ethically dubious", thus implying that there are ethical problems with them, but then go on to consider their worth. Even if you feel strongly that the study should not have been conducted on ethical grounds, you should always give clear reasons, rather than starting (and possibly ending) with a black-and-white judgement.
"This study was immoral because it upset the children."	The term "immoral" is not the same as unethical, so be careful with your use of language.

THE EXAM FORMAT

There are two exams, one for Unit 1 and one for Unit 2. Both are 1 hour 30 minutes, 50% of the AS marks, 25% of the A2 marks.

Unit 1	*Unit 2*
There will be structured compulsory questions based on Cognitive Psychology, Developmental Psychology, and Research Methods.	This unit consists of three compulsory structured questions, one based on the Biological Psychology content (stress), one based on the Social Psychology content (social influence), and one based on the Individual Differences content (Psychopathology—abnormality).
Questions will include short-answer questions, stimulus material, and one 12-mark question requiring extended writing in which QWC (quality of written communication—see below) will be assessed.	As in Unit 1, questions include short-answer questions, stimulus material, and one or more 12-mark questions requiring extended writing in which QWC will be assessed.

Let's see what the different types of question involve.
    Examples of *short-answer questions* are:

• Give one characteristic of short-term memory.
• Give an example of a behaviour shown by a securely attached infant.
• Give an example of Type A behaviour.

Questions involving *stimulus material* may involve a scenario. For example:

• In Unit 1 you may be presented with a scenario about a person who needed to improve his or her memory, and then be required to apply your knowledge of theories of memory to suggest appropriate strategies.
• In Unit 2 you could be presented with one or two people faced with a stressful situation and you could be asked for different strategies to help them cope.

The *12-mark questions* are obviously longer and will require both AO1 and AO2. You may be asked to describe and evaluate a particular theory (for example, the working memory model) or to describe and evaluate the use of drugs in treating abnormality.

QUALITY OF WRITTEN COMMUNICATION (QWC)

The 12-mark questions carry marks for QWC so make sure:

• Your writing is legible (can be read—this is more important than you may imagine!!) and that spelling, punctuation, and grammar are accurate so that the meaning is clear.
• You organise the information in your answer in a clear way, using appropriate psychological terms.

EXAM TECHNIQUE

So you know what each unit is about and how you will be assessed, you now need to think about exam technique. Passing the exam is as much about exam strategy as it is about intelligence and memory. Before you even start writing in the exam you need to THINK and ASK YOURSELF some questions that might help to guide you.

What is the question asking me to do?
Underline the KEY WORDS in the question and pause for a moment to check your answer is focused on the question and does not include irrelevant material.

Am I answering the question set?
There is a great temptation in exams to write down everything you know about a topic in the hope that the examiner will select the most relevant parts of your answer. This is referred to as the "vomit on the page" approach and will get you very few marks, so don't do it.

What about timing?
Before you start to answer the questions, you need to consider the issue of timing. The exams are an hour and a half.

In Unit 1 there are two main sections:
- SECTION A   COGNITIVE PSYCHOLOGY AND RESEARCH METHODS
- SECTION B   DEVELOPMENTAL PSYCHOLOGY AND RESEARCH METHODS

Each section is worth 36 marks out of 72 so you should divide your time equally between the two sections. This means spending NO MORE than 45 minutes on each section so STOP WRITING answers to Section A after 45 minutes. THIS IS EXTREMELY IMPORTANT. If you use 50 minutes on section A you will have only 40 left for section B—you cannot answer it properly in that time and you will seriously decrease your chance of doing well in the exam.

In Unit 2 there are three sections:
- SECTION A   BIOLOGICAL PSYCHOLOGY
- SECTION B   SOCIAL PSYCHOLOGY
- SECTION C   INDIVIDUAL DIFFERENCES

These sections are all of equal length (24 marks each, making 72 in total) so again, timing is crucial. **DO NOT SPEND MORE THAN 30 MINUTES ON EACH SECTION.** If you ignore every other piece of advice, do not ignore this one.

Planning your answers
For all your answers, but especially for the 12-mark ones, PLAN YOUR ANSWER carefully. Just take a few moments before you start writing to think through the key points you want to make. This will help you to be succinct and prevent you from falling into the trap of repeating the same point or missing out a vital piece of information. Write a brief plan if it helps.

Perhaps one of the best ways to think about exam technique is to analyse how people fail and determine not to make the same mistakes. The following list contains most of the strategies that you can use if you definitely want to fail an exam.

Take note and don't do any of these things in the exam:

TEN WAYS TO FAIL EXAMS

1. Spend 20 minutes answering a question that will only give you 3 marks.
2. On a one and a half hour paper of three sections, spend 40 minutes on section A, 40 minutes on section B, and leave only 10 minutes to answer section C.
3. Answer the question you wanted to come up, instead of the one that has been set.
4. Write down everything you know about the topic, preferably using your own personal experiences.
5. Repeat the same point and same study over and over again—the examiner will think you only know one study from the whole of the course.
6. Instead of planning your answer at the outset, just let it meander and develop in its own time.
7. Miss out a question.
8. Fall asleep in the exam due to having stayed up all night trying to revise.
9. Tell the examiner that you haven't revised the topic and you were taught very badly.
10. See a key word, such as stress, ignore the stimulus material and question, and just write about stress.

Finally, you need to get yourself in the right frame of mind when taking exams.

BEFORE THE EXAM

Ban all negative thinking, such as:

Replace these thoughts with the following:

IN THE EXAM

The most important thing you can do when you turn over the exam paper is to AVOID PANIC, so ban phrases like:

Instead, use your knowledge of psychology to help you in your time of need . . . think of the concept of context-dependent memory and imagine yourself back in the classroom or reading your textbook or revision guide. Something *will* come back to you.

Remember that it's not what you know, but how you use the knowledge, that counts. Can you use the information you have to support a viewpoint or argue against it? It is very important that you remember how to evaluate and criticise, and do this wherever you are asked to.

AFTER THE EXAM

Different people handle the after-exam experience differently. Some people like checking everything they think they've written (but don't forget the findings of Bartlett's work on reconstructive memory that suggests that our memories aren't always 100% accurate). Others prefer to discuss their answers with their friends, teachers, and anyone who is willing to listen. If this is your preferred course of action and it makes you feel better, fine—you've earned it! But for many people it's great to think it's all over and there's nothing that you need to do until the results come out.

 **Good luck!!!**

COGNITIVE PSYCHOLOGY
Memory

2

What's it about?

Cognitive psychology focuses on how we interpret the world around us. It includes exploring perception, thinking, language, attention, and memory.

Cognitive psychologists try to help us understand why we remember some things and not others, why our perception of the world is not always accurate, and why we think about the world in the way we do. In addition they are interested in how our memories, thoughts, and language influence our behaviour and experiences.

The cognitive psychologists were strongly influenced by the computer revolution and often use models to help aid our understanding of how we acquire, store, and retrieve information.

WHAT'S IN THIS UNIT?

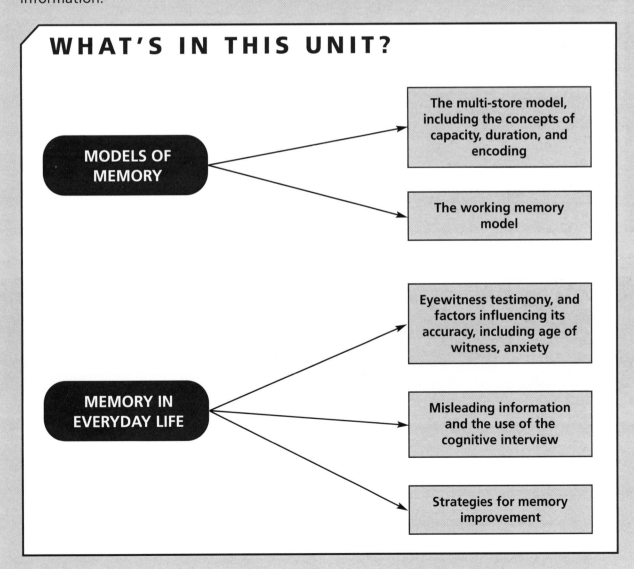

MODELS OF MEMORY

- The multi-store model, including the concepts of capacity, duration, and encoding
- The working memory model

MEMORY IN EVERYDAY LIFE

- Eyewitness testimony, and factors influencing its accuracy, including age of witness, anxiety
- Misleading information and the use of the cognitive interview
- Strategies for memory improvement

IMPORTANT TERMS AND CONCEPTS

In the AS exam:

- You may be asked to describe, explain, outline, or contrast different models of memory.
- You could also be asked to discuss their strengths and weaknesses.
- You will be expected to know what factors aid or inhibit the accuracy of eyewitness testimony.
- You will also need to be able to discuss how we can improve our memories.
- The examiner may ask you to apply your knowledge to real-life situations or explore how research into memory might be undertaken.

The following terms are important for understanding this module so it will help you in the exam if you understand what they refer to. Make a list of definitions of the following terms and if you get stuck there is a glossary at the end of this book to help you.

Acoustic coding	Memory	Repression
Chunking	Memory span	Retrieval
Chunks	Method of loci	Schema
Declarative knowledge	Mnemonic techniques	Semantic coding
Displacement	Multi-store model	Short-term memory
Dysexecutive syndrome	Pegword method	Story method
Encoding	Phonological loop	Stroop task
Eyewitness testimony	Procedural knowledge	Visuo-spatial sketch pad
False memory syndrome	Reading span	Working memory model
Long-term memory	Rehearsal	

OVER TO YOU

Outline key features of the working memory model.

6 MARKS

MODELS OF MEMORY

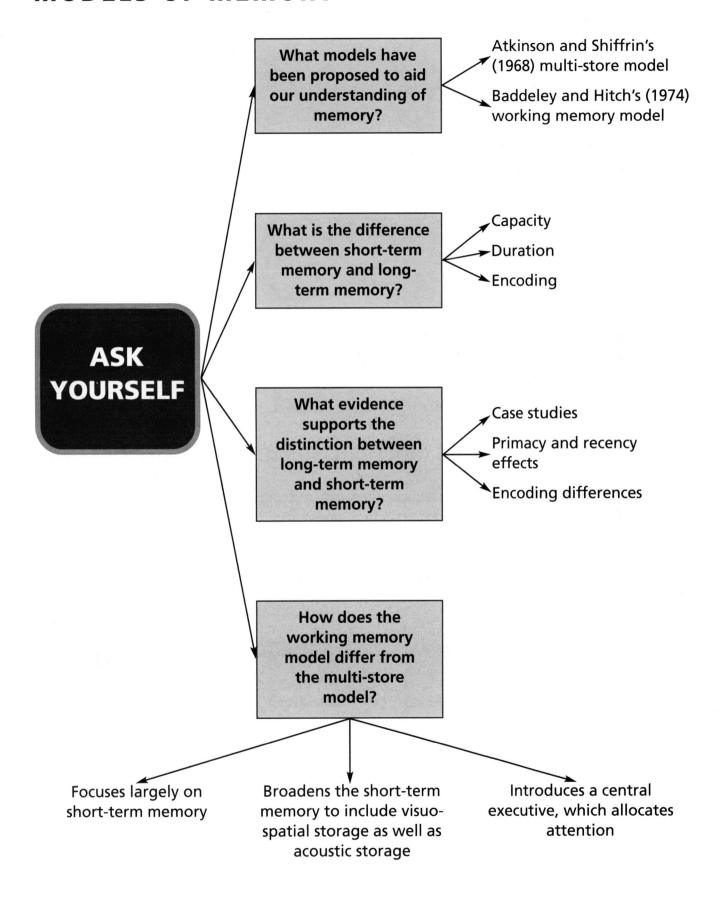

Some of the alleged differences between short-term memory and long-term memory are shown below.

ATKINSON AND SHIFFRIN'S MULTI-STORE MODEL: A BRIEF OUTLINE

This model suggests that incoming data passes through a sensory store into a short-term store. If active rehearsal takes place, the information is then transferred to the long-term store. Forgetting from the short-term memory may be due to interference or decay. Forgetting from the long-term memory may be due to retrieval failure or interference.

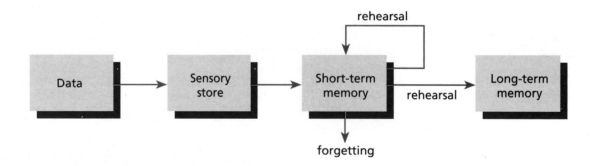

Supporting Studies

Differences between short-term memory (STM) and long-term memory (LTM):

- **Capacity**
  - Jacobs (1887; see ASP4 p.46) Early research into the memory span.
  - Miller (1956; see ASP4 p.47) 7 ± 2 chunks.

- **Duration**
  - Brown and Peterson (1959; see ASP4 p.48) 18 second duration in STM.
- **Encoding**
  - Baddeley (1966; see ASP4 p.50) STM—acoustic; LTM—semantic.

Other Supporting Research

- Glanzer and Cunitz (1966; see ASP4 p.48) Study on the primacy and recency effect.
- Bahrick et al. (1975; see ASP4 p.46) VLTM (very long-term memory)—recognition of classmates after 35 years.
- Tulving (1972) Broadened our understanding of the LTM by dividing it into semantic memory and episodic memory.
- Cohen and Squire (1980; see ASP4 p.51) Distinguished between declarative and procedural memory.
- Case study: HM (see ASP4 p.52) HM failed to form any new long-term memories, and attempts to reconstruct memories were unsuccessful.

EVALUATION

STRENGTHS

There is a lot of support for the distinction between the long-term store and short-term store.

- The capacity of the two stores is different (e.g. Jacobs/Miller).
- The duration of the two stores is different (e.g. Bahrick/Peterson & Peterson).
- The predominant mode of coding differs between short-term memory (acoustic) and long-term memory (semantic) (Baddeley).
- The model helps explain the primary and recency effect, in that the first items are recalled from LTM, having been rehearsed, and last items are still being held and actively rehearsed in STM. This is further supported by Glanzer and Cunitz's research demonstrating that the recency effect can be removed if an interference task (like counting backwards in threes) is given immediately after the information is presented.
- Case study: HM.

WEAKNESSES

- Rehearsal does not always lead to storage.
- If coding in the STM is predominantly acoustic, how do we understand language?
- How does acoustically coded information get transferred into semantic coding as it enters the LTM?
- Initial oversimplification of LTM store, but this was redressed by Tulving (semantic/episodic), and Cohen and Squire (procedural/declarative).
- How does it explain flashbulb memories?
- Posner demonstrated visual codes exist in the STM.
- Oversimplification of the STM. Studies on patients with brain damage suggest there is more than one store.
- Some types of information are not amenable to rehearsal, e.g. smells.

Developments of the Model

The multi-store model formed the basis for much research into memory, leading to other models being proposed. Baddeley and Hitch broadened the functions of the short-term memory with their working memory model, whilst Cohen and Squire (1980) argued that the long-term memory is divided into two memory systems:

Declarative knowledge	Procedural knowledge
KNOWING THAT e.g. I had cornflakes for breakfast	KNOWING HOW e.g. how to ride a bike

Evidence to support this division comes from research into patients with amnesia. Spiers et al. (2001; see ASP4 p.52) reviewed 147 cases of amnesia and found that all the patients had problems with declarative knowledge, but that none experienced problems with procedural knowledge.

How Does the Model Explain Forgetting?

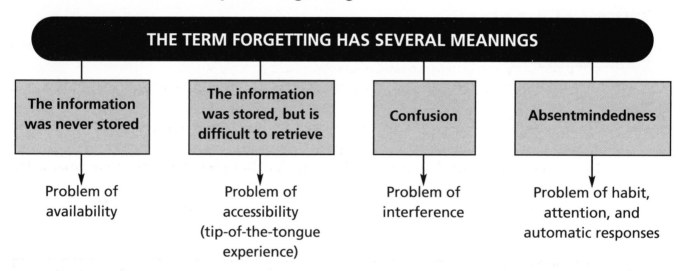

THE TERM FORGETTING HAS SEVERAL MEANINGS

The information was never stored	The information was stored, but is difficult to retrieve	Confusion	Absentmindedness
Problem of availability	Problem of accessibility (tip-of-the-tongue experience)	Problem of interference	Problem of habit, attention, and automatic responses

It has been suggested that forgetting from the short-term memory is different from forgetting from the long-term memory. If information is forgotten from the short-term store, it is often thought to be lost forever and hence is no longer available. Whereas it is often thought that forgetting from the long-term store is more like mislaying the information and with the appropriate cues, the information could be found. In this sense the information is still accessible.

Research has tried to establish whether forgetting from STM and LTM is due to retrieval failure or lack of availability. Let's examine some of the theories and supporting research.

Forgetting From:

Short-term memory
- **Trace decay**. Spontaneous disappearance of the memory trace. Peterson and Peterson (1959; see ASP4 p.48) found that memories were held in STM for approximately 18 seconds, after which they disappeared via trace decay. This occurs when the memories are not rehearsed.
- **Displacement**. New information pushes out or displaces the original information in the short-term memory, due to its limited capacity.

- **Interference**. New information interferes with, or disrupts, the information held in the short-term memory.
- **Diversion of attention**. If attention is diverted away from the information to be retained, it is likely to be forgotten.
- **Lack of consolidation**. An injury to the head prevents the memory trace being stored.
- **Insufficient level of processing**. Processing information at a shallow level prevents it from being stored.
- **Brain damage**. Damage to the brain causes a variety of effects on performance. Warrington and Shallice's (1972; see ASP4 p.53) study of KF found that his short-term forgetting of auditory letters and digits (things that were heard) was much greater than his forgetting of visual stimuli, suggesting that the STM is not just a single store, but consists of a number of different stores.

Long-term memory

- **Trace decay**. If a person does nothing during the time of initial learning and the retention interval, and they forget the material, it is probable that the memory trace has disappeared.
- **Retroactive interference**. New information interferes with the recall of previous information stored.
- **Proactive interference**. Old information interferes with the recall of new information.
- **Lack of retrieval cues**. Cue-dependent forgetting takes place due to lack of accessibility of the memory. The memory will pop up when an appropriate cue is given.
- **Context dependency**. You may need to be in the same context as learning took place to be able to recall information.
- **State dependency**. You may need to be in the same emotional or physical state as you were in when learning took place to recall the information.
- **Repression**. A defence mechanism that prevents emotionally threatening memories from being accessible to consciousness.
- **Brain damage**. Depending on the damage, there can be various impairments to LTM.

Confusion can occur when new information interferes with the information we are trying to remember.

BADDELEY AND HITCH'S WORKING MEMORY MODEL

The working memory model helps us understand how we use our memory in everyday life and broadens the function of the short-term memory beyond storage and rehearsal.

The model (see ASP4 pp.53–54) suggests that our memory consists of a central executive, which is described as a limited capacity modality-free attentional system, along with two slave systems—the phonological loop and the visuo-spatial sketch pad.

- The central executive has overall control and allocates attention and directs the operation of the slave systems. It is therefore involved in planning, shifting attention when doing more than one task, and organising and monitoring our actions.
- The phonological loop is described as a temporary storage system that holds verbal information in a speech-based form. It acts like an inner voice and an inner ear, and is primarily concerned with our perception and production of speech.
- The visuo-spatial sketch pad is an inner eye, and is responsible for visual spatial coding. It is a bit like a writing pad for remembering visual data, such as how to get back to where the car is parked.

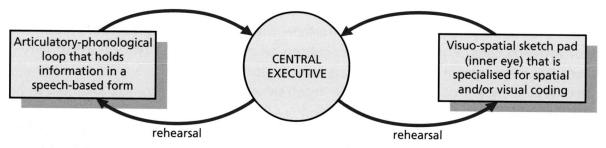

Research into the Working Memory Model

Research into the working memory model focuses on performing tasks that use either the same or different systems, sometimes known as the dual-task technique.

This technique assumes that the phonological loop and the visuo-spatial sketch pad have a limited capacity and therefore if people are asked to perform two tasks that use the same system, their performance on one or both will be affected. One of the most common techniques used to test this hypothesis involves getting the participants to repeat meaningless words like "the" over and over again or getting them to recite a list of digits while trying to read information or do verbal reasoning.

Supporting Studies

Research into the phonological loop using word length or the dual-task technique

- Baddeley, Thomson, and Buchanan (1975; see ASP4 p.56) Word length influenced recall in that participants' recall of five words was higher when shorter words were presented.
- Baddeley and Lewis (1981) Articulatory suppression led to difficulties in reading and understanding texts.
- Hitch and Baddeley (1976; see ASP4 p.55) Participants' performance on a verbal reasoning task was slowed down when they were required to repeat a random string of digits at the same time as doing the verbal reasoning.
- Gathercole and Baddeley (1990; see ASP4 p.55) Children with reading problems had an impaired memory span and had difficulties saying whether words rhymed, perhaps suggesting that there is a phonological loop deficit.

Research into the visuo-spatial sketch pad

This research often explores whether there are separate systems for spatial and visual information:

- Studies on people who have been blind from birth clearly suggest that the two systems are separate; although they have no visual awareness of their environment, they clearly have a spatial awareness of their environment.
- Smith and Jonides (1997; see ASP4 p.57) Differences in brain activation were studied when participants undertook visual and spatial tasks. It was found that there was more activity in the right hemisphere when participants were taking part in a spatial task, and more activity in the left hemisphere when they were doing a visual task.

Research into the central executive

Such research focuses on the use and complexity of the central executive by using experiments and case studies:

- Miyake et al. (2000; see ASP4 p.58) The central executive serves different functions:
  - inhibitory function—minimising distraction from other tasks
  - shifting function—allowing us to switch from one task to another
  - updating function—enabling us to take account of changes.
- Stuss and Alexander (2007; see ASP4 p.59) The central executive has three functions:
  - task setting (planning)
  - monitoring (checking one's own performance for quality control)
  - energisation (sustained attention or concentration).
- The Stroop Effect This demonstrates the need for the inhibitory function of the central executive, in that you are required to focus on the colour the word is printed in, and ignore the meaning of the word.
- Robbins et al. (1996; see ASP4 p.55) The quality of chess players' moves was reduced when they were given a second task to do that involved their using either the central executive or the visuo-spatial sketch pad. However, the quality of their moves was not affected if the second task involved the phonological loop.
- Dysexecutive syndrome Research on individuals with dysexecutive syndrome suggests that they have difficulties with planning, organising, monitoring, and initiating behaviour: all key functions of the central executive. This disorder is linked to damage within the frontal lobes at the front of the brain.
- Stuss and Alexander (2007; see ASP4 p.59) Rather than global dysfunction, such patients may have problems in only one of the three key functions of the central executive.

EVALUATION

STRENGTHS

- Broadens the role of the STM store, by emphasising its importance in active processing as well as storage.
- Emphasises the importance of the phonological loop in everyday life tasks such as reading, comprehension, verbal reasoning, and arithmetic tasks.

- Demonstrates that while rehearsal may lead to storage, it is optional and doesn't have to be used to remember information.
- The introduction of a central executive makes an important link between memory and attention.
- It has practical applications in helping children to read, by suggesting that the difficulties may reside in deficits with the phonological loop.

WEAKNESSES

- Not a great deal is known about the central executive.
- Perhaps it is oversimplistic to have a single central executive.
- The visuo-spatial store has not been explored in as much depth as the phonological loop.
- It is not entirely clear how the three main components of the model interact.
- It tells us very little about the long-term memory.

OVER TO YOU

Using the list below, complete the table to distinguish between the central executive, phonological loop, and visuo-spatial sketch pad.

- Use when giving someone directions
- Allocates resources
- Would use when reading
- Modality free
- Acts like an inner voice
- Useful for remembering visual data

Central executive	Phonological loop	Visuo-spatial sketch pad

3 MARKS

Explain one strength and one weakness of the working memory model.

4 MARKS

MEMORY IN EVERYDAY LIFE

This area looks at how our understanding of memory can be applied to everyday life. The first section looks at eyewitness testimony and then we look at how you can improve your memory.

EYEWITNESS TESTIMONY

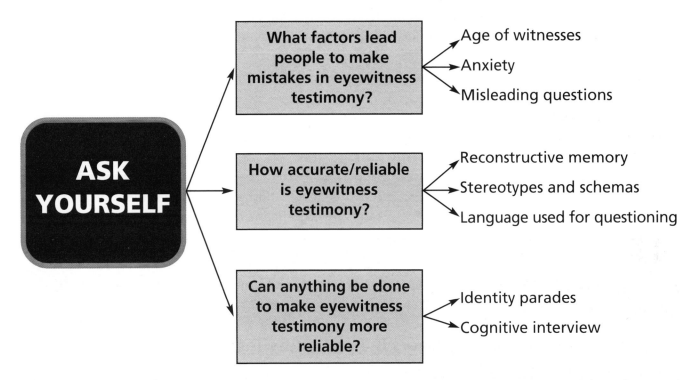

Although psychologists have strong reservations about the accuracy of eyewitness testimony, jurors have tended to find it "more persuasive than any other sort of evidence". With the development of DNA tests it has become clear that many people who were convicted of crimes, on the basis of eyewitness testimony, were in fact innocent.

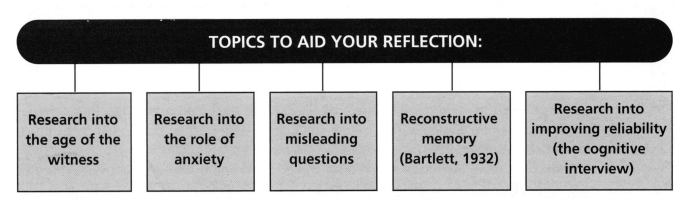

Does the Age of the Witness Affect Their Recall?

Research has shown that the age of the witness may influence the reliability of their evidence. Studies have shown that both children and older adults are more prone to making errors, and that the accuracy of witness accounts by children declines over time. This finding is very important as children may often have to wait several months before giving evidence in court.

Research on Children

- Pozzulo and Lindsay (1998; see ASP4 p.64) Using a meta-analysis of numerous studies, they reported that:
  - children under 5 were less likely to correctly identify a culprit from a line-up
  - children up to 13 were more likely to say that someone was the culprit in a line-up, even if the culprit was not there
  - children over 5 performed as well as adults in identifying a culprit if they were in the line-up.
- Keast et al. (2007; see ASP4 p.64) Children tend to be more overconfident than adults when making their decision.
- Flin et al. (1992) studied three groups of participants of different ages:
  - 5–6 years old
  - 9–10 years old
  - adults.

All participants saw a staged argument during a talk on foot hygiene. Whilst there was no significant difference between the three groups' recall after 1 day, there were marked differences in accuracy after a delay of 5 months. The 5–6-year-olds and the 9–10-year-olds forgot significantly more than the adults and there was also a significant difference between the accuracy scores of the 5–6-year-olds and the 9–10-year-olds, with older children gaining significantly higher accuracy scores.

For these reasons it would seem advisable to collect evidence from children as soon as possible after the event.

Explanations for Childhood Errors in Eyewitness Testimony

Social factors	Cognitive factors
Children may be more suggestible (Brofenbrenner, 1998).	Children's ability to attend to, and process, information may be limited.
Children may be more likely to yield to social pressure, especially since the interviewer is an adult.	Children may have limited linguistic ability, and so store information visually.

For these reasons, children may be more prone to believe their distorted memories. Indeed even when they have been warned that the interviewer may be mistaken, they continued to produce false memories (Bruck & Melnyk, 2004).

One strategy that has been introduced to reduce the errors made by children is to get them to draw what they remember. Gross and Hayne (1999; see ASP4 p.65) found that children who produced drawings recalled about 30% more information in their verbal reports on a visit to a chocolate factory than children who hadn't produced drawings.

Research on Older Adults

- Brewer et al. (2005; see ASP4 p.65) Older adults (60–80-year-olds) were more likely to choose someone from a line-up, even if the culprit was not present.

- Mueller-Johnson and Ceci (2004; see ASP4 p.65) Older people (average age 76) were more likely to be influenced by misleading questions. This older age group was compared with younger participants (average age 20). Both groups were given relaxation techniques, including body massage and aromatherapy. Several weeks later they were given misleading information, such as being told that they had been massaged in places that hadn't been touched. This information distorted the older groups' memories more.
- Wright and Stroud (2002; see ASP4 p.65) found there was an "own age bias" when people are asked to identify culprits from crime videos. Participants were better able to identify someone from their own age group.

These findings stress the need to make sure that older adults are not exposed to misleading information that could distort their memories. In addition detailed questioning is needed to check that their recollection of the event has not been distorted by the context or the circumstances in which the information was encountered.

The Role of Anxiety in Eyewitness Research

One major difference between eyewitness research undertaken in a lab setting and a real-life eyewitness account is that the person witnessing the event in real life may be experiencing greater anxiety. This anxiety might:

- Direct the victim's or witness's attention away from the perpetrator to focus on any weapon they might have.
- Lead to their thinking that the event lasted longer than it did.
- Lead to their experiencing flashbulb memories.

Personality factors could also contribute to how much they notice and store when experiencing great stress.

Three areas of research that have helped explore the role of anxiety in eyewitness accounts include:

The Effect of Anxiety and Stress on Face Recognition

Deffenbacher et al. (2004; see ASP4 p.67) carried out meta-analyses on numerous studies exploring the effects of anxiety and stress on eyewitness testimony. The average number of correct identifications fell by 12% from 54% (when it was a low anxiety/stress condition) to 42% (when it was a high anxiety/stress condition) suggesting that heightened anxiety decreased identification accuracy. Further research found that high anxiety led to participants recalling fewer details about the culprit and the scene.

The Weapon Focus Effect

The underlying idea of this research is that people will be so concerned by the weapon that they will be less likely to recall any other information.

Loftus et al.'s (1987; see ASP4 p.67) research supported this idea in that participants who viewed a person pointing a gun at a cashier had a poorer memory for details that weren't related to the gun, than participants who saw the person passing a cheque over the counter. However, this may be because it is unusual for us to see a gun. When studies are undertaken using a rifle range as the setting, the weapon focus effect is decreased (Pickel, 1999; see ASP4 p.67). Perhaps this is because we expect to see guns at a rifle range.

The Role of Individual Differences

- Bothwell et al. (1987; see ASP4 p.68) found a difference between people who scored high on neuroticism and people who scored low on neuroticism in identifying a culprit. When the stress level was low the people who scored higher on neuroticism were better at identifying the culprit, with 68% correct in comparison with 50% of the low neuroticism scorers. However, under high stress situations, this was reversed, with only 32% of the high-scoring participants identifying the culprit in comparison with 75% of those low in neuroticism.

Research Using Leading Questions

After witnessing an event, people are often asked questions about what they saw, who was involved, and what happened. Research, most notably by Loftus and colleagues, has shown that the language used when questioning eyewitnesses may alter what they remember. If the questions contain misleading information then the new information can influence the original memory. This may result in witnesses saying that they saw something or someone when in fact they did not. In some cases this is due to *post-event information*, where the person confuses information received outside the context of the witnessed event with the event itself. In other situations, *memory blending* occurs whereby details from various sources are combined with memories of the actual event.

An important study conducted by Loftus and Palmer (1974; see ASP4 p.69) investigates the effects of language on recall using a series of projected slides showing a car crash. They found that changing the description of how the cars went into each other resulted in participants perceiving the speed of the cars differently:

- "Smashed" led participants to estimate that the cars were going at 41 mph.
- "Collided" led them to say the cars were going at 39 mph.
- "Hit" reduced the perceived speed to 34 mph.
- "Contacted" reduced the perceived speed further to 32 mph.

What was more important than the initial speed assessment was the fact that there had not been any broken glass as a result of the crash. However, 1 week later the participants were asked if they had noticed any broken glass at the scene of the accident, with the following results:

- In the "smashed" condition, 32% of participants claimed to have seen broken glass.
- In the "hit" condition, 14% said they had seen broken glass.

These results show that at least some of the participants had been influenced by the initial wording used to describe the crash. This idea of broken glass would have been plausible at the scene of a car crash; however, if the misleading information is blatantly incorrect, and therefore implausible, it does not have the same influence.

Even changing the article from "a" to "the" can influence the participants' responses as Loftus and Zanni (1975; see ASP4 p.70) found. Despite the fact there was no broken headlight, 17% said they did see a broken headlight when asked, "Did you see THE broken headlight?" in comparison to 7% of the participants who were asked, "Did you see A broken headlight?"

Other research has shown that eyewitness testimony can be influenced by misleading information presented BEFORE and AFTER the event.

Information Preceding the Event

- Lindsay et al. (2004; see ASP4 p.70) showed eyewitnesses a video of a museum burglary. On the day before the burglary, they had listened to a narrative that was either similar or dissimilar to what they had seen. When the narrative was similar, more errors were made.

Information Given After the Event

- Eakin et al. (2003; see ASP4 p.70) Participants' memory of a man stealing some money from an office was impaired when they were given post-event misleading information.

Concerns about Research into Eyewitness Testimony

Whilst the psychological research into eyewitness testimony has highlighted the need to think carefully about the questions witnesses are asked and raised concerns about misleading information given both prior and post the event, it is clear that lab studies differ from real-life events.

In real life

- It is often the victim rather than the eyewitness giving testimony.
- It is much more likely to be stressful and anxiety provoking than watching a video of an event.
- The event may last much longer, in that the victim often has on average 5–10 minutes to view the crime in comparison to a few seconds in the lab.
- The consequences of identification are extremely important.
- Ihlebaek et al. (2003; see ASP4 p.69) compared participants' recall from a real-life (albeit staged) robbery with participants' recall from video footage of the same event. Both groups exaggerated the duration of the event, but interestingly participants who viewed the video of the robbery were more accurate in their descriptions of the robber and the weapons.

However, findings from another real-life situation revealed that important information about the crime was not easily distorted.

Yuille and Cutshall (1986; see ASP4 p.70) looked at witnesses' recall of a shooting that took place outside a gun shop in Canada, where one person was shot dead and one was seriously injured. The incident took place mid-afternoon in a busy area. Twenty-one witnesses observed the shooting. All were interviewed by the police, and thirteen of them also agreed to provide research interviews 4–5 months after the event.

Yuille and Cutshall analysed these eyewitness accounts and research interviews and suggested that:

- The witnesses were extremely accurate in their accounts of the event even when interviewed 4–5 months later.
- Errors were made in some aspects of colour memory, and age, height, and weight estimations. This means that even though witnesses can be accurate about an actual event, they tend to have difficulties remembering precise details. (Erikson, 1998, found that there was less memory distortion for central or important details than trivial ones.)
- There was a weapons effect, where participants did focus on the weapon rather than the details.

In this real-life study, the eyewitnesses resisted leading questions. However, in lab studies, people are likely to be misled if there is a delay between the event and being given false information. They are also misled by insignificant details.

"Well I know he was wearing tights."

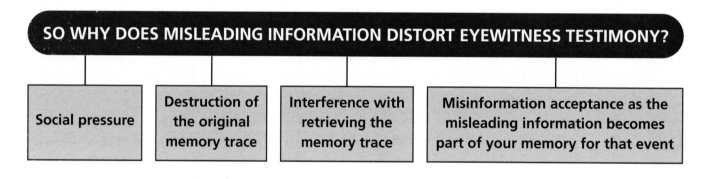

SO WHY DOES MISLEADING INFORMATION DISTORT EYEWITNESS TESTIMONY?

| Social pressure | Destruction of the original memory trace | Interference with retrieving the memory trace | Misinformation acceptance as the misleading information becomes part of your memory for that event |

Reconstructive Memory

Using stories, Bartlett (1932; see ASP4 p.71) demonstrated that people's recall of information was influenced by schemas—frameworks for thinking about the world based on one's experience and culture. Bartlett's work demonstrated that participants' recall of information was not only influenced by how they interpreted the information, but also that their recall of the information often changed over time. One of his famous studies involved asking participants to read a Native American folk tale called "The War of the Ghosts". The participants were asked to recall the story several times up to 1 year later and their versions were then analysed. From his content analysis Bartlett found that the following changes took place:

- **Omission** Information considered to be irrelevant is often omitted from recall.
- **Transformation of order/detail** Participants may change the order in which events occurred when retelling their story, or they might shift their focus of what is the most important aspect of the story.
- **Rationalisation** In an attempt to make sense of the story, people may try to explain what happened in a way that makes sense to them and is coherent, even if this is not accurate.
- **Cultural shifts** Both the style of the story and the content will be altered to be more appropriate to one's own culture.

Bartlett's work highlighted the importance of schemas and stereotypes. He demonstrated that humans often distort the information they receive to fit in with their own ways of looking at and understanding the world. He also clearly showed that we reconstruct our memories.

Schemas and Stereotypes

One study that clearly supports Bartlett deals with the effect of schemas and stereotypes on memory, and is detailed below.

Cohen's investigation into whether stereotypes influence memory

Cohen's (1981) study was designed to see whether being told that a woman was either a "librarian" or a "waitress" would influence participants' recall of her. However, Cohen was also interested to see whether receiving the information before or after seeing the woman made any difference.

In this experiment, participants were shown a 15-minute videotape of a man and a woman eating a meal and celebrating a birthday party. The participants were later asked to describe the woman's behaviour, appearance, and personality. There were two conditions. In the first condition the information about her occupation was given before the participants saw the video, and in the second condition the information about her occupation was given after participants saw the video.

In both conditions participants recalled more information that was consistent with the stereotype of "waitress" and "librarian" than information that was inconsistent. However, information that was received before the video was shown resulted in more accurate recall.

This study is clearly important, for it shows that schemas and stereotypes are not only important at the initial storage stage of memory, they are also clearly important at the retrieval stage of memory. This has clear implications for real life when people might be given information after an event has occurred, as was shown in a study of the witnesses called to the Oklahoma bombing trial.

Memon and Wright (1999) showed that information received subsequent to a trial could influence witnesses' recall of events. Two of the eyewitnesses, who initially stated that there was only one man who came into a garage to hire a van, changed their account when they heard another witness say that there were definitely two men. Days after their initial statement, these two eyewitnesses claimed to remember a second man. This showed that information received after a crime can, and does, influence memory.

Further support for the role of schemas comes from Tuckey and Brewer (2003; see ASP4 p.71) who obtained information about people's bank robbery schemas (e.g. robbers are male, wear disguises, dark clothes, demand money, have a getaway car). When participants had to recall details of a simulated crime they had observed, ambiguous information tended to be consistent with their crime schema.

Improving the Reliability of Eyewitness Testimony

To help prevent the conviction of innocent people, it is essential that steps are taken to improve the reliability of eyewitness testimony. Mistakes made by eyewitnesses may occur because of what was happening at the time of the crime or incident or what happens afterwards.

When considering identity parades, the following precautions should be taken:

- Place suspects in different places in the identity parade.
- Tell the witness that the suspect may not be in the identity parade.
- "Fillers" in the line-up should resemble the suspect, but not too much.
- Use sequential line-ups.

- Avoid post-identification suggestions (e.g. "Yes, well done").
- Avoid contact of the witness with members of the identity parade beforehand.

When considering interview techniques:

- Ask open-ended questions.
- Avoid encouraging guessing, as it may consolidate a false memory.
- Do not prompt the witness, but allow them to volunteer information.
- Establish a rapport with the witness so he or she feels comfortable.

THE COGNITIVE INTERVIEW TECHNIQUE

These ideas have filtered into the cognitive interview technique that was developed by Geiselman et al. (1985; see ASP4 p.72). With this approach the witness has to:

- Recreate the context mentally that existed at the time of the crime including environmental and internal (e.g. mood) information.
- Recall everything they remember whether they feel it is relevant or not, or fragmented.
- Recall details of the incident in different orders.
- Recall the event from a different perspective such as that of another witness.

Geiselman et al. found that using the basic cognitive interview resulted in a higher average number of correct statements produced by the eyewitness (41% compared to 29%).

Roy (1991; see ASP4 p.73) added some recommendations for the basic cognitive interview technique called the enhanced cognitive interview:

- Avoid making judgemental and personal comments.
- Encourage the witness to speak slowly.
- Tailor the complexity of your language to suit individual eyewitnesses.
- Try to minimise distractions.
- Follow up each bit of information with an interpretative comment.
- Allow a pause between the response and the next question.
- Try to reduce eyewitness anxiety.
- Always review the eyewitnesses' description of events or people under investigation.

Kohnken et al. (1999; see ASP4 p.73) did a meta-analysis of over 50 studies using the enhanced cognitive interview and found that eyewitnesses produced more correct items of information than 81% of eyewitnesses given a standard interview, but worryingly they also produced more errors than participants given the standard interview.

Concerns about the Cognitive Interview

- There is a small increase in incorrect information provided by the eyewitness.
- It is less effective at enhancing recall after longer intervals after the crime.
- It is not exactly clear which aspect of the interview contributes to its success:
  - context reinstatement
  - changing perspective
  - changing the order
  - reporting everything.

Milne and Bull (2002; see ASP4 p.74) suggested that all four components were equally beneficial.

OVER TO YOU

Mary has witnessed a robbery at her local post office. She is an important witness and the police need to get accurate information from her. Outline two strategies that will help the police obtain their information and explain why these strategies are thought to improve the reliability of eyewitness testimony.

3 MARKS + 3 MARKS

STRATEGIES FOR IMPROVING MEMORY

Several methods can be used to improve our memory. Many people remember the colours of the rainbow using **R**ichard **o**f **Y**ork **G**ave **B**attle **i**n **V**ain (RED, ORANGE, YELLOW, GREEN, BLUE, INDIGO, VIOLET) where the first letter is a cue for recall. Most methods for improving our memory stress the need for organising the material, both at the time of learning and storage, and at the time of retrieval and recall. The methods may require the use of previous knowledge of places (e.g. method of loci) or previous knowledge about meaning (e.g. hierarchical encoding). They may encourage you to link ideas to relevant cues (e.g. the pegword method). Encoding information may be improved by using visual strategies (e.g. using visual imagery) or verbal strategies (e.g. using rhymes).

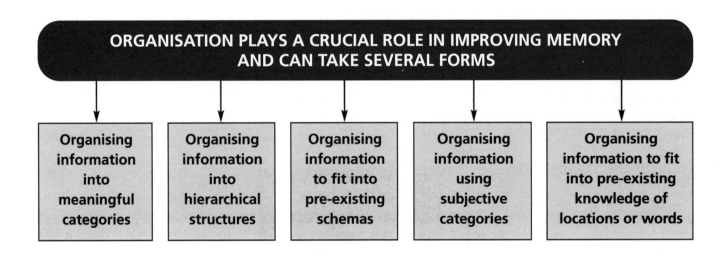

Research into the Role of Organisation

Research into organising information into meaningful categories

- Shuell (1969; see ASP4 p.75) used the classic research method of giving one group information, organised into categories such as girl's names or birds, while the other group was given the same words but randomly presented. The findings were as follows:
  - recall was higher in the group given the material organised into categories
  - participants tended to recall the information category by category
  - participants with the highest rate of categorical clustering recalled most words.

Research into organising information into hierarchical structures

- Bower et al. (1969; see ASP4 p.75) Organising words into hierarchical categories with MINERALS as the overarching category and METALS AND STONES as subheadings resulted in participants' recall being three and a half times greater than when the same words were presented unorganised.

Research into organising material using subjective organisation

- Mandler (1967; see ASP4 p.76) asked participants to sort 52 cards into piles using between 2–7 categories, until they used the same categorising system on two different occasions. It was found that recall was better for participants who used all 7 categories to sort the cards. This finding was robust when the study was replicated and participants were assigned randomly to using between 2 and 7 categories.

EVALUATION

STRENGTH

- Research evidence clearly shows that organisation can improve recall.

WEAKNESSES

- One major problem with using methods based on previous knowledge is that we may mis-remember information. As Bartlett suggested, we may recall information relevant to our schemas even if the information was not presented. Evidence supports this concern.
  - Deese (1959; see ASP4 p.78) found participants would often recall a non-presented, but related word when given a list like THREAD, PIN, EYE, SEWING, SHARP, POINT, PRICKED, THIMBLE, HAYSTACK, PAIN, HURT, INJECTION. Participants often reported hearing the word NEEDLE.
- The notion of organisation is somewhat vague in that it is hard to ascertain what previous knowledge participants are using.

Mnemonic Techniques

These are techniques thought to improve your memory and any glance in a bookshop will reveal there are numerous mnemonic strategies on offer. They also involve using previous knowledge and organising information. However, it needs to be pointed out that these techniques can be time consuming and may be more useful for remembering lists of concrete words rather than complex information.

Two major techniques used are:

- Mnemonics using visual imagery.
- Mnemonics using word-based strategies.

Mnemonics Using Visual Imagery

The method of loci

The words to be learned are associated with a series of well known locations, e.g. rooms in a house. Ross and Lawrence (1968; see ASP4 p.79) found that participants using the method of loci could recall more than 95% of a list of 40/50 items after a single study trial.

EVALUATION

STRENGTHS

- Evidence to support the benefits of this method, most notably when learning lists of unrelated words.
- Provides a detailed set of retrieval cues to aid memory.

WEAKNESSES

- You need to have reasonable visual imagery to use this method.
- Method not as easy to use with abstract material that does not lend itself to visual imagery or with information that needs to be integrated.
- Interference can occur when information is presented visually as was found by De Beni et al. (1997; see ASP4 p.79), who gave participants a 2000-word text. Whilst the method of loci increased recall when the text was presented orally, it had no effect when the information was presented in a written form.

The pegword method

With this method you remember peg words such as ONE . . . BUN, TWO . . . SHOE, etc. and then you associate the word to be remembered with the pegword, for example, given a list of words beginning with "sheep, car", you might visualise a sheep eating a bun and a car running over a shoe. Morris and Reid (1970; see ASP4 p.81) found that twice as many words were recalled when this system was used than when it was not.

EVALUATION

STRENGTHS

- There is evidence to support this method.
- Provides a set of retrieval cues to aid memory.
- Enables words to be learned in order.

WEAKNESSES

- It is time consuming and requires extensive training.
- It is less suited to learning abstract and integrated material.
- We rarely need to learn a random list of words in order.
- If participants are asked to relearn the list but using different pegwords, interference occurs.

Mnemonics Using Word-based Strategies

Verbal mnemonics: The story method

This method involves making up a story using the words to be remembered. For example, given the words DONKEY, WINE, COAT, CASTLE, DAFFODILS, you might make up a story like:

As the man took off his COAT to get on the DONKEY, a WINE bottle fell on the floor.
The man got off to pick up the bottle and the donkey galloped through
the DAFFODILS towards the CASTLE.

Bower and Clark (1969; see ASP4 p.82) found that the story method was beneficial. They gave participants 12 lists of 10 nouns to learn. Those who used the story method recalled 93% of words while those who didn't use this technique recalled only 13% of the words.

EVALUATION

STRENGTHS

- There is evidence to support this method.
- Elaboration of material may aid recall.

WEAKNESSES

- One problem with this method is you would have to work your way through the narrative to find the sixth word.
- Extensive training is needed to be able to use this method effectively
- It is difficult to create a story when the information is presented quickly.
- It is not particularly useful as a method.

Why Do Mnemonics Aid Our Memory?

- They aid encoding as the information is related to pre-existing knowledge.
- They aid retrieval in that information is stored with well known cues.
- They speed up encoding and retrieval since extensive practice is needed.

Other Strategies to Aid Recall

Mind maps

These involve representing information diagrammatically often linking to a central idea.

- Farrand, Hussain, and Hennessey (2002; see ASP4 p.84) When medical students used the mind map technique they recalled 10% more factual knowledge from a 600-word text than students who used ordinary study techniques.

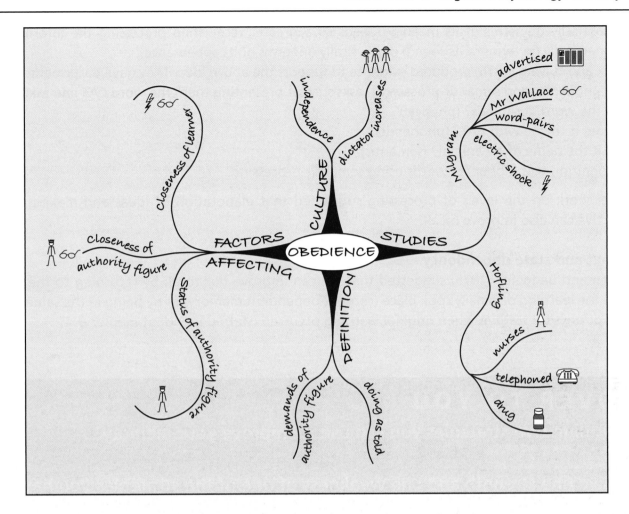

EVALUATION

STRENGTHS

- Students are actively involved when producing mind maps.
- The method emphasises links and connections between concepts, which aids organisation.
- The method reduces complex information to its essence by using key words.
- The method produces a striking visual image.

WEAKNESSES

- The method was not thought to be suitable for all people: students who favoured a "doing" approach to learning found mind maps useful, but students who preferred a "thinking" approach to learning did not.

Other Factors that Can Improve Our Memory

Deeper levels of processing information

- Craik and Lockhart (1972) Information that is processed at a deeper level is more likely to be recalled than information processed at a shallower level. Their research suggests that processing information semantically (in terms of its meaning) leads to a greater recall than processing the information phonemically (in terms of its sound) or physically (in terms of its appearance).

- Craik and Tulving (1975) produced evidence to support the above idea. They gave participants physical, phonemic, and semantic processing tasks such as presenting them the word CAT and asking:
  ○ Is the word in capitals? (physical)
  ○ Does it rhyme with BAT? (phonemic)
  ○ Is it the name of an animal? (semantic)
  Recognition was higher for words using semantic processing.

Further work on the levels of processing suggested that elaboration of ideas and making ideas distinctive can also improve recall.

Context and state dependency
Godden and Baddeley (1975) suggested that we can improve our recall by returning to the place where the learning originally took place (context-dependent memory) or by being in the same emotional or physical state as when original learning occurred (state-dependent memory).

OVER TO YOU
Outline two strategies you can use to improve your memory.
2 MARKS
Give one strength and one weakness of one of the strategies you have described above.
2 MARKS + 3 MARKS

RESEARCH METHODS AND MEMORY

Much of the research into memory follows the classical experimental method using independent samples design, such that one group might be asked to use one strategy to remember a list of words (e.g. making a story out of them) while the other group might be given the list of words without being given any strategy to use to recall them (Bower et al., 1969; see ASP4 p.75).

One major concern with using independent samples design is that one group may have a better memory than the other; so psychologists might try to match the groups on their intelligence, age, and memory.

Other research by Peterson and Peterson (1959; see ASP4 p.48) tested the same participants' recall of trigrams (e.g. BVM, CTG) under different conditions. They were asked to recall the trigrams after a delay of 3, 6, 9, 12, 15, or 18 seconds, having counted backwards in threes after the trigrams were presented. By using the same participants, Peterson and Peterson removed the problem of participant variability. However, the use of trigrams has been criticised as we don't memorise this sort of information in everyday life (an example of the problem of studies lacking mundane realism).

Loftus undertook numerous experiments into eyewitness testimony where she would manipulate the independent variable, which could be the word used to describe how two cars hit each other (e.g. "collided", "smashed") in order to see how it influenced the dependent variable, the speed at which participants said the cars were travelling. However, Loftus's research has been criticised for lacking mundane realism.

Some of her findings have been challenged by field studies using interviews with witnesses of gun crime. Yuille and Cutshall's research demonstrated that in real-life incidents, eyewitness testimony may remain robust over time.

Other psychologists have used other research methods to study our memory. Bartlett used serial reproduction of stories and then analysed the content of these stories to see how they changed over time to fit into the participants' schemas and culture.

One valuable research method used to explore memory involves case studies of patients who have experienced brain damage. Some well-known studies include HM and KF. This research has broadened our understanding of the distinction between short-term memory and long-term memory as well as demonstrating differences between procedural memory and declarative memory.

However, case studies involving brain damage clearly raise the problem of individual differences. Brain damage is rarely "precise in its nature", so it is often difficult to relate patients' difficulties to specific structures.

The Ethics of Research into Memory

At first sight you might think that research into memory rarely breaks ethical guidelines in that participants usually give consent when taking part in studies of memory. However, as with many studies in psychology, it could be argued that the consent given isn't always informed. If participants were not deceived they might respond differently. For example, if they were actually told that they were taking part in a study designed to see the effect of misleading questions on eyewitness testimony, they might give the answers they think the experimenter wants to hear (demand characteristics).

Research into memory does raise questions about how the results might lower participants' self esteem, especially if they think their scores are lower than other participants. For this reason it is important for participants' data to be kept confidential and for participants to be given the right to withdraw their data. In addition it is important for them to be reassured about their performance before they leave the study.

Research into eyewitness testimony has broadened psychology's role into ethical issues by raising our awareness about the unreliability of eyewitness testimony and stressing the need to exercise caution when someone is identified as the culprit. In this sense it may prevent innocent victims being sent to prison.

Research exploring ageing and memory raises ethical concerns about the publication of these research findings. Studies suggesting that people's memory is more easily distorted as they age could be seen as ageist in that it gives a somewhat negative image of ageing.

Research involving testing the eyewitness reports from young children may expose them to scenes that they could find frightening. Even if parental consent is given it still raises concerns as to whether the child really wants to take part in the study.

Finally memory research has involved the use of case studies and these should be considered from the point of view of the patient who may wish to remain anonymous, and who might feel distressed if they were to read about themselves.

SAMPLE QUESTIONS

? Outline three differences between short-term memory and long-term memory. **6 MARKS**

? Research into memory often involves the learning of word lists as part of the experiment. What methodological criticism can be made of such research? **4 MARKS**

? Outline and explain two ethical issues involved in undertaking research into the reliability of children as eyewitnesses. **2 MARKS + 2 MARKS**

3

DEVELOPMENTAL PSYCHOLOGY
Early Social Development

What's it about?

Developmental psychology (also known as lifespan psychology) is concerned with the changes that occur as humans move from infancy, to childhood, through adolescence, and on to adulthood. These changes include the development of thought processes, emotion, and social interactions. The changes that occur in the first 20 years or so usually result in behaviour being better organised, more complex, more competent, and more efficient.

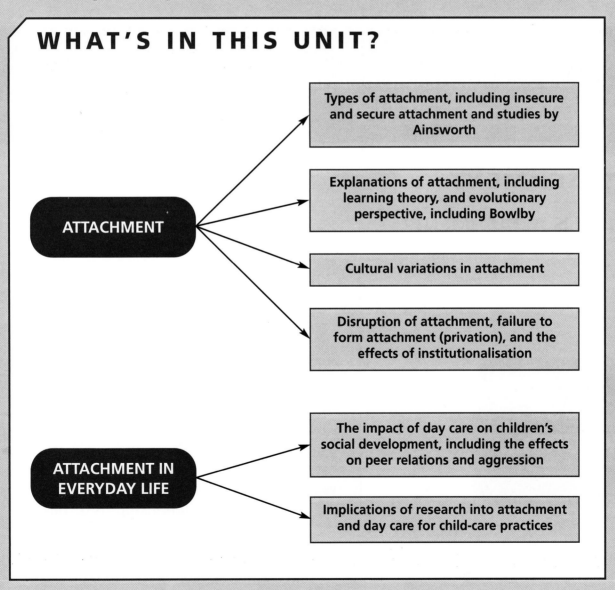

WHAT'S IN THIS UNIT?

ATTACHMENT

- Types of attachment, including insecure and secure attachment and studies by Ainsworth
- Explanations of attachment, including learning theory, and evolutionary perspective, including Bowlby
- Cultural variations in attachment
- Disruption of attachment, failure to form attachment (privation), and the effects of institutionalisation

ATTACHMENT IN EVERYDAY LIFE

- The impact of day care on children's social development, including the effects on peer relations and aggression
- Implications of research into attachment and day care for child-care practices

IMPORTANT TERMS AND CONCEPTS

The following terms are important for understanding this module so it will help you in the exam if you understand what they refer to. Make a list of definitions of the following terms, and if you get stuck, go to the glossary at the end of this book.

Anaclitic depression	Insecure attachment	Separation protest
Attachment	Maternal deprivation hypothesis	Social development
Bond disruption	Monotropy hypothesis	Strange Situation
Bonding	Privation	Stranger anxiety
Critical period	Secure attachment	Temperament hypothesis
Day care	Separation	
Deprivation	Separation anxiety	

OVER TO YOU

Outline two characteristics of an insecurely attached child.

2 MARKS + 2 MARKS

ATTACHMENT

WHAT IS ATTACHMENT?

ASK YOURSELF

When you were a small child, who did you go to if you were hurt?

Can you remember how you reacted to separation from your mother (or main caregiver) on your first day at nursery or school?

How does your relationship with your mother differ from that with your father? If you have brothers and sisters, how does your relationship with each differ? Think of all the reasons why each of these relationships is distinct.

Do you think your childhood relationships with your parents have affected your adult relationships? If so, how?

The study of attachment in infancy and childhood is of particular interest to developmental psychologists because of the effect it is believed to have on later relationships. But first, let's consider how we can define attachment.

Schaffer (1993) defines attachment as:

> *a close emotional relationship between two persons, characterised by mutual affection and a desire to maintain proximity [closeness].*

Attachments occur across the lifespan; they are a *reciprocal* emotional relationship in which both partners must be involved in order for a bond to be forged. Attachments depend on interaction rather than just two people being together.

Maccoby (1980; see ASP4 p.91) lists the characteristics of infant–caregiver attachment as:

- **Seeking proximity** Wanting to be near each other.
- **Separation anxiety (or distress)** A mutual feeling of upset if separated.
- **Pleasure when reunited.**
- **General orientation towards the primary caregiver** The infant is always aware of the attachment figure and seeks reassurance that they are there.

BENEFITS AND CONSEQUENCES OF ATTACHMENT

According to evolutionary theory, all behaviour has evolved so as to propagate genes. How does this operate with respect to attachment?

Immediate (Short-term) Benefits

The evolutionary approach says that behaviour is shaped by survival of genes. When animals help their offspring to survive, they propagate their own genes. The caregiver provides:

- Food and care (warmth etc.)
- Protection
- Education in survival.

Long-term Benefits

Attachment shapes various important long-term relationships:

- **Sexual relationships** These help to propagate genes. Attachment means that the father stays to help look after the young.
- **Attachment to infants** This ensures their survival.
- **Friendships and close-knit communities** Helps survival by mutual co-operation and reciprocal care (looking after each other).

Long-term Consequences

Bowlby (1969) hypothesised that the quality of early attachment relationships affects later ones. Evidence has been provided to support this theory:

- **Romantic relationships** Hazan and Shaver (1987; see ASP4 p.110) found that security or insecurity in early relationships was reflected in security or insecurity of adult romantic relationships.

- **Friendships** Grossman and Grossman (1991) found that quality of early attachment was reflected in quality of close friendships later in childhood.
- **Relationships with own children** Quinton et al. (1984) found that poor or inadequate attachment in early life due to institutionalisation led women in later life to have poor attachments with their own children.

When you evaluate the influence of early attachments, you have to ask the following question:

IS ATTACHMENT THE ONLY MAJOR INFLUENCE?

OTHER EXPERIENCES	INDIVIDUAL DIFFERENCES
There are several other factors that shape our later relationships, which include other childhood experiences, e.g. divorce of parents, or moving school frequently. The adult experiences within the relationships experienced will also have an effect.	Some psychologists believe that *temperament* rather than experience affects our most fundamental relationships. Thus, a "difficult" infant results in poor attachment, which results in poor later relationships, and vice versa. This shifts the emphasis from the caregiver to the infant.

STAGES OF ATTACHMENT

From their research, Schaffer and Emerson (1964; see ASP4 pp.92–93) list three stages in attachment:

Asocial stage (0–6 weeks)
Babies love human company but it makes no difference who the infant is with.
When smiling begins (4–6 weeks), it is directed at anyone.

Stage of indiscriminate attachments (6 weeks–7 months)
The child happily goes to anyone and enjoys attention from people in general.
However, he or she tends to smile more at familiar adults and children.

Stage of specific attachments (7–11 months)
The child typically, but by no means always, becomes attached to one individual, and this is the person who cares for them most of the time. The characteristics of this stage are:
- Distress if separated from that person, known as *separation protest*.
- Wariness and fear of people with whom they have had no contact at all, known as *stranger anxiety* or *stranger fear*.
- Formation of strong attachments to other familiar figures after about 10 months.
  Because of this, this stage is sometimes referred to as the stage of *multiple attachments*.

EVALUATION

STRENGTHS

- Observations in real life, and especially during Schaffer and Emerson's (1964) research, have demonstrated that these stages definitely exist. The attachment to a specific individual is demonstrated by *separation protest*. Up to this point, the infant has not shown distress at the absence of anyone.
- Stranger anxiety has also been demonstrated in several studies, including the Strange Situation study (see ASP4 p.97).
- Both of these responses indicate that the infant has formed *schemas* of familiar and unfamiliar people.

WEAKNESSES

- There is evidence that behaviour during the asocial stage may not be as asocial as suggested, as babies *do* respond differently to familiar and unfamiliar people.
- Carpenter (1975; see ASP4 p.93) showed that even infants a few days old respond differently to their mother than to others. For example, they spend more time looking at her, so they must recognise her face and voice, and they can become quite distressed if the face and voice do not match (if the mother mouths words spoken by someone else).
- Similarly, Bushnell et al. (1989; see ASP4 p.94) found that babies only 2 days old show a preference for the face of their mother over a stranger's face.

TYPES OF ATTACHMENT

There are considerable differences in the type of attachment that infants make. The main difference is between *secure* and *insecure* attachment.

- **Securely attached infants** A strong positive bond with the caregiver—although the infant is upset when briefly separated from their attachment figure, they are easily comforted when she/he returns.
- **Insecurely attached infants** A weak emotional bond with the caregiver—the infant feels anxious about the relationship.

Is Attachment Type Consistent Throughout Childhood?

This is an important question because, if attachment type changes over the years, then it is unlikely to be a major influence on later life. If, on the other hand, it is consistent, then it could significantly affect important influences, such as later relationships.

The answer is that in most cases the attachment type is consistent as demonstrated by much research including Wartner et al. (1994; see ASP4 p.96), who found that in 82% of children the attachment type was the same at 12 months as at 6 years. Nevertheless, Weinfield et al. (2004; see ASP4 p.96) found that, among high-risk children (born into poverty) there was little or no consistency in attachment type.

Advantages of Secure Attachment

Studies strongly suggest considerable advantages of secure attachment.

- Wartner et al. (1994) Securely attached preschool children are more competent in play, better at resolving conflicts, and had fewer behavioural problems.
- Szewczyk-Sokolowski et al. (2005; see ASP4 p.96) Securely attached preschool children got on better with their peers.
- Pauli-Pott et al. (2007; see ASP4 p.96) Securely attached children had fewer behaviour problems.
- Belsky and Fearon (2002; see ASP4 p.96) In a thorough study involving several thousand children, it was found that at age 3 securely attached children had greater social competence and school readiness, had better spoken language and understanding of language than insecurely attached ones, and, again, had fewer behavioural problems.

Note that these studies show a positive *correlation* between secure attachment and various positive behavioural characteristics. However, as with all correlations, we cannot infer cause and effect. So these findings do not demonstrate that secure attachment necessarily *causes* these behavioural characteristics. It is quite possible that children with an easy-going temperament are less likely to show behavioural problems, are socially competent, and get on better with other children. This type of temperament may also make secure attachment more likely to occur.

Effects of Attachment in Non-human Animals Including Monkeys

Research indicates that attachment has important long-term consequences in many species. One classic study demonstrates this.

Harlow (1959) kept newborn monkeys in total isolation and put them in a cage with a wire surrogate "mother" and a cloth one. He found that, regardless of which surrogate mother "fed" them (had the bottle attached to her), they preferred the cloth mother. They would cling to her, especially when frightened, and only go to the wire mother for food. The long-term consequences for these poor monkeys were dire. After about 6 months in isolation, they showed signs of serious disturbance such as:

- Biting themselves
- Curling up in a ball and rocking back and forth
- Making facial grimaces.

Adult female monkeys raised in this way were extremely poor mothers who neglected or abused their babies.

In later studies it was demonstrated that infants reared together without adults eventually suffered no ill-effects. This indicates that secure attachment is important but not the attachment figure; infant-infant bonding can be as effective as adult-infant bonding, at least in monkeys.

ATTACHMENT IN HUMANS

Ainsworth's "Strange Situation" Studies

The different types of attachment that infants have with their caregivers have been investigated by Ainsworth and her colleagues (Ainsworth & Bell, 1970; see ASP4 pp.97–98) using the Strange Situation set-up. The Strange Situation set-up uses a *controlled observation study* to see how infants, normally aged between 12 and 18 months, respond to various situations in unfamiliar circumstances.

The exact procedure is shown in the table:

Episode	What happens
1 (30 secs)	Researcher brings caregiver and child into room and leaves them alone together.
2 (3 mins)	The mother (or caregiver) sits quietly in a chair. She does not interact with the infant unless the child tries to attract her attention.
3 (3 mins)	A stranger enters, talks to the mother, and then approaches the baby with a toy. The mother leaves quietly without drawing attention to herself.
4 (3 mins)	Stranger attempts to interact with infant. If the infant seems bothered, the stranger tries to interact by talking to him or her and playing. If the child shows distress, the stranger attempts to comfort him or her.
5 (3 mins)	The stranger leaves and the mother returns and greets the infant. The mother tries to get the infant to play, then leaves, waving and saying "bye-bye".
6 (3 mins)	The baby is left alone.
7 (3 mins)	The stranger enters and interacts with the infant, offering comfort if the child is upset or a toy if the child is passive.
8 (3 mins)	The mother returns, greets the infant, and picks him or her up. The stranger leaves quietly.

Measurements made in the Strange Situation are as follows:

- **Separation protest** The response the child makes when the mother departs.
- **Stranger anxiety** The reaction of the child to the stranger.
- **Reunion behaviour** How the child behaves when the mother returns.

Ainsworth observed three different types of attachment behaviour. Later, Main and Solomon (1986; see ASP4 p.99) argued that a small number of infants display a fourth type of behaviour, which they called disorganised and disoriented attachment (Type D). Most infants seem to fit into one of these attachment types.

Secure attachment (Type B)

Infants explore freely when their mother is present and use her as a secure base when the stranger appears. They show distress when she leaves and greet her warmly when she returns. They are readily comforted by her, soon returning to a state of contentment, and show a clear preference for her over the stranger. This is the optimum form of attachment, and is present in about 70% of infants.

Anxious/resistant attachment (Type C)

Children do not explore the new toys with such confidence. Compared to secure infants, they remain closer to their mother, showing signs of insecurity even in her presence. They become very distressed when she leaves. When she returns they may cling to her but show ambivalent reactions, such as hitting her while still clinging. They are clearly angry and anxious. She does not provide a secure base.

Anxious/avoidant attachment (Type A)

Children show little or no concern when the mother leaves, and show little pleasure when she returns. There is no indication of stranger anxiety and the children show little preference for the mother over the stranger, often avoiding both.

Disorganised/disoriented attachment (Type D)

There are a few infants who lack any coherent strategy for coping with the Strange Situation and their behaviour is a confusing mixture of approach and avoidance. The children show no set pattern of reaction when the mother departs or when she returns (hence "disorganised"). This kind of behaviour is associated with abused children or those whose mothers are chronically depressed.

In the original research on infants in the US, the results showed:

- 70% of infants were securely attached
- 10% were resistant
- 20% were avoidant.

EVALUATION

STRENGTHS

- Provides a good measure of attachment that differentiates between different attachment types.
- Has been used successfully to explore cross-cultural variations in attachment.
- The research that comes from these studies clearly indicates that secure attachment is the preferred type in terms of healthy social and emotional development.

WEAKNESSES

- It does not detect a small number of cases of disorganised attachment as identified by Main and Solomon (1986).
- It may be culturally biased.
- It lacks ecological validity: it does not necessarily reflect the usual everyday behaviour between infants and caregivers.
- The attachment types may be crude. There is a lot of variation between children in the same category (e.g. anxious/avoidant attached) and differences in the degree to which they show that attachment behaviour (high/low).

EXPLANATIONS FOR INDIVIDUAL DIFFERENCES IN ATTACHMENT

Why are some children securely attached whilst others are insecurely attached? There are two main hypotheses:

Caregiver Sensitivity Hypothesis

The behaviour of the main caregiver determines whether children are securely or insecurely attached. Ainsworth advanced this hypothesis on the basis of her Strange Situation Studies. She and her colleagues found that the behaviour of the caregiver correlated with the type of security/insecurity of the child in the following ways:

- **Securely attached infants** Mothers showed *sensitive responsiveness*. This meant that they were sensitive to the infant's needs, effective at soothing them, gave them lots of cuddles, and spent time talking to them face-to-face.
- **Resistant infants** The caregivers were interested in the infant but often did not understand what the child required. They could not be relied on by the child to meet their needs.
- **Avoidant infants** The caregivers were uninterested in their infants and tended to be rigid in their behaviour, not varying it according to the child's needs. However, some were very different, interacting with their infants constantly and inappropriately even when they did not want it. Neither set of caregivers was responsive to the child's needs.

Research

- De Wolff and van IJzendoorn (1997; see ASP4 p.101) carried out a meta-analysis across many cultures and found a positive (but fairly weak) correlation between maternal sensitivity and security of infant attachment. They found that as well as sensitivity, the amount of interaction between caregiver and baby and the expression of positive emotion by the caregiver were important.
- Bakermans-Kranenburg et al. (2003; see ASP4 p.101) conducted a meta-analysis of research designed to increase caregiver sensitivity and found that these programmes consistently increased the security of the infant.
- De Wolff and van IJzendoorn (1997; see ASP4 p.101) looked at paternal sensitivity and found a positive correlation (but weaker than between main caregiver and infant) between paternal sensitivity and father–infant attachment.

- Baer and Martinez (2006) conducted a meta-analysis which suggested that insecure children are more likely to be maltreated than are securely attached children. This does not provide direct support for the caregiver-sensitivity hypothesis but does indicate that the behaviour of the caregiver towards the infant is important in influencing the security of their attachment.

The Temperament Hypothesis (Kagan, 1984)

It is the innate personality of a child that makes him or her attach securely or insecurely. Some babies are irritable, or simply quiet and passive, and it is difficult to form attachments with them. Others are alert, cheerful, and smile a great deal, making it easier to form attachments with these children. The implication is that genetic factors which influence temperament therefore influence attachment.

Research
In favour:

- Belsky and Rovine (1987; see ASP4 p.101) Newborns who show signs of tremors and shaking (signs of behavioural instability) were less likely than other infants to become securely attached.
- O'Connor and Croft (2001; see ASP4 p.102) Identical twins had slightly higher concordance rate than fraternal twins in attachment style, suggesting that genetic factors may influence attachment styles to at least a small degree.

Against:

- Bokhorst et al. (2003; see ASP4 p.102) Also comparing non-identical and identical twins, they found the role of genetics on attachment style negligible. They also believe that the concordance rate on attachment was not influenced by temperament.
- De Wolff and van IJzendoorn (1997) found very little relationship between attachment style with the mother and with the father, indicating that the temperament of the infant plays little part in attachment and that it is more dependent on the parents' characteristics.

Bringing Both Hypotheses Together

It is probable that both the sensitivity of the caregiver and the temperament of the infant influence attachment styles and that it is the *interaction* of the two that is crucial. A baby with an innately anxious disposition may be much more upset by a caregiver who is unpredictable in his or her attentions than an innately more confident child may be.

EXPLANATIONS OF ATTACHMENT

Learning Theory

- All behaviour is learnt, either by association (classical conditioning, CC) or consequences (operant conditioning, OC).
- By CC, the pleasure of feeding becomes associated with the person who feeds the infant and this person becomes a source of pleasure even when there is no feeding.
- Because the mother (or caregiver) is associated with positive reinforcement she becomes a *secondary reinforcer*.
- The attachment is not just one way; mothers are reinforced positively by smiles and general development, and reinforced negatively by cessation of crying.

EVALUATION

- This approach emphasises the role of "cupboard love", yet Harlow (1959) demonstrated that "cupboard love" is not a valid explanation for infant attachment behaviour—babies do not always attach to the person who feeds them. The attachment need is separate from the need for food.
- Schaffer and Emerson's (1964; see ASP4 p.92) study also showed that 39% of babies attached to someone other than the person who met their everyday needs.
- If this theory were correct, you would expect the attachment process to be gradual and steady, whereas the stage of specific attachment and the accompanying separation protest occur suddenly. This suggests a *maturational process* rather than a learning process.
- Later learning theorists emphasised the role of attention and affection rather than food as a positive reinforcer. There is more support for this but it does not get over the previous criticism of suddenness.
- It is a very *reductionist* approach in that it reduces the causes of complex human behaviour to such simple concepts as stimulus, response, and reinforcement.

Social Learning Theory

- Babies learn by imitation as well as by direct reinforcement.
- They learn by vicarious reinforcement, which is the effect on behaviour of seeing others reinforced.
- Hay and Vespo (1988; see ASP4 p.104) believe that parents deliberately teach their children to love them, e.g. by modelling affection, by direct instruction, by social facilitation (using others to model positive relationships).

EVALUATION

- Durkin (1995; see ASP4 p.105) pointed out that it is doubtful that strong emotions can be entirely learned.
- There is still the problem of timing (suddenness).
- However, it provides a much better model of parent–child interaction.

Evolutionary Perspective

The ethological approach: Imprinting

Ethologists explain behaviour in terms of its biological and evolutionary basis. They believe that attachment is related to a behaviour called *imprinting,* which is shown by ground-nesting birds who follow the first moving object they see (usually the mother).

The process of imprinting has certain important characteristics:

- It happens automatically without any obvious teaching or learning.

- It occurs only within a narrow time limit (usually within 36 hours of hatching) called the critical period.
- It is irreversible: once the bird follows an object, it will remain attached to it.

The ethological view is that human infants and their caregivers have evolved in ways that predispose them to feel positively towards each other and to form close attachments, thus enhancing survival chances.

EVALUATION

- Humans are more complex that young birds and you cannot necessarily generalise from one to the other. In general, non-human behaviour is far more likely to be innate and less influenced by learning (including culture) than is human behaviour, which is liable to be much more flexible.
- The original characteristics of imprinting have been somewhat modified. The concept of a critical period was shown to be too rigid in that, although imprinting is more likely to occur during a certain limited period, it does still happen outside this time. For this reason, the term *sensitive period* is now more popular.
- It has also been demonstrated that the effects of imprinting are not necessarily irreversible. Guiton (1966) found that, in certain circumstances, chickens imprinted on inanimate objects can engage in sexual behaviour with their own species.

Bowlby's theory
Bowlby was greatly influenced by evolutionary theory and believed that attachment behaviour was an innate, adaptive response that serves to promote survival. Here are his main points:

- Something akin to imprinting occurs in human infants and is a tendency to attach towards one human being.
- Babies are born with certain *social releasers*—actions that release a social response in adults, such as smiling and crying.
- Attachment behaviour is *reciprocal* (two-way), and mothers or carers are preprogrammed to respond to the infant's needs.
- Attachment does not need to occur until about 7 months as it is synchronised with crawling. Before that, the baby cannot move far from the carer. It is as if a physical "stayclose" mechanism is replaced by a psychological one.
- The bond made with the main carer is a very special one that is different from all other attachments. The tendency to bond with one main person is called *monotropy*.
- The first attachment serves as an *internal working model* that is the basis of all expectations and rules regarding relationships in later life.
- In the short term, babies use the attachment figure as a *secure base* from which they can explore. If the attachment is poor, exploration will not occur as the child will not move far from this base.
- The consequences of poor attachment are *dire* and possibly *irreversible*.

EVALUATION

STRENGTHS

- Bowlby's theory has formed the basis of a large body of research into the care of children. His research highlighted a crucial influence in healthy infant development.
- His theory was the first comprehensive theory of attachment and served as the basis of later theories.
- It demonstrated why attachment is so important.
- The theory has certain important practical applications.

WEAKNESSES

- Schaffer and Emerson's (1964; see ASP4 p.92) study indicates that attachment may not be monotropic. Most babies attach to more than one person and some psychologists believe that although these attachments may be different, no single one is more important than another.
- He may have over-emphasised the need for a single attachment. Thomas (1998) argues that a network of attachments provides a psychologically healthier start in life. Nevertheless, evidence from cross-cultural research indicates that infants do have a hierarchy of preferences in attachment and one particular person is usually preferred over others.
- Correlations between the quality of a child's various relationships are actually quite low (Main & Weston, 1981; see ASP4 p.111), so attachment is not necessarily the template for future relationships, and where a positive correlation exists it may be simply because some infants are better than others at forming relationships.
- The evolutionary approach appears on the surface to be sensible and valid, but the arguments are post hoc (after the event). They are based on observing behaviour and then proposing a survival function to account for it. The problem with this is that any behaviour can be explained in this way (could you think of an advantage of not being attached to one person, but being quite content to be with anyone?). The evolutionary explanation is plausible but there's no proof that it's correct.

CHARACTERISTICS OF ATTACHMENT

Is There a Critical Period for Bonding?

The biologically programmed, innate behaviour of imprinted geese occurs only during a *critical period* soon after birth. Is human attachment the same? Generally, researchers refer to a *sensitive period*, when attachment occurs most easily, but it is not the *only* time it can occur.

- Bowlby (1969; see ASP4 p.107) A sensitive period that ends between 1 and 3 years of age, during which infants orient towards, and attach to, a single individual.
- Klaus and Kennell (1976; see ASP4 pp.108–109) The *skin-to-skin hypothesis* in which there is a sensitive period immediately after birth when bonding occurs through skin contact.
- However, cross-cultural research suggests that the amount of early physical contact makes little difference to bonding (Lozoff, 1983; see ASP4 p.109).

- De Chateau and Wiberg (1977; see ASP4 p.109) Mothers who immediately suckled and had skin-to-skin contact with their babies after birth engaged in more kissing and embracing, and breast-fed on average for 2½ months longer than "traditional contact" mothers.

So, bonding may start with early skin-to-skin contact but attachments change over time. It is unlikely that any experiences immediately after birth can have irreversible effects in humans.

Is There One Attachment or Many?

The question arises as to whether infants become attached to one person or many people.

- Bowlby (1953; see ASP4 p.110) Infants have one main attachment, referred to as the *monotropy hypothesis*, and multiple attachments occur in a hierarchy.
- Schaffer and Emerson (1964; see ASP4 p.92) The first main attachment occurs around 6–7 months, followed by *multiple attachments*.
- Tronick et al. (1992; see ASP4 p.111) Children of the African Efe tribe showed primary attachment by 6 months of age, even though they were cared for by many people.

However, different attachments may serve different purposes:

- Thomas (1998; see ASP4 p.111) Multiple attachments are desirable as each relationship satisfies different needs.

Quality or Quantity of Attachments?

There is also the question of whether the strength of the attachment is due to how long someone spends with the infant, or how caring and sensitive they are.

- Fox (1977) Attachment in a kibbutz situation was usually still to the mother. Also, it has also been found that children in day care attach well to their mothers.
- Harlow (1959; see ASP4 pp.103–104) In this study, the isolated monkeys "attached" to cloth mothers, but they became maladjusted as the cloth mothers were unresponsive. Schaffer and Emerson (1964; see ASP4 p.92) showed that babies attach to those most sensitive to their needs.

It seems that quality of care is far more important than the amount of time spent with the infant. Babies attach to those who are responsive to their needs, and who offer them love and attention.

Do Early Attachments Affect Later Relationships?

Hazan and Shaver (1987; see ASP4 pp.110–111) conducted research that suggested the following relationship between early attachment and later romantic relationships:

Secure attachment	Happy, friendly, trusting
Ambivalent	Jealous, anxious, obsessive, great need for partner to demonstrate love, fear of abandonment
Avoidant attachment	Distant, feared intimacy, did not recognise need to be loved in order to be happy, emotional highs and lows

Problems with the research:

- Information of infant attachment may not be accurate.
- Self reports were used to assess adult relationships and these may not be honest.
- It is possible that attachment styles change as a result of experiences of romantic relationships. So adult relationships may affect attachment as well as vice versa.

CROSS-CULTURAL VARIATIONS IN ATTACHMENT

When considering attachment types, it is important to remember that findings from studies conducted in one country might not generalise to other cultures. There have been a number of studies that have looked at how children outside the USA have reacted to the Strange Situation and a summary was produced by Sagi et al. (1991; see ASP4 pp.114–115).

- **American children** Findings were similar to those reported by Ainsworth and Bell, in that 71% were secure, 12% were anxious/resistant, and 17% were anxious/avoidant.
- **Israeli children** The Israeli children were raised in a kibbutz and therefore saw few strangers but were used to separation from the mother. Secure attachment was shown by 62%, with 33% being anxious/resistant, and only 5% being anxious/avoidant. The fact that they were not used to the presence of strangers may account for the high percentage of resistant attachment, where their anxiety was shown not when the mother left but when the stranger entered.
- **Japanese children** The Japanese children showed similar attachment styles to the Israeli children, but probably for very different reasons. Secure attachment was shown by 68%, 32% were anxious/resistant, and there were no anxious/avoidant children. Japanese children are rarely left by their mothers, so the Strange Situation may have been particularly stressful when the mother leaves. Such children are likely to show avoidant behaviour. The Japanese children's anxious/resistant attachment behaviour was more likely to be due to the mother leaving rather than a stranger arriving.
- **German children** The German children showed a different pattern of attachment from the other children. Only 40% were securely attached, but 49% were anxious/avoidant, and the remaining 11% were anxious/resistant. German children are encouraged to be independent and not clingy, and the relatively high percentage of avoidant infants may reflect the ethos of encouraging independence (Grossman et al., 1985; see ASP4 p.115).

In sum:

- Secure attachment was the most common in all cultures except Germany.
- In Western cultures the dominant insecure attachment is avoidant.
- In non-Western cultures, with the exception of China, the dominant insecure attachment is resistant. In China, both forms of insecure attachment are equally common.

Conclusions from Cross-cultural Variations

- **The universal nature of attachment** The fact that the same attachment styles occur in all cultures indicates that attachment is universal and probably innate.
- **Child-rearing practices are influential** Differences in the rates of attachment styles between cultures indicates that attachment styles may be due to child-rearing practices.

- **Sub-cultures may be influential** Variations *within* cultures were found to be 1½ times greater than variations *between* cultures. In every culture there are liable to be several sub-cultures, so we must be cautious of generalising, and be aware that cross-cultural comparisons may lack validity.
- **Sample sizes make it difficult to generalise** Although there were many children studied overall, some sample sizes were too small to make safe generalisations. For example, only 36 Chinese children were used—not a representative sample from a population of hundreds of millions!
- **The methodology** The Strange Situation set-up assumes that reactions to separation indicate secure or insecure attachment, which is an American interpretation. The Israeli and Japanese children show that this is not the case, as behaviour does not always have the same meaning in all cultures, and is therefore an invalid measuring tool. The use of a technique developed in one culture to study another is known as an *imposed etic*, and it makes the methodology inherently flawed.

DISRUPTION OF ATTACHMENT, FAILURE TO FORM ATTACHMENT (PRIVATION), AND EFFECTS OF INSTITUTIONALISATION

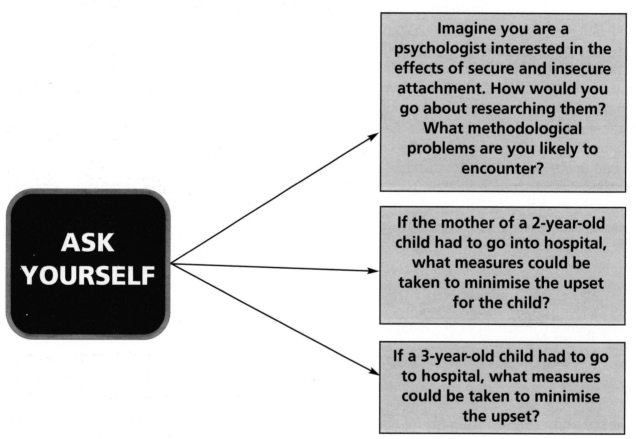

ASK YOURSELF

Imagine you are a psychologist interested in the effects of secure and insecure attachment. How would you go about researching them? What methodological problems are you likely to encounter?

If the mother of a 2-year-old child had to go into hospital, what measures could be taken to minimise the upset for the child?

If a 3-year-old child had to go to hospital, what measures could be taken to minimise the upset?

Some Important Concepts

- **Separation** Involves distress when separated for a relatively short time from a person to whom there is an attachment bond.
- **Deprivation** Occurs when a bond has been formed and is then broken by separations that are frequent and long lasting or even permanent. Separation can be seen as a mild form of deprivation.
- **Privation** Occurs when a child has no opportunity to form an attachment bond.

Short-term Effects of Separation

Even short-term separation can have seriously upsetting effects on a child. Robertson and Bowlby (1952; see ASP4 p.116) documented the protest-despair-detachment (PDD) model. This model, also known as the syndrome of distress, consists of three stages that a child goes through when separated from its main caregiver:

Protest
The child attempts to follow the mother, cries and screams, and does everything he or she can to recover her. This lasts for a long time after she has gone.

↓

Despair
The child sobs in a desperate, helpless way. He or she shows a distinct loss of hope.

↓

Detachment
The child appears calm and settled. However, the calm masks underlying distress. There is emotional flatness, a lack of response, and a lack of curiosity (which could have effects on cognitive development). There may be occasional spats of temper, revealing the underlying desperation.

Evaluation and Application of the PDD Model

Are all children equally affected?

Barratt (1997; see ASP4 p.117) argued that there is no strong evidence for the PDD model and that it does not take into account individual differences in coping. Insecurely attached children may be far more affected than securely attached children, or may reach the protest and despair stages almost immediately and become quite disoriented. Barratt argued that, in general, children are more able to cope with separation than the model implies. Nevertheless, the research by Robertson and Robertson (1971; see ASP4 pp.116–117) does indicate considerable harm is done by separations of several days as demonstrated by the case studies of John and Laura.

Is separation inevitably harmful?

In the 1950s it was not uncommon for children to go into hospital and be visited only briefly, or for children to be placed in a residential nursery whilst their mother went into hospital (e.g. to have another baby). Robertson and Robertson made amateur films to highlight the children's distress and indicate the damage done to attachment. They also showed how it could be avoided.

Minimising the effects of separation

Robertson and Robertson were instrumental in putting psychological theory into practice and took separated children into their home to try to establish the best way to minimise the effects of separation. They recommended:

- Children should be introduced to their new home before the separation in order to be familiar with their new surroundings.
- Children need to be given a daily routine as close as possible to their familiar one.
- The carer should talk to them about their mother.

The separated children the Robertsons cared for fared much better than children who were not given such care.

Long-term Effects of Separation

Prior to the development of Bowlby's (1969) theory of attachment he proposed a version called the *maternal deprivation hypothesis* (1953; see ASP4 p.117), which focused more on the effects of deprivation rather than the benefits of attachment. The hypothesis states that children have an innate need for a warm, continuous relationship. If the main attachment bond is broken in the early years then it will have an adverse effect on the child's emotional, social, and cognitive development. If many separations are experienced, behaviour patterns such as detachment or despair may persist into future life and develop into psychopathy or depression. Research showed that maternal deprivation of this kind can have the following effects:

- Emotionally disturbed behaviour such as bed-wetting (*enuresis*).
- Physical underdevelopment in children; a condition known as *deprivation dwarfism*.
- Depression.
- Intellectual retardation.
- An inability to make relationships; a condition known as *affectionless psychopathy*.

Evidence Supporting the Maternal Deprivation Hypothesis

Institutionalisation

Many of the important studies on institutionalisation and its effect on attachment behaviour were conducted during the 1940s, around the time of the Second World War. All the research pointed to the fact that early separations were associated with severe consequences:

- Bowlby (1944; see ASP4 p.117) Maternal deprivation can lead to a lack of emotional development and *affectionless psychopathy*.
- Spitz (1945; see ASP4 p.118) Some deprived orphanage children developed *anaclitic depression*.
- Spitz and Wolf (1946; see ASP4 p.118) Many hospitalised children were seriously depressed; if they were in hospital for more than 3 months, complete recovery was unlikely.
- Goldfarb (1947; see ASP4 p.118) Orphanage children fostered after 3 years were lower in IQ, less socially mature, poorer at language skills, more likely to be aggressive, and had poorer relationships than children who had been fostered before 3 months.
- Rutter (1998; see ASP4 pp.117–118) Romanian orphans who were adopted at age 2 showed marked improvement by age 4, but those adopted later in life fared less well.

All these effects could have been caused by poor physical care. However, Widdowson (1951) demonstrated the importance of emotional care. Children in an orphanage run by a harsh, uncaring supervisor suffered *deprivation dwarfism* until a more humane person took over, despite there being no change in diet.

Hospitalisation

Children experience separation as a result of being hospitalised, and when children are hospitalised for prolonged periods it may lead to the breaking of attachment bonds and later maladjustment.

• Douglas (1975) An analysis of data from the National Survey of Health and Development on 5000 children born in 1946 showed that the longer they had spent in hospital, the more intellectual and behaviour problems they had.
• Quinton and Rutter (1976) Repeated hospitalisation was associated with later problems, but single admissions rarely had later difficulties.

However, Clarke and Clarke (1976) argue that it may not be separation that is the problem but another factor such as general home problems. Perhaps children from disadvantaged homes are more likely to need hospitalisation because of poor living conditions. Also, the experience of being in hospital is likely to create anxiety and the lack of caregiving at such a critical time may lead to long-term problems. However, Bowlby et al. (1956) studied children hospitalised due to TB who were visited by their families every week so bond disruption was minimised and found few differences between them and their school peers in terms of intellectual and emotional development. It would therefore appear that hospitalisation does not inevitably have harmful effects, so long as bond disruption is minimised.

EVALUATION

STRENGTHS

• The studies of hospitalisation and institutionalisation previously mentioned are generally in support of the maternal deprivation hypothesis.
• Likewise, Harlow's (1959; see ASP4 pp.103–104) study of infant monkeys supports this theory.

WEAKNESSES

• The hypothesis is similar to the concept of imprinting and is therefore subject to the same criticisms.
• There may be a sensitive period for attachment formation but it is unlikely that there is a critical period. Clarke and Clarke (1976) propose that early childhood is no more important than middle or later childhood. However, the work of Goldfarb (1947) and Rutter (1998) indicates that early life *is* more crucial than later childhood.
• The damage caused by deprivation may be reversible; with very good care, children can recover.

Note: The work of Rutter and his colleagues (presented in more detail later) is essential to any evaluation of the maternal deprivation hypothesis. His work recognised the importance of the hypothesis, but extended and modified it. Rutter (1972; see ASP4 p.118) pointed out that Bowlby had assumed that all experiences of deprivation were the same, whereas in fact there are differences, and he went on to introduce the distinction between *deprivation* and *privation*.

Applications of the Maternal Deprivation Hypothesis

Bowlby's maternal deprivation hypothesis has led to some important real-life applications:

- **A positive change in attitudes towards infant care** Bowlby's ideas were quite revolutionary. At the time he started publishing his work, physical care was considered to be the only important factor in rearing children. Back in 1928, J. B. Watson's recommendation to parents was that affection should be avoided. Bowlby's work changed attitudes for the better, and child care manuals started to strongly recommend plenty of love.
- **Humanising child-care practices** The theory led child-care practices to be reviewed and improved. The care in orphanages was improved to take account of emotional needs. Wherever possible, fostered children were kept in one foster home rather than being moved around. In maternity units mothers spent more time with their babies. Finally, provision was made for parents to stay in hospital with young children and much longer visiting time was allowed.
- **Controversial applications** The most controversial interpretation of Bowlby's work was that mothers were encouraged to stay at home with children under 5 years of age. In fact this was not a direct recommendation from Bowlby, but an interpretation made by the government who may have wished to discourage women from working outside the home once the war was over and jobs were required for returning soldiers. Nevertheless, even if the advice did not come direct from Bowlby, he thought that very young children were better off spending most of their time with their mother or primary caregiver.

Distinguishing Between Deprivation, Privation, and Institutionalisation

The work of Rutter
Rutter pointed to key differences in separation experiences, and distinguished between:

- **Deprivation** A bond is formed and broken, usually through separation.
- **Privation** No bond is ever formed, as with many institutionalised children.

He also pointed out that the circumstances of deprivation can be very different and must be taken into account. We need to consider:

- How many changes of caregiver are experienced
- If the child was in an institution, the quality of it
- The general quality of any substitute care
- The length of separation.

Long-term Effects of Privation

Studies of privation and key findings include:

- Hodges and Tizard (1989; see ASP4 pp.119–120)
  - If children can form attachments then the experience of institutionalisation can be ameliorated (not be so bad).
  - The effects of privation can be very long lasting.

- Koluchová (1976; see ASP4 p.120) Twins who suffered very severe deprivation for the first 7 years of their life showed that with good quality care:
  - Intelligence can be normal
  - Excellent relationships can be established.
- Curtiss (1989; see ASP4 pp.120–121) Genie, who was kept in one room for 13½ years:
  - Initially learnt around 200 words but could not put them together in meaningful sentences
  - Progressed quite well with good quality care but regressed when subsequently given poor quality care again.
- Soutter (1995; see ASP4 p.121) Tom, who was kept in one bare room for first 10 years of life and then received 8 years of treatment:
  - Studied at university
  - Made meaningful friendships
  - Showed behaviour appropriate to his age.
- Freud and Dann (1951; see ASP4 pp.121–122) Six war orphans who suffered extreme deprivation and traumatic experiences for first 3–4 years of life:
  - Bonded with each other
  - Eventually became attached to adult carers
  - Developed rapidly in terms of social skills and use of language
  - However, one received psychiatric help as an adult; another felt lonely and isolated.

EVALUATION

- **Reversibility of effects** A lot of evidence indicates that the effects of privation can, under certain circumstances, be reversed. It requires good quality care and, probably, fairly early intervention.
- **Reactive attachment disorder** If children suffer from this, the outcome is poor.
- **Many studies need to be considered** Studies of deprivation and privation are case studies, involving very few individuals, so it is difficult to generalise from them.
- **Recovery requires good quality care** The work of Hodges and Tizard indicates that recovery requires loving relationships.

OVER TO YOU

Why do the studies by Tizard and colleagues (see ASP4 p.119) provide a better body of evidence than case studies by which to judge the effects of deprivation and privation?

4 MARKS

Long-term Effects of Institutionalisation

- Rutter et al. (1998; see ASP4 p.123) With 111 Romanian orphans brought up in extremely deprived orphanages and adopted before the age of 2:

- ○ There was reasonable recovery in all following adoptions
- ○ The later the adoption, the slower the improvements in educational and emotional development.
- O'Connor et al. (2000; see ASP4 p.124) Romanian orphans had been exposed to severe neglect and deprivation, then adopted. Early adoptees (6 months–2 years) were compared with late-placed adoptees:
  - ○ Both showed good recovery
  - ○ Early adoptees had fewer difficulties in achieving good cognitive and social development.
- Gunnar and van Dulmen (2007; see ASP4 p.124) Institutionalised children from various countries who had then been adopted:
  - ○ Had higher rates of attention and social problems than children brought up in families
  - ○ Had more behavioural problems if they had been adopted after 2 years of age than those adopted earlier.
- Smyke et al. (2007; see ASP4 pp.124–125) Children being raised in Romanian orphanages were compared to those raised at home. Institutional children:
  - ○ Showed severe delays in cognitive development
  - ○ Had poorer physical growth
  - ○ Had inferior social competence.
    The researchers concluded that the crucial factor in determining cognitive and social competence was the quality of caregiving they received.
- Sigal et al. (2003; see ASP4 p.125) Middle-aged adults who had been placed in institutions very early in life:
  - ○ Were far less likely to have married than a random control group
  - ○ Had fewer social contacts
  - ○ Suffered high rates of depression
  - ○ Had higher rates of physical illness.

ATTACHMENT IN EVERYDAY LIFE

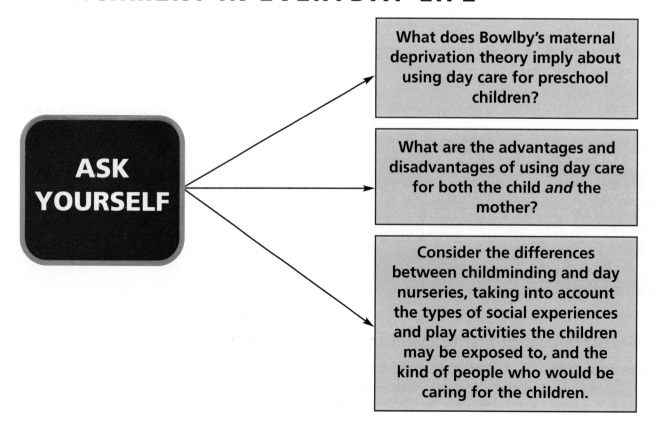

ASK YOURSELF

What does Bowlby's maternal deprivation theory imply about using day care for preschool children?

What are the advantages and disadvantages of using day care for both the child *and* the mother?

Consider the differences between childminding and day nurseries, taking into account the types of social experiences and play activities the children may be exposed to, and the kind of people who would be caring for the children.

IS DAY CARE HARMFUL OR BENEFICIAL?

Is it harmful?	Is it beneficial?
• In 1951 the World Health Organization stated that day nurseries would cause "permanent damage to the emotional health of a future generation". • They used Bowlby's research and theory of maternal deprivation to support this view.	• In America in the 1960s day care schemes were instigated to improve the preschool opportunities for disadvantaged children so they could start school on a par with their peers. • The best known was a large-scale programme called Headstart.

Kagan et al. (1980; see ASP4 p.127) suggested a double standard was being applied: day care is good for lower-class children (it improves cognitive abilities), but not for middle-class children (due to maternal deprivation).

TYPES OF DAY CARE

The main forms of day care are for preschool children in either day nurseries or with childminders.

Childminding

This is a form of day care that some feel is preferable to day nurseries because it is apparently more similar to home care. However, studies have proved that this is not always the case:

• Mayall and Petrie (1983; see ASP4 p.128) Care by London childminders was often not very good. Many children were exposed to an unstimulating environment and failed to thrive. As there was no control group, maybe children at home would be equally deprived.

- Bryant et al. (1980; see ASP4 p.128) 75% of the children cared for by childminders in a middle-class Oxfordshire area were passive and detached, and 25% were disturbed and had bad speech. Bryant believes that these behaviour patterns are not an inevitable consequence of childminding, but some of the minders were untrained, and did not view it as part of their job to stimulate the youngsters in their care.

Day Nurseries

There are some important studies that involved day nurseries:

- Kagan et al. (1980; see ASP4 p.128) 33 nursery children were compared with a control group of "home" children. The children were about 3½ years old and were assessed for 2 years. No significant differences were found in attachment, cognitive abilities, or general sociability. The use of a control group meant that the effects of day care could be reliably measured, and the study concluded that day care is not harmful.
- Vandell and Corasaniti (1990; see ASP4 p.128) American children in day care from infancy had poorer peer relationships and emotional health than those in home care. However, this could be due to the poor quality of the day care since carers were not highly trained and the staff–child ratios were high. It does not necessarily indicate that day care is inevitably damaging.
- Headstart (see ASP4 p.127) This was not a "minding" service but intended to improve opportunities for disadvantaged children. Those attending these "enrichment" programmes were cognitively more advanced when starting school than their counterparts from similar backgrounds. Lazar and Darlington (1982) found that by adolescence fewer Headstart children were on welfare, more were in college, and fewer were delinquent. It is difficult to evaluate the findings because the programme was so large and varied, but it showed no detrimental effects of intensive preschool education.

The NICHD (National Institute of Child Health and Human Development) has carried out very large scale research on the effects of day care. This was important for the following reasons:

- It distinguished between effects of *quality* of care, *quantity* of care, and *type of* care.
- It was a longitudinal study so it looked at long-term effects (initially early infancy–4½ years, then up to 12 years in some cases).
- Quality of home care was taken into consideration.
- It looked at five different types of day care: father care; grandparent care; child care outside the home (excluding grandparent care); in-home care by caregiver other than mother, father, grandparent; group care.

IMPACT OF DAY CARE ON CHILDREN'S SOCIAL DEVELOPMENT

Effects on Attachment

Day care can affect emotional development, sometimes in a negative way:

- Belsky and Rovine (1988; see ASP4 p.129) There was an increased risk of an infant developing insecure attachments if they were in day care for at least 4 months and if this had begun before 1 year of age, but there were no negative effects on children who started after they were 1 year old.
- Sroufe (1990) The first year of life is vital for mother–child attachment and day care should be delayed until the second year.

Day care may not, however, have an adverse effect on emotional development and some effects can be positive in that children become more active, sociable, outgoing, playful, and less aggressive.

- Clarke-Stewart et al. (1994; see ASP4 p.129) investigated the relationship between time spent in day care and quality of attachment in over 500 children, and found that 15-month-old children who had experienced "high intensity" child care (30 hours or more a week from 3 months onwards) were equally distressed when separated from their mothers in the Strange Situation as children who had experienced "low intensity" child care (less than 10 hours a week). This suggests that attachment was not affected by the experiences of separation.
- Roggman et al. (1994; see ASP4 p.130) In a comparison of infants who were cared for at home with those who attended day care before the age of 1, both were equally securely attached when assessed by the Strange Situation set-up.
- Erel et al. (2000; see ASP4 p.130) In a meta-analysis of the effects of day care on social development, they found day care had virtually no effect on the measures listed below even if children spent a great deal of time in day care:
  - Security of attachment to mother
  - Attachment behaviours of exploration, avoidance resistance
  - Mother–child interaction
  - Self-esteem and behaviour problems
  - Social interaction with peers
  - Social interaction with adults who were not their parents.

Effects on Peer Relations

The opportunity to interact with other children can have positive effects on some children but not all:

- Shea (1981; see ASP4 p.130) Videotapes of children in day nurseries were used to assess them on aggression, rough-and-tumble play, frequency of peer interaction, distance from teacher, and distance from the nearest child. They found that children became more sociable over time. This was greater for those attending nursery 5 days a week than those attending 2 days a week, indicating that it was the nursery setting rather than normal maturation that was producing the changes.
- Clarke-Stewart et al. (1994; see ASP4 p.131) In a study of 150 children from Chicago aged 2–3 years, they found that the day care children had more advanced peer relationships and could negotiate with them better than children brought up at home. They also learnt how to cope in social situations earlier than the home group.
- Pennebaker et al. (1981; see ASP4 p.131) Some children might not benefit from day care. Those children who are shy and unsociable can find nursery school very frightening, making them even more withdrawn.
- Erel et al. (2000) As mentioned before, they found no effect on social development in different forms of day care.

Taking into account the effects of home life

Marshall (2004; see ASP4 p.131) points out that any relationship between day care and social development may not indicate that day care *causes* the effect. We return again to the possibilities of a correlational relationship. It could be that children in good quality day care have very enriched home lives and vice versa, so the home life could be as important as the day care.

The NICHD study (2003) (referred to earlier) considered this issue and found that when the effects of home environment was controlled the influence of day care on peer relations was very small but was associated with less social competence (in other words, when home life was similar, children of 4½ years were slightly less sociable). However, higher quality care was associated with higher cognitive skills.

Effects on Aggression

- Vandell and Corasaniti (1990; see ASP4 p.132) 8-year-olds who had started full-time day care in their first year were more non-compliant than other children.
- Bates et al. (1994; see ASP4 p.132) Day care children were generally more aggressive and had more behavioural problems than children who had not experienced day care.
- Belsky (1999; see ASP4 p.132) Similarly, children who had spent more time in day care tended to be more aggressive.
- Borge et al. (2004; see ASP4 p.132) In a study of a large number of children, they found lower levels of physical aggression in 2- and 3-year-olds attending day care than those looked after by their mothers. When they separated the children into those who came from very disadvantaged homes as opposed to those who did not, they found higher levels of aggression in those disadvantaged children who were at home full time compared with those in day care. However, this did not apply to non-disadvantaged children.
- NICHD (2003; see ASP4 p.132) Distinguished between assertive behaviour (e.g. boasting, demanding attention) and aggressive/disobedient (e.g. cruelty) behaviour. They found higher levels of both in 4½-year-olds in day care.
- Belsky et al. (2007; see ASP4 p.133) Looking at long-term effects of day care on 12-year-olds, they found that long periods in day care involving large groups were associated with behavioural problems but this was not true of other types of day-care setting.

EVALUATION

- There is, overall, a positive correlation between time spent in day care and physical aggression. This does not necessarily mean that day care *causes* children to be physically aggressive. There are other possibilities, e.g. that children in day care may have be physically aggressive due to other factors such as problems within the family.

IMPLICATIONS OF RESEARCH INTO ATTACHMENT AND DAY CARE FOR CHILD-CARE PRACTICES

Implications for Child-care Practices

Features of high quality care

It is essential that any sort of care should be of high quality. The two crucial variables that affect day care are *consistency* and *quality*. The less consistent the care and the poorer the quality of care, the more harmful the experience is for the child.

Good quality care involves the following:

- **Consistency**
  The research of Tizard and Hodges (1989), Kagan et al. (1980), NICHD (1997), and many others demonstrates that children need consistency of care and that frequent changes in caregivers can have serious effects. Recommendations are:
  - Minimal turnover of staff.

- ○ Infant-to-caregiver ratio no more than 1 : 3.
- ○ One staff member assigned to each child.
- ○ Consistent routines and physical environment.
- **Quality**
  It is not always easy to define quality but some features are obvious. Recommendations for good quality care:
  - ○ High-quality verbal interaction between carer and child.
  - ○ Child–child interaction and interaction with the task. Ridley et al. (2000; see ASP4 p.135) found that good quality day care afforded opportunities for children in these respects. Tizard (1979) found mothers had more complex conversations with their children than did nursery teachers.
  - ○ A good number of toys and activities: stimulation is important.
  - ○ Carers sensitive to children's needs. NICHD found that only 25% of carers gave highly sensitive infant care and one fifth were emotionally detached.
  - ○ Regular discussions with parents.

Improving the quality of care

- Howes et al. (1998; see ASP4 p.135) Carers were given minimal training in sensitively handling children—there was an improvement in the children's security and general happiness.
- Howes et al. (1995; see ASP4 pp.135–136) In Florida efforts were made to reduce child–carer ratios and use more highly qualified carers. Teachers became more responsive, there was less negative interaction between teachers and children (telling off etc.), and there was an improvement in children's emotional and cognitive development.
- Phillips et al. (2000; see ASP4 p.136) Quality of care in three American states was better in those with more stringent regulations on child care.

Implications for Attachment

The relationship between attachment and day care

- Good quality care is even more important for insecurely attached than securely attached children for two main reasons:
  - ○ Insecurely attached children have greater problems coping with peers and are less socially competent therefore will find it more difficult to cope with day care, so it needs to be of good quality (sensitive care, low child–carer ratios) in order to develop good social skills.
  - ○ Insecurely attached children have more behavioural problems (Belsky & Fearon, 2002) and are poorer at conflict resolution so they are likely to be more disruptive and aggressive in day care. Good quality care should reduce these problems.
- Since attachment at 12 months predicts attachment at 6 years, the quality of care can have long-lasting effects on children, so it needs to be of good quality in order to foster secure attachment.
- Training to enhance sensitivity of carers will have significant beneficial effects on children in day care by enhancing the security of their attachment.

Child–environment fit
Some types of day care are likely to be better suited to certain children than others. The following recommendations are based on research:

- Children showing aggression are better in a home environment than in a centre-based one.

- Very socially disadvantaged children are better in group day care than being looked after full time by their mothers as they tend to be less aggressive in these circumstances (Borge et al., 2004; see ASP4 pp.136–137). This is not true of less disadvantaged children.
- In order to enhance positive relations with other children (peer relations), it might be better for children with little opportunity to mix with other children (e.g. only children) to spend some time in day care.

Effects of separation on parents

It is important to consider parents as well as children. Harrison and Ungerer (2002; see ASP4 p.137) found that mothers who returned to work in the first year of the child's life were unhappy if they were anxious about the care. It is useful to have good parent-carer links such as workplace nurseries.

Parents need to be reassured that day care is not always associated with negative effects. Brown and Harris (1978; see ASP4 p.137) found that full-time mothers with several young children were more likely to be seriously depressed than working mothers.

Children of working mothers tend to be more socially confident so perhaps working outside the home makes women better mothers.

RESEARCH METHODS AND ATTACHMENT

Observations

The main research method for studying attachment in young children is by observation studies, both naturalistic observation and controlled observation. An example of a naturalistic observation study is that of Schaffer and Emerson (1964). Naturalistic observations such as this one are particularly useful in looking at the behaviour of infants and young children in their ordinary everyday environments. It enabled Schaffer and Emerson to see which adults the children attached to and the very different relationships they had with each of the adults in their life. It has the advantage of high ecological validity (of reflecting everyday behaviour). On the other hand, the findings cannot be generalised across populations because all the circumstances are different.

Controlled observations are particularly useful when researchers want to compare how different children respond in an identical situation. A classic example of the use of the method of controlled observation is the Strange Situation devised by Ainsworth. Because the situation is controlled (the same for every participant), it allows researchers to generalise to other children. However, it has much lower ecological validity than naturalistic observation because the children are placed in an unfamiliar situation and may behave differently from the way they would to a similar series of events that happened in their own home.

Case Studies

Sadly, there are cases in which children have suffered severe neglect and abuse. These children can be investigated by using the case study method—the in-depth study of one or a small number of individuals. Examples of such studies are listed earlier and include Koluchová (1976—the Czech twins), Curtiss (1989—Genie), Soutter (1995—Tom), Freud and Dann (1951—war orphans). Case studies provide rich, detailed, insightful information into the individuals concerned and allow researchers to look at the effects of situations that could never be engineered. Nevertheless, because each child's experiences are unique, the effects cannot be generalised to other people. They can, however, provide limited support or criticism for already formulated theories.

Interviews

Another method used to study attachment and its effect includes interviews (for example, of parents and teachers) to try and assess the child's level of social and intellectual functioning. Interviews may also be done with children themselves once they've reached adolescence, to find out about their early childhood. Interviews can be a very useful means of gathering information in a relatively quick and straightforward manner. They are particularly useful with people who have no reason to lie or exaggerate, such as teachers and people working in day care. However, they also have the disadvantage that people may not always tell the truth, either because they deliberately lie or because their memory is inaccurate.

The Ethics of Research on Attachment

Most research on attachment has been conducted on young children. There are several ethical issues that need to be considered when conducting research on children:

- Young children are unable to give informed consent so this must be obtained from parents, guardians, or caregivers.
- In any research it is essential to consider the amount of distress that might be caused to participants and this is even more important with respect to young children. It is sometimes easy to cause distress without necessarily anticipating it, so researchers need to keep an eye on the children and be ready to stop the study if they see any signs of discomfort, embarrassment, or anxiety. After all, the children cannot give informed consent so they have not agreed to take part in a study and neither can they ask to withdraw if they become upset by what is happening.
- It is also essential in all research to consider issues of confidentiality and again, this is especially true of research on young children. Nothing should be published without consent of the appropriate adults. This applies even if the children are not named if it is possible to identify them from the descriptions given in the study. This of course includes case studies of severely neglected and abused children.
- As with all ethical issues, it is important to consider the costs and benefits. Any distress that is caused (e.g. in the Strange Situation studies) must be weighed against the benefits (e.g. having an improved knowledge of how children form attachments) and this is often difficult to gauge in advance of the study.

For ethical reasons, some research on attachment has been done on animals. A classic example is Harlow, who raised rhesus monkeys in isolation with the result that they showed signs of severe disturbance and were permanently damaged by the experience. In terms of costs and benefits, the costs are the considerable suffering of the animals and the permanent damage they sustained whilst the main benefit is the knowledge that can be gained about the long-term damage done by neglect and failure of attachment in a species closely related genetically to that of humans.

SAMPLE QUESTIONS

? Outline the evolutionary explanation of attachment behaviour. **4 MARKS**

? Some research on attachment has used the structured (controlled) observation method. Explain one advantage and one disadvantage of using a structured observation to study attachment. **2 MARKS + 2 MARKS**

? Outline two ethical issues in conducting research on young children. **2 MARKS + 2 MARKS**

RESEARCH METHODS

4

What's it about?

Everyone has theories about what causes behaviour. The difference between these "common-sense" ideas and theories in psychology is that psychological theories are tested to see if they are true. In order to systematically test theories, psychologists conduct research. As behaviour is so variable, psychologists need to use a wide variety of methods. The research methods available include experiments, questionnaires, interviews, observations, and methods using correlations.

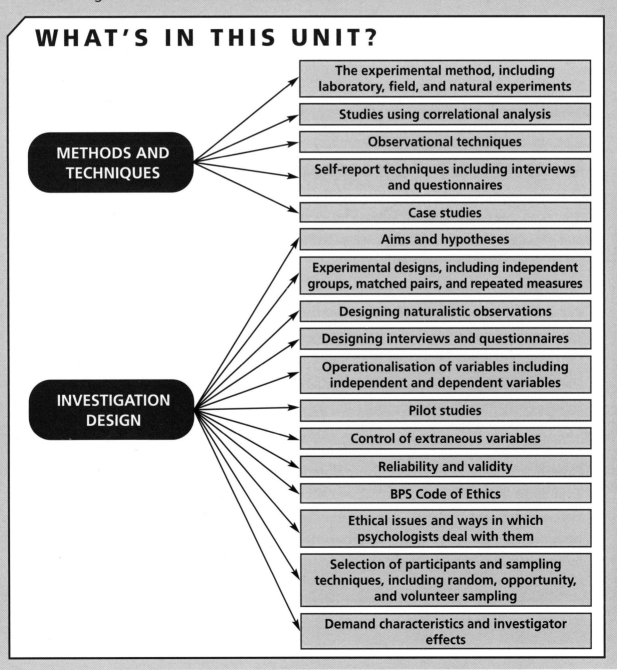

WHAT'S IN THIS UNIT?

METHODS AND TECHNIQUES

- The experimental method, including laboratory, field, and natural experiments
- Studies using correlational analysis
- Observational techniques
- Self-report techniques including interviews and questionnaires
- Case studies

INVESTIGATION DESIGN

- Aims and hypotheses
- Experimental designs, including independent groups, matched pairs, and repeated measures
- Designing naturalistic observations
- Designing interviews and questionnaires
- Operationalisation of variables including independent and dependent variables
- Pilot studies
- Control of extraneous variables
- Reliability and validity
- BPS Code of Ethics
- Ethical issues and ways in which psychologists deal with them
- Selection of participants and sampling techniques, including random, opportunity, and volunteer sampling
- Demand characteristics and investigator effects

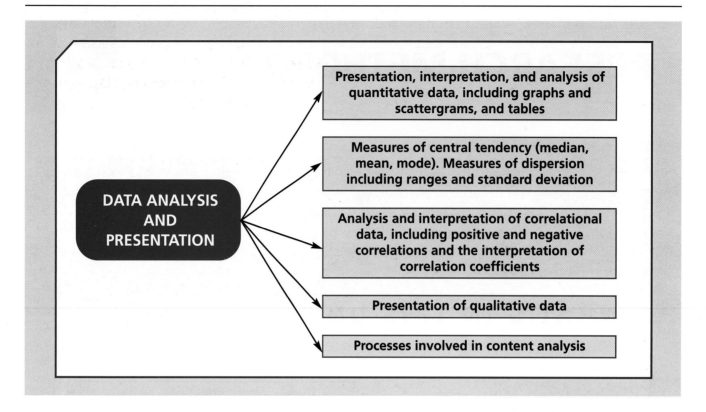

DATA ANALYSIS AND PRESENTATION

- Presentation, interpretation, and analysis of quantitative data, including graphs and scattergrams, and tables
- Measures of central tendency (median, mean, mode). Measures of dispersion including ranges and standard deviation
- Analysis and interpretation of correlational data, including positive and negative correlations and the interpretation of correlation coefficients
- Presentation of qualitative data
- Processes involved in content analysis

IMPORTANT TERMS AND CONCEPTS

The following terms are important for understanding this module so it will help you in the exam if you understand what they refer to. Make a list of definitions of the following terms, and if you get stuck, go to the glossary at the end of this book.

Alternative hypothesis	Interview	Positive correlation
Bar chart	Investigator effects	Qualitative data
Confounding variables	Laboratory experiment	Quantitative data
Correlational analysis	Matched pairs design	Quasi-experiment
Demand characteristics	Mean	Questionnaire
Dependent variable (DV)	Median	Random sampling
Directional (one-tailed) hypothesis	Mode	Range
Experiment	Mundane realism	Reliability
Experimental hypothesis	Natural experiment	Research
Field experiment	Naturalistic observation	Scattergram/scattergraph
Histogram	Negative correlation	Standard deviation
Independent groups design	Null hypothesis	Validity
Independent variable (IV)	Opportunity sampling	Volunteer sampling
	Pilot study	

You may be asked for a brief explanation and then required to explain this in the context of a described study. For example, "Explain what is meant by a pilot study and give one reason why it might be appropriate to use a pilot study as part of this investigation" (1 MARK + 2 MARKS). Or you may simply be expected to describe the concept in the context of the study. For example, "Describe one way that demand characteristics might influence your findings" (2 MARKS).

OVER TO YOU

Explain one way in which participant reactivity might have influenced the results obtained in this study. (Answer this with reference to any study you know.)

2 MARKS

METHODS AND TECHNIQUES

THE SCIENTIFIC APPROACH

- Science aims to discover facts about the world by using *systematic and objective methods of investigation*.
- Theories about people's behaviour come from casual observations. *These theories then generate specific expectations*, e.g. Watching violent role models makes people act aggressively; organised material is better remembered than unorganised material.
- The expectations can be tested to see whether or not they are correct but first the predictions need to be stated in terms of *a research hypothesis*. This is a formal and unambiguous statement about what is believed to be true, e.g. Children who watch a violent adult model will be more aggressive than children who do not watch a violent adult model. More information will be remembered when material is organised in a meaningful way than when it is not organised.

To sum up: scientists generate research hypotheses that they then test in order to prove or disprove them. They then adjust and refine their theories accordingly. They use many methods in order to do this, not simply experiments. We will take a look at some of these methods.

THE EXPERIMENTAL METHOD

The experimental method is the only method that allows us to draw conclusions about cause and effect. In order to illustrate how an experiment would be designed, we will consider an experiment to see if loud noise reduces performance on a memory test.

The hypothesis
Loud continuous noise reduces performance on a memory test.

The independent and dependent variables (IV and DV)
Another way of expressing this is to say that memory *affects* performance, or performance *depends* on memory. The variable that we believe has an effect (noise) is called the IV, the one that is affected is called the DV because, if our hypothesis is correct, it *depends* on the IV. The DV is therefore the amount of material that is remembered.

The IV is manipulated while all other variables (the room, the material to be memorised, the time of day, and so on) are kept the same. These variables must be kept the same for both groups or they may affect the result. They are known as *extraneous variables* and they must be controlled.

Experimental group
A group of people perform a memory task against a background of loud noise.

Control group
A similar group of people do the same task in peace and quiet.

The same test of memory is given to both groups and the results are compared.

EXPERIMENTAL CONTROL

The most important principle of the experimental method is control; the IV is manipulated, the DV is free to vary, but all other variables must be controlled.

Controlling Confounding Variables

The variables that need to be controlled are known as *extraneous variables*. It is crucial that they are controlled because they have the potential to become *confounding variables* that bias the results of the study. The IV is manipulated and the DV is measured, but the only way we can be certain that any changes in the DV are caused by the IV is to keep everything else constant. This is really basic common sense and if you were setting up an experiment you would control certain things as a matter of course. For example, in the experiment on the effect of noise on memory, every participant should be given the same time to learn the material to be memorised; they should be tested in a similar room; they should be tested at the same time of day; and so on.

Matching the Participants

When experiments are conducted it is also essential to ensure that, if two different groups of participants are used, they are *matched* on any important variables. What variables are important? Well, think of what we are measuring (the DV) and start with any factors that might influence this. In our example, the DV is amount of material remembered, so we need to try to match on ability to remember things. It would be wise, for example, to match them on intelligence. Other variables on which it is common to match are age and sex. However, if you are asked what factors you should match on in an exam question, don't just automatically say "age and sex". Think about what is being measured (the DV) and match on that.

Randomisation

Often the matching of participants can be a problem, so you are more likely to use randomisation. It's easy to match on sex and not too difficult on age, but as for intelligence and other traits, it's not so straightforward. One way around this is to split the whole group of participants randomly into two (or three or four) groups. In this way, the groups should hopefully be fairly similar. Alternatively, you can simply take participants in the order of their arrival. The process of splitting the groups randomly is called *randomisation*. Randomisation is fundamental to any controlled experiment.

OVER TO YOU

In our example of the effect of noise on memory, can you think of any other confounding variables that might need to be controlled? (See ASP4 p.143 where others are mentioned.)

If you were designing a study to see if watching violent television affected the amount of aggression that children displayed, what confounding variables would you need to control during the study? What is the most essential trait on which to match the two groups of child participants? (Think about what you are measuring; about what the DV is.)

When planning an experiment, what would be the easiest way to split participants randomly into two groups?

There are a number of advantages and disadvantages of the experimental method that you need to be aware of as they will help you to evaluate experimental studies.

EVALUATION

STRENGTHS

- **Cause and effect** The experimental method is the only method that establishes cause and effect. If a behaviour (e.g. decrease in performance) follows an event (e.g. intense noise) it is reasonable to assume that the noise caused the poor performance. However, caution is needed when inferring cause and effect. For example, if we selected a group of people in a hot country and asked half to sleep with the window open and half with windows closed, the first group is more likely to be bitten by insects. However, it is not the open window that causes the bites but the greater opportunity for insects to enter. Mistaken assumptions of cause and effect are not always so transparent, so beware! Nevertheless, information from experiments provides a starting point for further research.
- **Replication** Because everything is carefully controlled, it's possible for other researchers to repeat the study. Replication is important because if it confirms the original findings, then there is greater confidence in the validity of the theory being tested.
- **Objectivity** This is a more objective method than others. However, total objectivity is impossible since the experimenter's interests, values, and judgements will always have some influence, and the control of all confounding variables is impossible. Nevertheless, the experimental method offers the best chance of objectivity.

WEAKNESSES

- **Artificiality** The major criticism of experiments is that they are artificial and do not measure "real-life" behaviour. In other words they lack *ecological validity*. This is a particular problem with social behaviour. However, there may be times when artificiality is required in order to isolate the behaviour in which the researcher is interested. There is a distinction between *mundane realism* (where the situation is made to resemble everyday life) and *experimental realism* (where the situation is artificial but still interesting enough to produce full involvement from participants), and it seems that experimental realism may be more important than mundane realism in producing findings that generalise to real-life situations.
- **Demand characteristics** Orne (1962; see ASP4 p.145) found that there are features of the experiment that give clues as to what is being studied, and people try to guess what the study is about and will then act accordingly. They often try to act in a way that supports the hypothesis.
- **Evaluation apprehension** When people are watched and/or they know their behaviour is being recorded they may not act as they normally would. Sigall et al. (1970; see ASP4 p.145) used a test of copying numbers out of a telephone book and found that participants did not comply with their request to repeat the task taking more time, thus showing that they would avoid any behaviour that might cause them to be evaluated negatively by the researcher.

TYPES OF EXPERIMENTAL INVESTIGATION

All experiments investigate the effect of an IV on a DV, but there are a number of different ways in which this can be done, depending mainly on how rigorous the controls are.

Laboratory Experiments

What is a laboratory experiment?
Laboratory experiments are conducted in a laboratory or other contrived setting that is not the participant's natural environment. *The independent variable is set up by the researcher in an artificial situation with as many confounding variables as possible controlled.*

EVALUATION

STRENGTHS

- The researcher can precisely manipulate the IV and carefully measure the DV, using measuring instruments if necessary. Considerable control can be exercised over any potential confounding variables.
- They are replicable—a laboratory study can be repeated and therefore the reliability can be checked.
- Of all the experimental methods, this is the one that gives most confidence that the IV has caused changes in the DV.

WEAKNESSES

- They lack ecological validity.
- There may be problems of evaluation apprehension and demand characteristics (see later in this section).

Field Experiments

What is a field experiment?
Field experiments are experiments in *which the IV is manipulated in a natural setting*. They are conducted anywhere where people live, work, or gather, such as schools, factories, hospitals, or on a train.

EVALUATION

STRENGTHS

- Since they use an experimental design, cause and effect can occasionally be established to some extent, but note the limitations listed in the disadvantages section.
- As the study is in a natural setting it has high ecological validity.
- There is control over the IV.
- Studies can, within reason, be replicated.

> ## WEAKNESSES
>
> - Random allocation of participants to experimental and control conditions is difficult, if not impossible, and this threatens the ability to establish cause and effect relationships.
> - There is less control over extraneous variables, so cause and effect are less certain.
> - When considering ethics, most field experiments cannot involve informed consent, cannot offer the right to withdraw, nor can involve a debriefing.

Quasi-experiments

ASK YOURSELF

> The local school is about to introduce a completely new reading scheme into one of its two Year 1 classes while the other Year 1 class keeps the old scheme. How could a psychologist investigate whether the new scheme is better or worse than the old one? The head teacher is quite happy to release data on reading ability but on no account can the psychologist influence any organisational aspects of the school.

What problems might there be in drawing conclusions from the data provided?

> In one maternity ward of the local hospital, newborn babies stay with their mothers all the time and are never removed by nurses for feeding, even at night. In another ward, babies stay with their mothers in the day but are put in the nursery from midnight until 8 o'clock the next morning, during which time they are cared for by nurses. The choice of which ward to go in is largely the choice of the mothers, space permitting.

How could a psychologist investigate whether this affects mother–child bonding? What problems might there be in drawing conclusions from any data?

What is a quasi-experiment?

True experiments based on the experimental method provide the best way of being able to establish cause and effect (to establish whether or not the IV is having an effect on the DV). In other words, it is the best method from which to draw causal inferences. However, it is often the case that there are practical or ethical reasons why it is not possible to carry out a true experiment, and in such situations, investigators often carry out what is known as a *quasi-experiment* ("quasi-" means "almost but not really").

Quasi-experimental designs are like experiments, but are weaker in some ways. The essence of a true experiment is that the IV is manipulated and everything else is controlled. Two essential features of a true experiment are:

- Direct manipulation of the IV by the experimenter.
- Random allocation of participants to the different groups.

Often this is impractical with psychological research in the real world and instead the psychologist will look at naturally occurring variables by using a quasi-experimental design. Quasi-experiments tend to fall short of being true experiments in the following ways:

- The manipulation of the IV is often not under the control of the experimenter.
- It is usually not possible to allocate the participants randomly to groups.

Both the examples in the Ask Yourself section involve independent variables that occur naturally. When investigating these variables, neither of the two essential elements of a true experiment can be met, so a quasi-experiment can be used instead. In the case of the school, the classes are not necessarily the same. In the case of the hospital wards, the new mothers are definitely not matched as they have, for the most part, chosen to be in a particular ward. This means that there are already differences in the two groups even before the effect of the IV is investigated.

The type of quasi-experiment that would be used to investigate a naturally occurring independent variable is known as a natural experiment, and these are discussed next.

Natural Experiments

What is a natural experiment?
Natural experiments are a type of quasi-experiment. *They are studies in which a naturally occurring IV is investigated, and the IV is not deliberately manipulated by the researcher.*

EVALUATION

STRENGTHS

- People behave fairly naturally as they are usually unaware that they are taking part in an experiment, even if they know they are being observed.
- They allow us to study the effects on behaviour of IVs that would be impractical or unethical to manipulate.

WEAKNESSES

- Findings can be difficult to interpret.
- Observed differences in behaviour between groups may be due to individual differences rather than to the effect of the IV, as participants are not assigned randomly to groups.
- Cause and effect are more difficult to establish, as it is difficult to ascertain which aspects of the IV are having an effect.
- Raises the ethical issue of voluntary informed consent, and requires ethical sensitivity.

TYPES OF NON-EXPERIMENTAL INVESTIGATION

Investigations Using Correlational Analysis

What is a correlation?
Studies using a correlational design investigate whether there is an association or relationship between two variables. For example, whether there is a relationship between aggression and amount of violent television watched, or whether people in the same family have similar IQs.

You have seen how to use the experimental method to investigate whether, for example, exposure to intense noise levels *causes* a drop in performance. In a correlational study no causal relationship can be determined. As an example, to investigate the relationship between violent behaviour and watching violent television, we would simply measure the amount of violent television a particular person watches and how aggressive they are, and then compare the two. If there is a relationship, we cannot say that one causes the other as there are other possible explanations. As well as the possibility that watching violent television causes aggression, it is possible that aggressive people like watching violent television, or that children from disadvantaged homes watch lots of television and are violent.

EVALUATION

STRENGTHS

- The greatest use of correlation is in prediction. If two variables are correlated, you can predict one from the other.
- It is a useful method when manipulation of variables is impossible.
- Establishing no relationship between variables is useful in eliminating cause and effect.
- It is often possible to obtain large amounts of data on a number of variables more rapidly and efficiently than with experimental designs.

WEAKNESSES

- Cause and effect is impossible to establish.
- Interpretation of the results is difficult.
- Other variables may be involved.
- Direction of causality is uncertain.

Positive and negative correlations
- **A positive correlation** This is when one variable increases as the other variable increases. If we are told that there is a positive correlation between health and optimism, it means that in general people high in optimism are also healthy, while those low in optimism are less healthy.
- **A negative correlation** This is when one variable increases as the other decreases. A negative correlation between work productivity and stress means that the *more* stressed a person is, the *less* work they produce; conversely, the *less* stressed they are the *more* work they do.
- **A correlation co-efficient** This is a number that expresses the degree to which two things are related, and ranges from +1 to –1. If two variables are very closely related, the co-efficient will be close to 1, say 0.9; if they are weakly related it will be low, say 0.13. A positive correlation is expressed as a positive number (+0.7) and a negative correlation is expressed as a negative number (–0.6).

OBSERVATIONAL TECHNIQUES

Naturalistic Observation

Naturalistic observation involves looking at behaviour without interfering with it in any way. A crucial element is that the observer should not influence behaviour but remain inconspicuous.

EVALUATION

STRENGTHS

- They have high ecological validity so they tell us something about real-life situations.
- There are no problems of demand characteristics or evaluation apprehension.
- A richness of behaviour can be observed, far more so than in lab experiments.
- They are particularly useful when researching children or animals.

WEAKNESSES

- They only provide descriptions of behaviour rather than explanations for it.
- There may be problems of reliability due to observer bias or imprecise recording of data.
- Such studies are difficult to replicate.

Controlled Observation

A controlled observation involves placing participants in a certain environment in which they encounter a series of events and recording their reaction to these events. There is far more control than in the naturalistic observation study and there is a scientific element because all the participants encounter the same conditions, so it is replicable. One of the most famous is the series of studies known as "The Strange Situation" by Ainsworth et al. (see ASP4 pp.97–98).

EVALUATION

STRENGTHS

- If used within a laboratory experiment, you can infer cause and effect while still gaining the rich, detailed information you obtain from an observation.
- You have some control over extraneous variables, so you have fewer confounding influences than in a naturalistic or participant observation.
- Since you can set up a certain situation, you can observe behaviour that may occur only rarely in a natural setting but which is important.
- You gain richer more detailed information about people's behaviour than by simply using a lab experiment in which only a tiny sample of behaviour is recorded.

WEAKNESSES

- Participants are in an artificial environment so they do not act as they normally would, so there is a lack of ecological validity. This means that the results cannot be generalised to an everyday situation.
- The researchers may expect certain findings, so there can be problems with investigator effects.
- The participants are in an artificial environment so they may act in a way they think is expected of them, that is, they may be affected by demand characteristics.

Participant Observation

A participant observation is an observation study in which the investigator becomes part of the group they are observing. In some studies the participants are aware of the observer's role; in others they are entirely unaware. Sometimes this is not an issue (such as an observer being part of a football crowd and joining in the chanting etc.).

EVALUATION

STRENGTHS

- Some such studies are conducted over a long period of time so a great deal of rich information is gained.
- Observers can gain information that could not be obtained if they remained outsiders, as in naturalistic observations.

WEAKNESSES

- The observers influence the behaviour of the group.
- The observers may become involved in the group and this can bias their interpretation of the behaviour.
- The observers often record their findings later so they may not record them accurately.
- There are ethical problems if the observers do not inform the participants.
- There is no fully informed consent.

Techniques for collecting observational data

There are various techniques that can be used in order to collect data from an observation:

Event sampling	Focuses only on events that are of interest to the observer
Time sampling	Observations are made at specific intervals, e.g. every 10 mins
Point sampling	One person is observed for a while then another individual and so on

SELF-REPORT TECHNIQUES

Interviews

Psychologists often want to talk to people, to find out about their experiences and opinions. There are many types of ways in which interviews can be conducted, and these have been detailed below together with strengths and weaknesses. Before that we can consider weaknesses common to all interviews:

- **Social desirability bias** It is also possible that people may not tell the truth in order to give a good impression.
- **You only gain information of which the interviewee is consciously aware** You don't get information through body language etc.
- **Lack of interviewing skills** Many interviewers are not skilled at gaining good quality, accurate information from people.

TYPES OF INTERVIEW			
Name	*Description*	*Strengths*	*Weaknesses*
Non-directive interview	The person is free to discuss anything. The interview guides the discussion.	Provides rich in-depth information. Particularly useful in a case study.	Not replicable, but not intended for that.
Informal interview	Similar to non-directive but there are general topics explored in depth.	Provides detailed information on general areas of interest.	Not replicable.
Semi-structured or guided interview	The interviewer identifies issues to be raised and decides during the interview when and how to raise these issues.	Provides detailed information on specific topics.	Difficult, but not impossible, to replicate.
Clinical interview	All interviewees are asked the same question initially, then their answers determine subsequent questions. The name comes from its original use in a clinical setting.	Very useful in talking to people about mental health problems.	Can be problems of "leading" the interviewee. Piaget was accused of this in his early work in his use of clinical interviews with children.
Fully structured interview	A standard set of questions in a fixed order. There is a restricted number of answers (e.g. yes/no; agree/disagree).	Allows replication and comparison between people. Quick and easy to collect data.	You don't get a richness of response, simply the answers to set questions.

Questionnaires

These are a set of questions with instructions that the participant answers. They are used for many purposes including personality assessment and measuring life events. There are two main types of questions:

TYPES OF QUESTIONNAIRE				
Question type	**Description**	**Example**	**Strengths**	**Weaknesses**
Fixed-choice	The question is followed by a fixed number of choices, e.g. yes/no; agree/disagree. Provide quantitative data.	Do you have any recollection of your first day at school? Yes/no.	1. Easy to score. 2. Produce reliable and consistent data, i.e. replicable. 3. Allows for numerical comparison between groups (e.g. 40% of women and 50% of men drink alcohol every day).	Provide a very limited amount of information.
Open-ended	Questions require a descriptive answer.	Write down everything you can remember about your first day at school.	Provide rich, detailed information.	1. Difficult to score accurately. 2. People need to be literate and willing to fill out forms, so the sample may be biased.

Questionnaires may be a combination of *fixed-choice* and *open-ended* questions. See the Questionnaire Design section for a consideration of when each is appropriate.

EVALUATION

STRENGTHS

- They provide a lot of information at relatively little cost.
- They can explore attitudes and beliefs—this is difficult by any other means.
- They usually have high reliability and reasonable validity, in that they reflect the true attitudes of people.

- People may not give truthful answers. They may remember wrongly or give socially desirable answers.
- The design of questions can be problematic. Questions may be leading, ambiguous (able to be interpreted in more than one way), or difficult to understand.
- On personality questionnaires, people need to have insight into their own attitudes and values.
- People may need to be very literate in order to understand the questions. This limits the sample of people who can complete the questionnaire.

Questionnaires have the same disadvantage as interviews in that people may give socially desirable answers or simply have poor memory for events.

CASE STUDIES

A case study is a detailed investigation of a single individual or a small group of individuals. There are several types of individual who may be seen by a psychologist—those suffering early abuse, those with brain damage from, for example, a stroke, those with other problems, or those with unusual skills. Data can be collected by various means, for example:

- interview
- psychometric test (e.g. a memory test for a brain damaged patient)
- brain scans
- observations.

EVALUATION

STRENGTHS

- Can provide very detailed information.
- Can provide useful data on the effects of unusual experiences such as extreme deprivation, hospitalisation, or unusual educational experiences.
- Help refine, refute, or question a theory.
- Can indicate routes of future research into theories.

WEAKNESSES

- The results cannot be generalised to other individuals. No single individual is typical of others and, in addition, case studies are often of people with unusual experiences.
- The psychologist may be influenced by his/her own theories and therefore may be biased.
- The psychologist may only investigate and/or report certain behaviour patterns (those that tie in with their own theoretical perspective) so samples of reported behaviour may be biased.
- The psychologist may become emotionally involved, especially if the case study has lasted a long time, and this can also result in bias.

Case Studies Featured in *AS Level Psychology, Fourth Edition*

- Curtiss (1989; see ASP4 p.120) Study of Genie.
- Watson and Rayner (1920; see ASP4 p.331) Study of Little Albert.
- HM (see ASP4 p.52).
- Freud's study of Anna O (see ASP4 p.351).

INVESTIGATION DESIGN

AIMS AND HYPOTHESES

An aim is a general statement of *why* the study is being carried out. To illustrate this, we will use the multi-store model of memory, specifically the capacity of short-term memory with or without chunking (see ASP4 pp.162–163).

- **FOR EXAMPLE:** To investigate the effect of chunking on short-term memory.

A hypothesis states precisely *what* you expect to show. You need two of these: an alternative (experimental) hypothesis and a null hypothesis. The alternative (experimental) hypothesis states that some difference or effect will occur.

- **FOR EXAMPLE:** "More items will be recalled when chunked than when not chunked."

The null hypothesis states that the IV has no effect on the DV.

- **FOR EXAMPLE:** "Chunking will have no effect on the amount of items recalled."

◾ **The term "experimental hypothesis" only applies when using the experimental method. Otherwise, you should use the term "alternative hypothesis".**

The experimental (alternative) hypothesis can be directional or non-directional:

DIRECTIONAL
One-tailed
States the *direction* in which the results are expected to go. A one-tailed (directional) hypothesis is used in the example above because all research done beforehand indicates that chunking leads to better recall.

NON-DIRECTIONAL
Two-tailed
Sometimes we think the IV will affect the DV but we are not sure how, so we do not state the direction. For example, if we say that "arousal affects performance", we are not predicting whether it will make it worse or better.

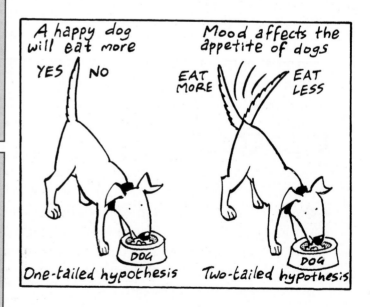

RESEARCH DESIGNS

When conducting experiments, there are three research designs that are available to use. We will carry on using the chunking example to explain the features of each one.

Independent groups design
Different participants are used in each of the conditions. One group of participants processes words semantically (e.g. by thinking of another word that means the same). The other group processes words physically (e.g. by counting the number of letters in each word).

Matched pairs (matched participants) design
This design uses two separate groups of people who are matched on a one-to-one basis on important variables, such as age or sex. This controls for some individual differences.

Repeated measures design
The same group of people is used in each of the two conditions. Each participant is tested on free recall after semantically processing some words and then tested on free recall after physically processing some words. This controls for all individual differences.

STRENGTHS AND WEAKNESSES OF DIFFERENT RESEARCH DESIGNS

You will need to be familiar with the various advantages and limitations of the different research designs that can be used.

Independent Groups Design

EVALUATION

STRENGTHS

- There are no problems of order effects (see below).
- No participants are lost between trials.
- It can be used when a repeated measures design is inappropriate (e.g. when looking at gender differences).

WEAKNESSES

- There may be important individual differences between participants to start with. To minimise this there should be randomisation (for explanation see earlier).
- You need more participants than you do with a repeated measures design.

Matched Pairs (Matched Participants) Design

EVALUATION

STRENGTHS

- It controls for some individual differences between participants.
- Can be used when a repeated measures design is inappropriate.

WEAKNESSES

- It is quite difficult to match participants in pairs. You need a large pool of participants from which to select.
- You need more participants than you do with a repeated measures design.

Repeated Measures Design

EVALUATION

STRENGTHS

- It controls for all individual differences.
- It requires fewer participants.

WEAKNESSES

- It cannot be used in studies in which participation in one condition affects responses in the other.
- Participants are likely to guess the purpose of the study, thus introducing problems with demand characteristics.
- There are problems of *order effects* (see next section).

ORDER EFFECTS AND COUNTERBALANCING

When a repeated measures design is used there may be problems that result from participants doing the same task twice. The second time they carry out the task they may be:

- Better than the first time because they have had practice.
- Worse than the first time because they are tired or bored.

The problems are known as *order effects* because they arise due to the order of the conditions, but we cannot tell whether differences are genuinely due to the IV or to the order effects.

Solution

Use a technique called *counterbalancing*, where the group is split into two:

- Half the participants do Condition A (e.g. semantic processing) followed by Condition B (e.g. physical processing).
- Half the participants do Condition B followed by Condition A.

So, any order effects are balanced out. Counterbalancing can only be used when the total number of participants in the study is known. If this is not known, you will have to allocate participants to either Condition A followed by Condition B, or Condition B followed by Condition A, on a random basis (known as *randomisation* of order presentation).

DESIGN OF NATURALISTIC OBSERVATIONS

Behavioural Categories

In order to cope with the huge amount of potential information that could result from a naturalistic observation study, observers use behavioural categories and record the number of times a particular behaviour occurs. Examples of behavioural categories in playground play may be running and chasing, games with balls, hopscotch, marbles.

How behavioural categories are developed
1. Define the behavioural categories: as in the example above for playground play.
2. Decide whether behavioural categories should be based on simple recording or on interpretation so that each category is unambiguously defined. For example, participant raises hand (based on simple recording) or participant made a threatening gesture (based on interpretation). Most behavioural categories will involve some interpretation.

3. Ensure observers are properly trained in use of the categories. This is done by checking *reliability* (consistency) by seeing how similar the records of any two observers are by correlating them. This correlational measurement is known as inter-observer (or inter-rater, or inter-judge) reliability.

4. Test validity of the categories. It is necessary to make sure the categories actually measure what they are intended to measure, i.e. that they are valid. This can be done by comparing the observers' records with other evidence. For example, records from observation of aggression in a group of children could be compared to teachers' ratings of how aggressive these particular children are.

DESIGN OF INTERVIEWS AND QUESTIONNAIRES

Types of Interviews and Questions to Use

The various types of interviews were discussed earlier in this section.

- **Open** Non-directive interviews with open questions are appropriate when the following applies:
  - The aim is to obtain rich, in-depth, personal information from each person.
  - The aim is to make the individual feel involved in the interview.
  - The aim is to gain a general impression of opinions and views rather than specific, detailed information on a particular topic.
  - It is not important to compare responses of different people.
  - The interviewer is well-trained to cope with such interviews.
- **Closed** Structured questions with closed questions are appropriate when the following applies:
  - The aim is to obtain information that is easy to analyse.
  - The aim is to compare directly the answers given by different interviewees.
  - There are specific topics in which the interviewer is interested.

The influence of the interviewer and interviewer bias
The gender, ethnicity, accent, age, and other personal qualities (such as how relaxed they make the interviewee feel) of the interviewer can all influence the responses given to interview questions.

Views expressed by the interviewer can influence the interviewee: this is known as *interviewer bias*. This can be minimised by the interviewer remaining impassive (neutral) when answers are given.

Questionnaire Design

Questions on questionnaires may be *fixed choice* (also known as closed) or *open*. See earlier for examples, with strengths and weaknesses.

Constructing a questionnaire
- Construct an attitude scale, e.g. strongly agree, agree, neutral, disagree, strongly disagree.
- Decide on fixed choice or open-ended questions. Open-ended questions do not allow comparisons between people or statistical analysis. You would not, for example, be able to say that 30% of people believe it is wrong to smack children. Open-ended questions do, however, give more information.
- Avoid leading questions. A question like "Do you agree that students' grants should be increased?" tends to imply that the person should agree with it.
- Avoid long, complex questions that may be misunderstood.
- Make sure questions are straightforward and can be answered. For example, a question like "How many times have you been to the doctor in the last year?" is very difficult to answer.

- Avoid emotive questions that may put people on the defensive, for example, when interviewing students, "How do you feel about students receiving public money to further their education?"
- Do not ask too many questions.
- Do not invade people's privacy. Do not ask questions that can cause embarrassment or annoyance.

Characteristics of a good questionnaire

- **Standardisation** Standardised questionnaires (and tests) are those that have been given to a large representative sample so any individual's scores can be compared against others. This allows us to say, for example, how prejudiced someone is in comparison to an average derived from many other scores.
- **Reliability** This always refers to consistency so it's a measure of how consistent attitudes (or anything else being measured) are. You would expect some variation over a long time period, but little over a short one. The more consistent the scores, the more reliable the questionnaire. This can be measured by the test–retest method in which a lot of people are given the same (or a very similar) questionnaire on two occasions and the scores are correlated. The higher the correlation, the higher the reliability.
- **Validity** This refers to the extent to which the questionnaire measures what it is supposed to measure. The results of the questionnaire are correlated with another means of obtaining the same data. For example, scores on an anxiety questionnaire for schoolchildren could be compared with teacher ratings on their anxiety levels.

OPERATIONALISATION OF VARIABLES

Some variables such as "performance" are very general so we need to decide on a precise way to measure them. For example, we could measure "performance in LTM" by the number of words remembered. This is known as *operationalising* the variable because it is defined in terms of the operations taken to measure it.

It is necessary to operationalise both the independent and the dependent variable. For example, if we wanted to see if people perform better in quiet than in noisy conditions, we need to decide exactly what will constitute "quiet" and what will constitute "noisy" (the IV) (Music playing? Traffic noise outside? TV on? etc.).

Psychologists use very different means of operationalising variables and this can strongly influence results. For example, think about how different researchers have operationalised conformity (Asch used line length; Zimbardo used a simulated prison etc.).

EVALUATION

STRENGTH

- It generally provides a clear and objective definition of even complex variables.

WEAKNESSES

- Operational definitions can be arbitrary or artificial. For example, memory is often oper-ationalised by learning specific information such as lists of words but there are very many other ways in which memory could be measured.
- Operational definitions often cover only part of the meaning of the variable or concept, e.g. operationalising verbal ability by measuring the number of anagrams a participant can solve. There are many types of verbal ability not covered by this.
- Everyone is not always agreed on the accuracy of the operationalisation.

PILOT STUDIES

A pilot study is a small-scale study carried out before the main one in order to check procedures, de-sign, and so on. It helps sort out problems and allows for adjustments, thereby saving time and money.

Purposes (Advantages) of Pilot Studies

- To check the standardised procedure and general design to see if it's worth investing time and money in the main study.
- To check the practical details, for example, that measurement can be made accurately, that the procedure is neither too quick nor too slow.
- To ensure that the instructions can be understood.
- To decide between two alternative ways of conducting a study, for example, face-to-face or tele-phone interview.
- To decide on the approximate number of participants to use in order to obtain meaningful results.

CONTROL OF EXTRANEOUS VARIABLES

Earlier we discussed the possible effects of extraneous variables. In any study there are likely to be variables that affect the results. The researcher is only interested in the effect of the IV on the DV—any other variables that may affect the DV are called extraneous variables. If these variables cause problems they are called confounding variables.

As far as possible, confounding variables must be controlled, as they mask the effect of the IV.

Types of Confounding Variable

- **Controlled variables** It is important to control, or keep constant, certain variables such as time of day and location. These are known as controlled variables.
- **Constant error** Any variables that change between conditions, such as participants becoming more tired, or being more motivated in one condition than another, are difficult to control. Such confounding variables are known as a constant error.

RELIABILITY AND VALIDITY

Reliability

One of the most important aspects of measurements is that they should be reliable. If measurements are taken on more than one occasion they should be *consistent* or they are meaningless. If a speedometer gave different readings at the same speed it would be useless. The same applies to measuring behaviour. We can consider reliability in terms of *internal reliability* and *external reliability*.

- **Internal reliability** How consistently a method measures *within itself*. For example, a ruler should measure the same distance between 0cm and 5cm as it does between 5cm and 10cm.
- **External reliability** How consistently a method measures over time, population, or location when repeated. Results from an IQ or personality test should not differ markedly from one occasion to another.

We considered earlier how to measure reliability of observers (inter-observer, inter-rater, inter-judge reliability).

Ways of establishing reliability of tests
- **Split-half technique** The participant does the whole test, then the answers are split in two (either odd/even items or randomly) and scores of the two halves are correlated. This measures internal reliability.
- **Test–retest method** The same test is given to participants on two separate occasions to see if their scores remain relatively similar. The interval between testings must be long enough to prevent a *practice effect* from occurring, but not so long that the measures may have changed anyway (e.g. reading ability may change over a period of 6 months). This measures external reliability.

 For *reliability* read *consistency*. When exam questions ask about "reliability", substitute the word "consistency" and you will be on the right track.

Validity

Validity refers to whether a technique can achieve the purpose for which it was designed. "Valid" means "true", and measures are valid if they measure what they are supposed to measure. We will look at the validity of research studies, especially experiments, and ask whether the measurements taken will be a true reflection of what they are supposed to be measuring. For example, did the technique used by Milgram *really* measure obedience? One of the major problems with establishing validity in psychological research is that the more precisely and carefully you control conditions (by using a laboratory-type set up), the less valid the measures are likely to be in terms of how they generalise to the real world.

We need to distinguish between two types of validity: *internal validity* and *external validity*.

Internal validity
Internal validity refers to the validity of an experiment within the confines in which it is carried out. It is the extent to which the measurements are accurate and the extent to which they measure what they are supposed to measure; thus it refers to the extent to which it is possible to establish *causality*.

Internal validity establishes whether the IV really caused the results. Experiments may lack internal validity because of experimenter effects (see ASP4 pp.194), demand characteristics (see ASP4 pp.145), and participant reactivity (see ASP4 p.240). In order to be valid, it is necessary to have standardised instructions (see ASP4 p.64) and randomisation (see ASP4 p.144).

External validity
External validity refers to the validity of a study outside the research situation itself. Thus, it provides some idea of the extent to which the findings can be *generalised*. It can be referred to as *ecological validity*. When considering the issue of external validity and generalisability, it is necessary to consider four main aspects:

Populations	Is the sample representative? Do the findings obtained from a given sample of individuals generalise to a larger population from which the sample was selected?
Locations	Does the setting and/or situation created in the study generalise to a real-life setting and/or situation?
Measures or constructs	Do the measures used generalise to other measures? For example, does a measure of long-term memory based on remembering word lists generalise to everyday memory?
Times	Do the findings generalise to the past and future? For example, are people as obedient today as they were 30 years ago?

Meta-analyses are a means of determining whether results generalise outside of a particular population. All the results of studies in a particular area (such as obedience studies across time and culture) are combined into a single analysis to see which of the results remain consistent and which vary.

 Laboratory experiments have high internal validity, but fairly low ecological validity. Field experiments have high external validity, but fairly low internal validity.

AWARENESS OF BRITISH PSYCHOLOGICAL SOCIETY CODE OF ETHICS

Ethical issues arise when there is a conflict between the rights and dignity of participants and the goals and outcomes of research. Professional bodies in psychology have drawn up guidelines to protect the participants. These include BPS (the British Psychological Society) and APA (the American Psychological Association). These are standards of conduct adopted by psychologists and are designed to preserve "the well-being and dignity of research participants". However, there are variations in the ethical codes of different countries, and there is some concern as to how these ethical codes are actually enforced.

Ethical Guidelines

Here is a brief summary of the 2006 BPS Ethical Guidelines for research with human participants (see ASP4 p.183; and for the full, unabridged 2006 BPS guidelines, please visit The British Psychological Society website at http://www.bps.org.uk/the-society/code-of-conduct/code-of-conduct_home.cfm):

General

- Investigators must always consider the ethical implications of their research and the psychological consequences for their participants.

Consent

- Whenever possible, the investigator should inform all participants of the objectives of the investigation. If this is not practical, there should be additional safeguards to protect the welfare and dignity of the participants.
- Whenever possible, real consent should be obtained from people under 16 and those of any age with impairments in understanding and communications. For children under 16, permission should also be obtained from parents or teachers.
- Payment of participants must not be used to induce them to risk harm.

Deception

- The withholding of information or the misleading of participants is unacceptable if the participants are likely to object or to show unease once debriefed.
- Intentional deception of the participants over the purpose and general nature of the investigation should be avoided whenever possible. Before conducting a study in which withholding of information is considered unavoidable, the investigator has a responsibility to:
  - Determine that no alternatives procedures that avoid this are possible
  - Ensure that participants are provided with sufficient information at the earliest stage
  - Consult appropriately upon how the deception is likely to be received by the participants.

Debriefing

- After any study in which participants are aware they have taken part, the investigator should provide them with necessary information for them to understand the nature of the research.
- If a verbal description is not enough, the debriefing should include active intervention.

Confidentiality

- Information obtained about a participant is confidential unless otherwise agreed in advance. Participants in psychological research have a right to expect that information they provide will be treated confidentially and, if published, will not be identifiable as theirs.

Protection of participants

- Participants should be protected from physical and mental harm during the investigations. The risk of harm should be no greater than in everyday life.
- Participants should be given ways of contacting the investigators if stress or concern arises after the research.

Observational research

- Unless the people observed give their consent to being observed, observational research should only be carried out in situations where those observed would expect to be observed by strangers.

Giving advice

- If, during the investigation, the researcher obtains knowledge of any physical or psychological problems of which the participant is unaware, they should tell them about it if their future well-being may otherwise be endangered.

Colleagues

- A psychologist who believes that another psychologist is not correctly following these guidelines should encourage that investigator to re-evaluate the research.

THE COST–BENEFIT ANALYSIS

Psychologists face a dilemma when investigating some topics in psychology, such as social influence. On the one hand they want to use their research skills to advance our knowledge and understanding of humanity, but on the other hand they have a responsibility to the people who are willing to take part in their research. The participants are not objects of study, but human beings.

Preventing psychologists from undertaking any research that might involve stress or conflict would necessarily result in a somewhat "lopsided" view of psychology. However, if psychologists do undertake such research they can be accused of abusing their power and being disrespectful towards fellow human beings.

It has been suggested that psychologists should do a *cost–benefit analysis* of the research, with the benefits (or strengths) focusing on the gains for both psychology and in some cases the participants, whilst the costs (or weaknesses) focus on the perceived harm to the participants or the profession.

Ethics are determined by a balance between benefit and cost, or a cost–benefit analysis. Some things may be less acceptable than others, but if the ultimate end is for the good of humankind then psychological researchers may feel that an undesirable behaviour, such as causing stress to an animal or deceiving participants as to the nature of the study, is acceptable.

EVALUATION

STRENGTHS

- The results may make us more aware of our own and others' behaviour and raise consciousness about important issues.
- Milgram's study may result in people taking more responsibility for their own actions and not blindly obeying others.
- Asch's research may make us challenge group norms and stand up for our own beliefs, and the rights of others.

- Zimbardo's research may help us understand why some of the atrocities that take place in prisons occur, and how being given power can change people in a negative way.
- Hofling et al.'s research may encourage people working in institutional settings like hospitals to check whether the orders given are in the best interest of the patient.
- Such obedience research can also benefit the participants by giving them insight into their own behaviour.

WEAKNESSES

- Participants may be distressed at finding out something about themselves that they would have preferred not to know.
- Participants may feel that they have been "tricked" or lied to.
- Participants may have lowered self-esteem as a result of taking part in the study.
- Participants are not given the opportunity to give informed consent.
- Participants may say that they are pleased that they took part in the study because they feel obliged to, rather than because they did (demand characteristics).
- It may bring the psychological profession into disrepute as an "institutionalised candid camera".
- Diener and Crandall (1978; see ASP4 p.184) suggested the following drawbacks to the cost–benefit approach:
  - It is almost impossible to predict both costs and benefits prior to conducting a study.
  - Even after the study, it is hard to quantify costs and benefits, partly because it can depend on who is making the judgements. For example, a participant may judge the costs differently from the researcher, and benefits may be judged differently in years to come.
  - It tends to ignore the substantive rights of individuals in favour of practical, utilitarian considerations.

KEY ETHICAL ISSUES

The key ethical issues are:

- The use of deception
- Informed consent
- Protection from harm.

The Use of Deception

One major concern revolves around whether deception should take place. Without deception, it is argued that participants' behaviour in a research situation would not be an accurate portrayal of how they would behave in a real-life scenario. Often, if the psychologist reveals the purpose of the study, then it becomes pointless. An example would be Asch's study of conformity by judging line length (see ASP4 p.145). In order to cope with necessary deception, participants should be debriefed. This means that at the end of the study the participants should be told the true nature and purpose of the research, provided with information about the research findings, and offered the opportunity to have their results excluded from the study if they wish.

Informed Consent

It is considered the right of participants to provide *voluntary informed consent*. This means several things:

- Being informed about the purpose of the research.
- Being informed about what will be required.
- Being informed about your rights as a participant, e.g. the right to confidentiality, and the right to withdraw.
- Giving your full consent to take part in the study.

However, there are many situations where it is just not possible to obtain full informed consent prior to the study commencing. In an attempt to resolve the difficulty of obtaining informed consent when participants are being deceived, other methods of obtaining consent have been proposed, and we will now consider each one in turn.

Presumptive consent

This involves asking members of the population, who are similar to the participants, whether they would consider the research to be acceptable.

Prior general consent

This involves asking people who volunteer to take part in research general questions before they are chosen.

- **FOR EXAMPLE:** "Would you mind taking part in a study that involved your being misinformed about its true nature?"

    "Would you mind being involved in a study that might cause you stress?"

Participants who agree may later be chosen, since it is assumed that they have agreed in principle to take part. This consent is sometimes referred to as *partially informed consent* for obvious reasons.

Retrospective consent

Some psychologists suggest that by fully debriefing the participants and giving them the opportunity to withdraw their data, the participants have provided retrospective consent. The assumption is that giving them the right to withdraw their data gives them the same power as if they had refused to take part in the first place.

However consent is obtained, you need to remember that people sometimes agree to take part in a study without really thinking through exactly what it involves. In other cases, the consent is given by another person, such as a parent or other authority figure.

Protection from Harm

Participants should be protected from both physical and psychological harm as far as possible.

It could be argued that Milgram's research involved physical as well as psychological harm—some of them were sweating profusely and biting their lips.

Psychological harm is harder to measure but some of Milgram's participants may have experienced lowered self-esteem from the knowledge that they could have harmed (even killed) an innocent person just because they were told to. Nevertheless, many felt grateful for their increased self-awareness and believed the research to be important.

Some of the guidelines are designed to protect participants, especially those of confidentiality and right to privacy.

There are no easy answers in ethics and, ultimately, judgements have to be made as to whether the end justifies the means.

Ethical Considerations of Different Methods

It is of paramount importance that studies are conducted in an ethical manner. Listed below are some of the ethical issues raised by the different types of research methods.

- **Experiments**
  - Participants may feel that they should do things they would not do normally. Milgram's research demonstrates this.
  - Participants should be given the right to withdraw but they may feel reluctant to do so.
- **Field experiments**
  - Most do not lend themselves to obtaining informed consent from participants.
  - It is difficult for participants to know that they have the right to withdraw.
  - It is also difficult to offer debriefing.
- **Natural experiments**
  - There are problems of informed consent since this cannot be obtained.
  - Researchers need to be sensitive if investigating the effects of an unpleasant event, such as a natural disaster.
- **Naturalistic observations**
  - If participants do not know they are being observed—a situation called an *undisclosed observation*—then there are issues of invasion of privacy and intrusion. This would apply if, for example, one-way mirrors were used or if people were observed in public places.
  - There may be issues of confidentiality if the place in which the psychologists made their observations (such as a hospital or school) can be easily identified, or if it was known they were visiting it.
  - If the observer participates in a group (participant observation), he or she may influence the group behaviour without prior consent.
- **Correlational analysis**
  - There can be problems with the way in which the public interpret the results of correlations, where they might think that correlation equals causation. This is especially true with socially sensitive issues such as the relationship between race and IQ.
- **Interviews**
  - *Confidentiality* should always be respected, especially where personal issues are involved. It may not be sufficient to simply withhold someone's name since they may still be identifiable. Interviewers should take great care to avoid material getting into the wrong hands.
  - Interviewees should not feel obliged to answer questions that they find embarrassing, and should be reassured that they do not have to answer any questions they do not want to answer.

SELECTION OF PARTICIPANTS

The *target population* is the whole group to which a researcher wishes to generalise the findings. Obviously the whole target population cannot be used so it is necessary to select just some of them.

The *sample* of participants is the actual group of participants that take part in a study. A *representative sample* is a sample that is typical (representative) of the target population. There are several ways in which to select a sample:

Random sampling	Involves having the names of the target population and giving each one an equal chance of being selected. This can be done by using a computer or drawing names from a hat.
Systematic sampling	A modified version of random sampling that involves selecting, say, every one-hundredth name from a phone book.
Opportunity sampling	Involves using whoever is available and willing.
Volunteer sampling	Involves using participants who volunteer to take part in a study, perhaps by replying to an advertisement.

Problems with random and systematic sampling

It is almost impossible to obtain a truly random sample because obtaining a total list of the target population is difficult, not all of the target population may be available, and some people may refuse to take part, thus giving a *volunteer bias*.

Problems with opportunity sampling

Opportunity sampling can be an *ad hoc* affair, and the sample really depends on who is available at the time, such as friends of the researcher, students, or people in a particular workplace. This type of group is unlikely to be representative and almost certainly constitutes a *biased sample*.

Problems with volunteer sampling

Some researchers believe that people who volunteer may be different from non-volunteers, for instance in personality, so may not be a truly representative sample.

Random sampling

Opportunity sampling

 Only if we have a representative sample can we generalise to the target population but such a sample is difficult to obtain. The best we can do is try to reduce *sampling bias*.

The Sample Size

When considering the ideal number of participants for each condition, there is no definite answer. Each study needs to be designed in such a way as to reduce *sampling bias*, and the following factors need to be taken into consideration:

- The sample should be large enough to be representative.
- The sample must not be so large that the study becomes very costly or time consuming.
- If the target population is large then it is probably going to have quite a lot of variation, so a fairly large sample will be required in order to be representative.
- If the target population is very small, it may be wise to use the whole population. This may apply to some very unusual disorders, or to people over the age of 105.
- If the research has important implications and will be used in policy making (e.g. testing a new biological therapy) then the sample size should be larger than a less important study such as an undergraduate research project.

If there is a general rule of thumb that applies to deciding on sample size, it is the following:

"The smaller the likely effect being studied, the larger the sample size needed to demonstrate it."

Remember that not all the participants who volunteer to take part in a study are eligible. This adds to the number who need to be approached by the researcher. More importantly, not all participants who start a study will finish it (particularly with longitudinal studies) and this may leave you with a *biased sample*. This was true of Hodges and Tizard's (1989; see ASP4 pp.149–150) study of privation.

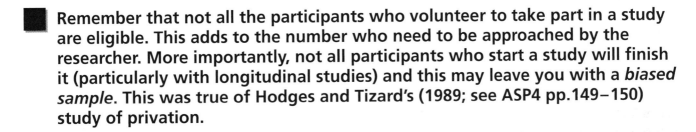

OVER TO YOU

Many famous psychological studies have used a biased sample. For example, Asch used students for his conformity studies (see ASP4 pp.265–267), as did Zimbardo in his prison study (see ASP4 pp.275–277). Can you think of any other examples where a biased sample was used? Try to think of examples that did not deal with students.

One of the reasons why students are not representative of the general population is that their mean age is low. Suggest two other ways in which students are not representative of the general population.

Would you need to use more participants in an independent measures design than in a repeated measures design? If so, why?

DEMAND CHARACTERISTICS AND INVESTIGATOR EFFECTS

Interaction between researchers and participants can cause certain problems. These can be due to the behaviour of the participants or the behaviour of the researcher.

Participant Reactivity

Knowing you are being studied affects behaviour, and this is known as participant reactivity, or the Hawthorne effect. People's behaviour changes when an interest is shown in it, regardless of any other variables being manipulated. Two examples of participant reactivity are demand characteristics and evaluation apprehension:

Demand characteristics

Orne (1962; see ASP4 p.145) found:

- Most people do their best to comply with what they perceive to be the demands of the experimental situation, so they try to guess what is expected of them.
- Others may look out for "tricks" so they can avoid being caught out.
- Some may try to do the opposite of what they think is expected.
- Their interpretation of the situation affects their behaviour in some way.

Demand characteristics can be reduced by using a *single blind* procedure, where participants do not know which condition they have been allocated to. Instead they are given a false account of the experiment so they will not discover clues as to the nature of the research. This can be problematic ethically as fully informed consent cannot be obtained.

Evaluation apprehension

This is when concern by participants that they are being judged can alter their behaviour.

Investigator effects

The researcher can inadvertently affect the results of an experiment. The main problem is *experimenter expectancy*, whereby the investigator's expectations can affect the behaviour of participants being tested. This was shown by Rosenthal's (1966; see ASP4 p.193) research with flatworms and rats. He demonstrated an expectancy effect when students were training rats to perform tricks, and found that those students who were told their rats had been bred for intelligence managed to teach their rats more tricks than those who had been told that their rats had been bred for dullness.

Investigator effects can be reduced by using a *double blind* procedure, where neither the investigator nor the participants know what the research hypothesis being tested is. However, this is often either impractical or too expensive.

DATA ANALYSIS AND PRESENTATION

PRESENTATION AND INTERPRETATION OF QUANTITATIVE DATA

Graphs, Scattergrams, and Tables

Quantitative data involves data that is in *numerical form* (e.g. how many words were remembered; what percentage of people agreed with a certain statement; the correlation co-efficient between two variables).

It is helpful to use visual displays to summarise information and to get a feel for what it means. Information presented in a graph or chart makes it easy to understand what has been found. The different types of graphs and charts include histograms, bar charts, and scattergrams, each of which will be considered in turn.

Histogram

Histograms provide a way of showing *frequencies*. The histogram below gives information on the number of athletes that can run at each speed from 45 to 94 seconds in 5 second intervals. Notice that the vertical axis on a histogram always shows *frequency* (either as actual numbers or as a percentage).

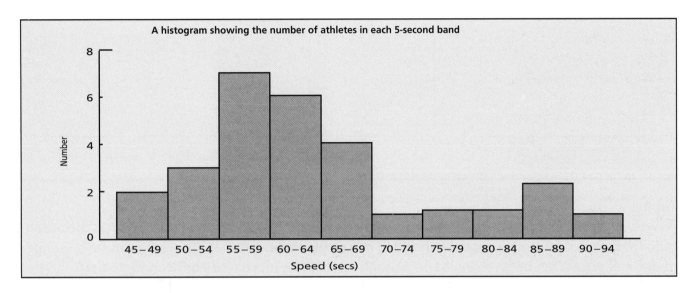

Bar chart

Bar charts are used when scores are in *categories*, such as how many people are categorised as Type A, Type B, or Type C personality, or, as in the bar chart below, what people's favourite leisure activities are.

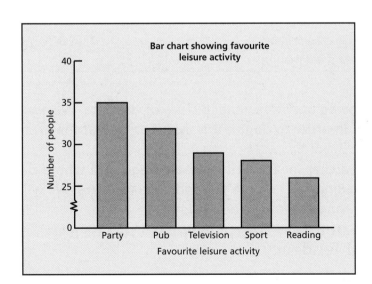

In a bar chart the categories are shown along the horizontal axis, and the frequencies are indicated on the vertical axis, as in a histogram. However, in contrast to the data contained in histograms, the categories in bar charts cannot be ordered numerically in a meaningful way. Instead, they are arranged in ascending or descending order of popularity. Another difference from histograms is that the rectangles (bars) do not usually touch each other.

Scattergrams

Scattergrams (also known as scattergraphs) are used to express *correlations*. To draw such a chart, one variable is put on the horizontal axis, and the other is put on the vertical axis. Then each pair of scores is placed as a dot or cross where the two scores meet.

Scattergrams enable you to see at a glance whether a correlation is positive, negative, or if there is no relationship. The different graphs are shown below.

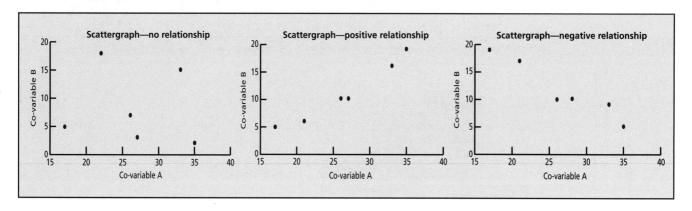

Tables

As well as graphs and charts, it is useful to summarise the data in terms of a table. This has the advantage that a lot of information can be included in a single table and that precise figures (to a number of decimal places) can be given whilst on a graph it would be much more difficult to do that.

Mean number of correct items recalled in different conditions		
	Group 1: Loud noise	*Group 2: No noise (control)*
No. of participants	15	15
Mean correct items	23.5	29.5
Standard deviation	4.7	4.9

Graphs and charts provide us with a visual picture of the data. We also need to look at the raw scores and analyse them. In order to do this it is useful to look at the averages, the variability, and so on.

For example, if a researcher measured the reading age of a whole class, of particular interest would be the average reading age and the top and bottom scores. We will look at summarising, in terms of *central tendency* and in terms of *dispersion*.

Measures of Central Tendency

The mean

The mean is obtained by adding the scores and dividing by the total number.

- **FOR EXAMPLE:** The mean of the scores 2, 6, 8, 5, 7, 6, 3, 3 = 5 (40 ÷ 8).

EVALUATION

STRENGTH

- It is the only measure of central tendency that takes account of *all* scores.

WEAKNESS

- It can give a distorted impression if there are any very unusual scores.

Example of a misleading mean
Scores
25
27
28
29
34
39
42
288
512 ÷ 8 = **64**

The median

The median is the halfway point that separates the lower 50% of scores and the upper 50% of scores. If there is an odd number of scores, this the middle value. If there is an even number, it's halfway between the two middle scores.

- **FOR EXAMPLE:** The median of 2, 4, 6, 7, 8, 9, 26 = 7 (the middle score), and the median of 2, 4, 6, 10, 12, 13 = 8 (halfway between 6 and 10).

EVALUATION

STRENGTH

- It is unaffected by extreme scores. Here 26 is an extreme score, but it does not distort the measure.

WEAKNESS

- It does not take account of most of the scores. It can be especially misleading if there are only a few scores.

The mode

The mode is the most frequently occurring score (remember this by thinking of the mode as "the fashionable one"!).

- **FOR EXAMPLE:** The mode of 2, 5, 7, 8, 5, 4, 2, 7, 8, 7 = 7 (as 7 occurs most frequently). Sometimes there is more than one mode. When there are two, it is called a *bimodal* distribution.

EVALUATION

STRENGTHS

- It is unaffected by extreme scores.
- It is useful when we want to know how most participants behaved. For example, in Milgram's study we want to know the modal value of where on the voltage scale most people went up to. Likewise, we may want to know the most frequent grade that students attained in an exam, or what most people's opinion is of a proposition.

WEAKNESSES

- It tells us nothing about all the other scores.
- It is often not very "central".
- It tends to fluctuate from one sample to another.

Measures of Dispersion

Suppose you measured the reading ages of a class of children. Apart from wanting some indication of the average reading age, you also want to know the dispersion of scores. It would be possible to have two classes in which the mean reading age was 7 years, with one ranging from 6.5 years to 7.4 years and the other ranging from 5 years to 10.5 years. The classes are therefore quite different and would require different teaching methods. There are three principal measures that can be used (the *range*, the *interquartile range*, and the *standard deviation*), and these have different levels of sophistication.

The range

The range is the top value minus the bottom value plus 1. When using whole numbers, we add 1 to the value because they have probably been rounded up and down from fractional values, so this makes it more accurate. When the numbers are not whole, simply take the lowest from the highest.

- **FOR EXAMPLE:** The range of 2, 5, 8, 6, 9, 3, 7, 4, 2, 7 = 8 (9 − 2 + 1). The range of 2.3, 3.4, 5.5, 6.7, 7.2, 8.9, 9.9 = 7.6 (= 9.9 − 2.3).

EVALUATION

STRENGTHS

- It is easy to calculate and see at a glance.
- It takes full account of extreme values.

WEAKNESSES

- There are limitations, as it can be distorted by only one extreme score. If there had been one value of 25 in the first list above, the range becomes 24, three times what it was without that single score.
- It only takes account of two scores (the highest and lowest) so it provides no indication of the overall spread of scores.

The interquartile range

This is another means of measuring variation, which uses the range of the middle 50% of scores. Suppose you had the following 12 scores: 1, 3, 4, 6, 6, 8, 8, 8, 9, 10, 15, 19. In order to calculate the interquartile range, you start by using the middle six scores, those underlined. The lower boundary of the interquartile range is between the lowest of these six scores and the score below that, in this case the number between 4 and 6, i.e. 5. Similarly the upper boundary is between 9 and 10, i.e. 9.5. The interquartile range is the difference between the upper and lower boundaries, 9.5 − 5 = 4.5.

EVALUATION

STRENGTH

- It is not influenced by a single extreme score, so it provides a more accurate reflection of the spread of scores than the range.

WEAKNESS

- It does not take account of most of the top and bottom 25% of scores.

Standard deviation

The standard deviation is a measure of dispersion of scores around the mean. It is a very useful measure especially when scores are normally distributed (i.e. fit a normal distribution curve, such as IQ or height; see ASP4 p.314) because about two-thirds of scores will lie within one standard deviation of the mean. If you don't have a good head for numbers DON'T GIVE UP, as this really is quite simple. Suppose the mean reading age of a group is 7 years and the standard deviation is one year. This means that two-thirds of all children will have reading ages between 6 years and 8 years (one year either side of the mean of 7).

EVALUATION

STRENGTHS

- It takes account of all scores, so it provides a very accurate measure of the spread of scores.
- It is especially useful with normal distributions because it gives a very precise measure of variation.

WEAKNESS

- It is more difficult to calculate than other measures of dispersion.

ANALYSIS AND INTERPRETATION OF CORRELATIONAL DATA

A correlational study involves looking at two variables and measuring the extent to which as one varies, so does the other. For example, we can look at the correlation (association) between the amount of violent TV programmes watched and the amount of aggression shown, or we could look to see whether there is a relationship in intelligence between parents and children. For each variable we have a pair of scores. In the case of the violent TV and aggression, each pair of scores comes from the same individual. In the case of intelligence, one of the pair comes from a parent and the other from a son/daughter. In each case there is a related *pair* of scores such that, when presented in a table, the pairs would be together.

There are two important facts to remember about correlations;

- They do NOT allow you to draw conclusions about cause and effect.
- They can be used to make predictions. If you know there is a correlation between two variables, knowing the value of one of these variables allows you to predict the other.

We can, within reason, predict that children who watch a lot of violent TV are likely to be more aggressive than those who watch little of it. That isn't to say that the violent content of the TV programmes has caused the aggression (there may be other factors operating) but it does mean that prediction is possible over a large group of people.

Positive and Negative Correlations

- **Positive correlation** High values of one variable are associated with high values of the other. For example, in the section on stress we saw that there is a positive correlation between stress and illness: people who scored high on the Holmes–Rahe scale also took more time off sick (1967; see ASP4 p.233).
- **Negative correlation** High values of one variable are associated with low values of the other. We may expect to see a negative correlation between work productivity and stress, in that the higher your stress level the lower your work productivity and vice versa.
- **No correlation** There is no relationship between them. This can be as important a finding from research as finding a positive or negative relationship.

Correlation Co-efficients

Some correlations are strong whereas others are weak. It is very useful to have a means by which the strength, as well as whether the relationship is positive or negative, can be expressed. This is done by means of a number called a correlation co-efficient. These numbers vary from +1 to –1.

We said earlier that correlations allow you to make predictions about the other variable if you know the value of the one of them. The correlation co-efficient allows you to judge the confidence to which this prediction can be made.

A correlation of 1 (+ or –) means that there is a perfect correlation; obviously this is rare. The closer the value is to 1 (whether positive or negative) the stronger the correlation and the more confidently you can predict one from the other. So a correlation of +0.87 is stronger than +0.34; a correlation of –0.68 is stronger than –0.29, and so on.

Interpretation of correlations

As mentioned earlier, you cannot infer cause and effect from a correlation. Nevertheless, there must be a reason for the relationship. If we call the variables A and B and there is an association between them, then are three possible ways in which they may be related (or possibly a combination of all three):

1. A may cause B.
2. B may cause A.
3. X (a third factor) may cause both A and B.

Let's take the example of watching violent TV (factor A) and levels of aggression (factor B). It's possible that watching violent TV causes children to become aggressive (A causes B); that aggressive people choose to watch violent TV (B causes A); or that people from violent backgrounds (factor X) are aggressive and enjoy watching violent TV.

OVER TO YOU

Using the guidance above, try to think of three separate reasons why there is a positive correlation between stress and illness.

PRESENTATION OF QUALITATIVE DATA

Qualitative data are descriptive data—data that express meanings and explanations rather than numbers. Some methods that psychologists use yield both qualitative and quantitative data; others provide only quantitative data; whilst yet others give qualitative data only. The main methods that yield qualitative data are case studies and discourse analysis.

Presentation of Data from Case Studies

We discussed case studies earlier in this section. The data are usually detailed and are often presented by:

- Direct quotes from the participants.
- Main categories of behaviour, sometimes divided into sub-categories. An example in *AS Level Psychology, Fourth Edition* is that of a set of case studies of people with a phobia of going to the dentist. They were placed in categories of threat to self-respect and well-being; avoidance; readiness to act; ambivalence in coping.
- Whether the data support pre-existing hypotheses. For example, Lau and Russell (1980) divide data into whether wins and defeats in sporting events are interpreted differently, that wins are interpreted as caused by internal factors (we played well; we are good players), while losses were interpreted as caused by external factors (the pitch was in poor condition; we had a lot of injuries).

Presentation of Data from Discourse Analysis

Discourse analysis involves focusing on the (hidden) meaning of a particular piece of material. An example is that of Burns (1998) who analysed the meaning of the lyrics to a no.1 hit in the UK, "Barbie Girl" by Aqua. This included the verse by Barbie (talking to Ken)

"You can touch
You can play
If you say
I'm always yours."

Burns considered that the hidden meaning was that Barbie was quite willing to be a possession, a sexual plaything on condition Ken made a lasting commitment to her. In essence, it expresses the view that men want sex and control while women want love and commitment.

The presentation of discourse analysis is, therefore, in the form of the hidden meaning of the material and depends to some extent on the interpretation of the person doing the analysis.

Content Analysis

A content analysis involves analysing the content of any piece of communication. It often involves analysing the content of newspapers, books, and television but has been carried out of a huge variety of sources propaganda, advertising, nursery rhymes, diaries, and even graffiti in men's and women's toilets.

Content analysis usually involves both qualitative and quantitative data, in other words, both description and numbers (often percentages) in each category.

STAGES INVOLVED IN CONTENT ANALYSIS	
Stage	*Example*
The researcher puts forward a hypothesis.	TV advertisements are sexist.
The researcher identifies relevant categories.	Who does voice over? Who gives technical advice? Who is in the main role? Do the characters act in gender stereotypical ways?
The researcher decides which sources of information to use for his/her sample. (This is important as there could be bias in the choice.)	There is a huge number of adverts on TV. The choice must not be too biased, you would not choose only adverts that were during programmes that mainly appeal to women or mainly appeal to men.
After training, two or more judges or coders assign the information into categories to ensure that the coding is reliable. These coders must not know the hypothesis.	Some categories are easy to score, e.g. whether the voice over is male/female. Others are more difficult, e.g. it may not be clear-cut who is the main character or whether the actors are in gender-stereotypical roles.
The results must be related to the hypothesis.	The researcher considers the results and decides whether or not the alternative hypothesis is supported.

Here is an example of what a content analysis table may look like:

Content analysis of TV advertisements					
	Number of advertisements with this feature		Total	% Male	% Female
	Male	Female			
Voice over					
Main character					
Persons shown in traditional role					
Persons shown in non-traditional role					

EVALUATION

STRENGTHS

- Qualitative techniques allow us to see people as rounded individuals in a social context.
- They allow us to formulate hypotheses that can be tested by subsequent research.
- They can reduce complex forms of behaviour to a manageable number of meaningful categories.
- Content analysis and discourse analysis have shown that the way we write or talk is strongly influenced by the immediate social context.

WEAKNESSES

- The data obtained from discussions/interviews may be affected by social desirability bias: people lie to be seen in a good light and don't necessarily tell the truth.
- The data may come from an unrepresentative sample. For example, many case studies are of people who have had unusual experiences.
- If a lot of material is collected (e.g. in a case study) the researcher may show bias in selecting certain parts of the information.
- It is inappropriate and/or meaningless to use qualitative data in some areas of psychology. There are times when a researcher needs to use numbers, for example, when looking at the capacity of short-term memory.

OVER TO YOU

A psychologist wishes to conduct an observation study of children's play in an infant-school playground to see if there any differences in the way that boys and girls play. Suggest two categories of play that the psychologist could use.

2 MARKS

Explain two ethical issues relevant to observational studies in a school playground.

2 MARKS + 2 MARKS

Explain how the psychologist could deal with these ethical issues.

2 MARKS + 2 MARKS

BIOLOGICAL PSYCHOLOGY
Stress

5

What's it about?

Biological psychology focuses on the physiological causes and explanations of behaviour. Biology is a very important influence on our behaviour but human behaviour is so complex that very little can be explained by physiology alone. Instead, we have to look at how psychological and social factors interact with physiology. Explanations that consider this interaction offer a biopsychosocial approach.

The topic areas of interest in the physiological approach include the way the nervous system, including the brain, operates, how hormones affect our body, and how our bodily rhythms affect our mood and behaviour. It also includes the topic area of this section; what constitutes stress and the effects it has on us.

WHAT'S IN THIS UNIT?

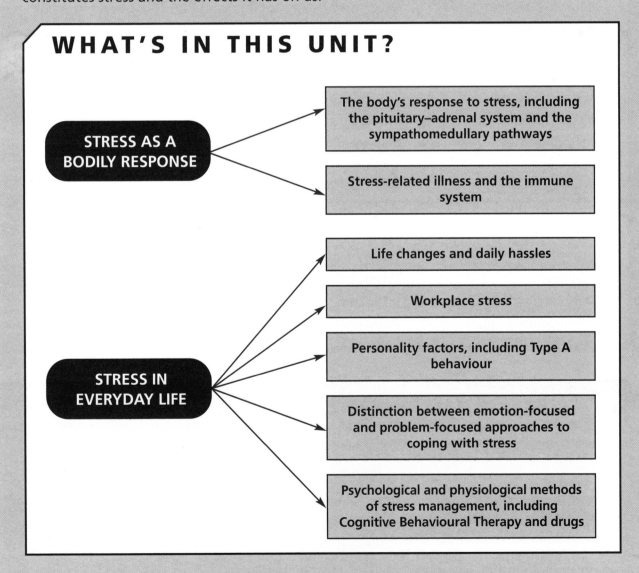

STRESS AS A BODILY RESPONSE
- The body's response to stress, including the pituitary–adrenal system and the sympathomedullary pathways
- Stress-related illness and the immune system

STRESS IN EVERYDAY LIFE
- Life changes and daily hassles
- Workplace stress
- Personality factors, including Type A behaviour
- Distinction between emotion-focused and problem-focused approaches to coping with stress
- Psychological and physiological methods of stress management, including Cognitive Behavioural Therapy and drugs

IMPORTANT TERMS AND CONCEPTS

As part of the AS exam:

- You may be asked to describe, explain, or outline the body's responses to stress.
- You may need to explain how stress is related to various illnesses and what effect it can have on your immune system.
- You will be expected to know what factors in our daily lives can be stressful and how this is related to personality.
- The examiner may also ask you to apply your knowledge to real-life situations or explore how research into stress has enabled us to understand the causes of stress and provide therapies for it.

The following terms are important for understanding this module so it will help you in the exam if you understand what they refer to. Make a list of definitions of the following terms, and if you get stuck, go to the glossary at the end of this book.

Adrenal glands	Emotion-focused coping	PNS (peripheral nervous system)
Adrenaline	Endocrine system	
ANS (autonomic nervous system)	General Adaptation Syndrome (GAS)	Problem-focused coping
Benzodiazepines	Hardiness	Psychological approaches to stress management
Beta blockers	Homeostasis	Psychoneuroimmunology (PNI)
Buffering effect	Hypothalamus	
Burnout	Immune system	Stress
Cardiovascular disorders	Life changes	Stress inoculation training
CNS (central nervous system)	Life events	Stress management
	Noradrenaline	Stressor
Cognitive Behavioural Therapy	Parasympathetic branch	Sympathetic branch
	Physiological approaches to stress management	Sympatho-medullary pathway (SAM)
Daily hassles		
Effort–reward imbalance	Pituitary–adrenal system	Type A personality

OVER TO YOU

Distinguish between emotion-focused and problem-focused approaches to dealing with stress.

3 MARKS + 3 MARKS

Give one strength and one weakness of using non-human animals in research on stress.

3 MARKS + 3 MARKS

STRESS AS A BODILY RESPONSE

WHAT IS STRESS?

There are several definitions of stress. Selye (1950) provided a general definition of stress:

"The non-specific response of the body to any demand."

"Demands" are called stressors—these are events that throw our body out of balance and force it to respond. Examples of stressors are cold, pain, and viruses.

The stress response originally evolved to help animals (including humans) react QUICKLY. When a mouse sees a cat, for example, the sequence of events goes like this:

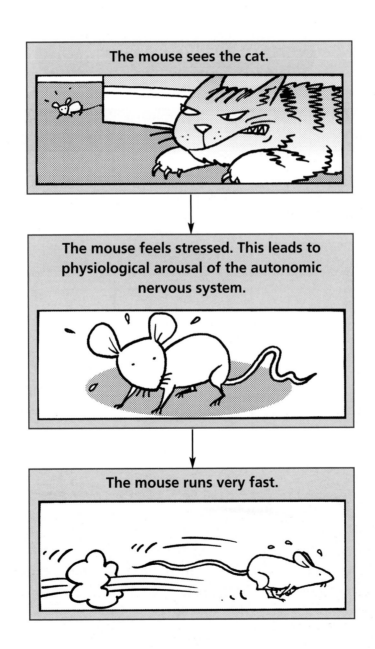

Stress is therefore an *innate, defensive, adaptive* reaction that promotes survival. The example used above is typical of the type of stress with which non-human animals have to cope. However, most stressors with which humans have to deal require a less immediate reaction, such as the stress of taking an exam, money worries, or having to get an assignment completed for the next day. This can make you physiologically aroused but not as much as in the pictures above. The arousal is not as intense but it lasts much longer.

THE NERVOUS SYSTEM

The nervous system is a complex network:

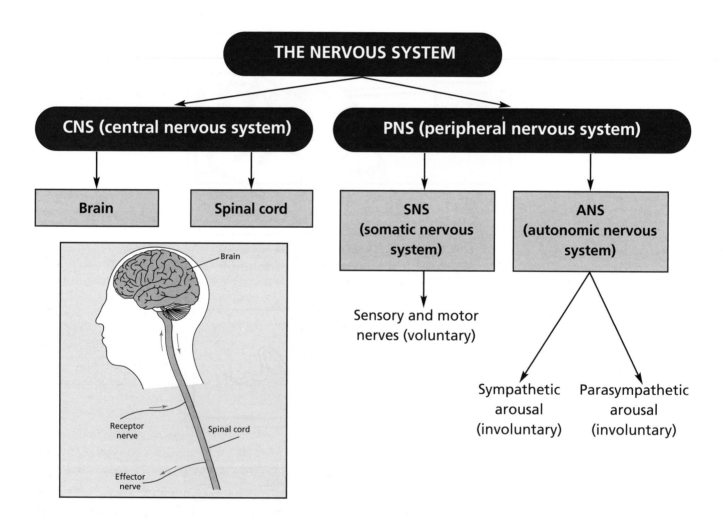

The central nervous system (CNS) consists of the brain and spinal cord. Receptor nerves transmit information to the brain via the spinal cord, and instructions from the brain are sent via the effector nerves. The autonomic nervous system (ANS) plays a vital role in stress:

ACTIVITIES OF THE AUTONOMIC NERVOUS SYSTEM

SYMPATHETIC BRANCH	PARASYMPATHETIC BRANCH

Activates internal organs in situations needing energy and arousal

- Increases heart rate
- Reduces stomach activity
- Pupils become dilated (expanded)
- Bronchi of lungs relax
- Glucose is released
- Expends (uses) energy
- Acts as a troubleshooter ("fight or flight" response)

Involved in trying to conserve and store resources—the opposite effects of the sympathetic NS

- Decreases heart rate
- Increases stomach activity
- Pupils become contracted (smaller)
- Bronchi of lungs constrict
- Glucose is stored
- Conserves (saves) energy
- Acts as a housekeeper ("test and digest" response)

THE BODY'S RESPONSE TO STRESS

Higher brain centres respond to changes in the environment—even mild but unexpected ones such as someone knocking over a cup, or a door slamming. The body has an immediate shock response to a stressor, and if the person is exposed to the stressor for some time a countershock response follows. The initial response depends on the sympathetic adrenal medullary system (SAM), whereas the second response involves the hypothalamic–pituitary–adrenocortical axis (HPA). Both responses originate in the hypothalamus, which is the first link in a chain that also includes the pituitary and adrenal glands.

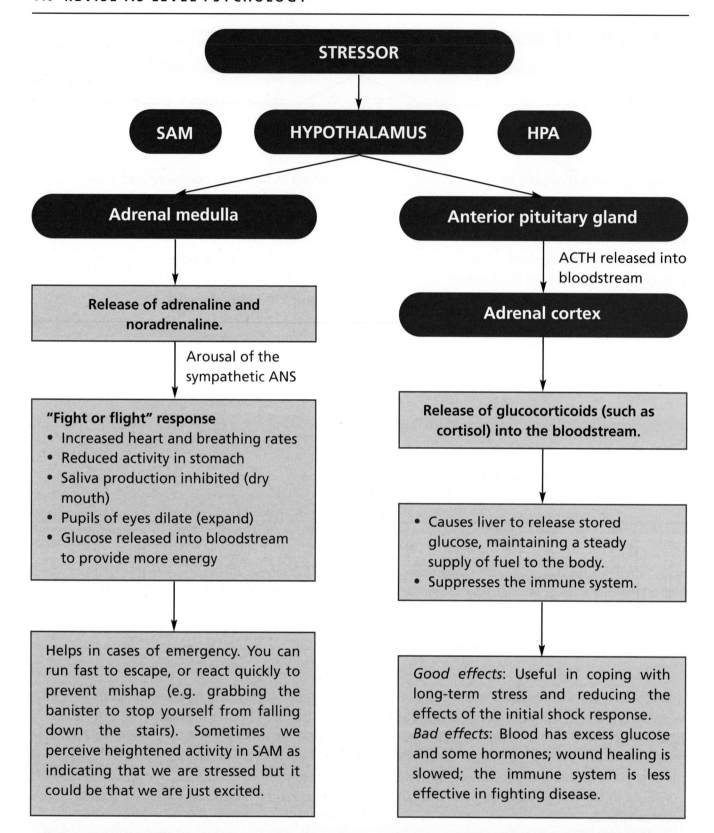

STRESSOR

SAM · **HYPOTHALAMUS** · **HPA**

Adrenal medulla → **Anterior pituitary gland**

ACTH released into bloodstream

Release of adrenaline and noradrenaline.

Arousal of the sympathetic ANS

Adrenal cortex

"Fight or flight" response
- Increased heart and breathing rates
- Reduced activity in stomach
- Saliva production inhibited (dry mouth)
- Pupils of eyes dilate (expand)
- Glucose released into bloodstream to provide more energy

Release of glucocorticoids (such as cortisol) into the bloodstream.

- Causes liver to release stored glucose, maintaining a steady supply of fuel to the body.
- Suppresses the immune system.

Helps in cases of emergency. You can run fast to escape, or react quickly to prevent mishap (e.g. grabbing the banister to stop yourself from falling down the stairs). Sometimes we perceive heightened activity in SAM as indicating that we are stressed but it could be that we are just excited.

Good effects: Useful in coping with long-term stress and reducing the effects of the initial shock response.
Bad effects: Blood has excess glucose and some hormones; wound healing is slowed; the immune system is less effective in fighting disease.

OVER TO YOU

Make a list of the sort of situations that might induce a "fight or flight" response. Do you think you can prepare for such reactions? If so, how?

THE GENERAL ADAPTATION SYNDROME

Selye (1936, 1950; see ASP4 pp.219–220) put rats under enormous stress to assess their responses. He called their overall reaction the *General Adaptation Syndrome* (GAS). There are three stages of GAS, detailed below.

Stage 1: Alarm reaction stage

The ANS responds to the stressor:
- Activation of the sympathetic adrenal medullary system
- Activation of the hypothalamic–pituitary–adrenocortical axis, with associated release of ACTH
- Release of glucocorticoids and adrenaline and noradrenaline
- The individual is ready for "fight or flight"

Stage 2: Resistance stage

All alarm systems are at full capacity, so the parasympathetic nervous system calls for a more cautious use of resources. Coping strategies, such as denial, are used, and the "fight or flight" response is less effective. When the stress reduces there is a period of adjustment when:
- Adrenaline levels return to normal
- The body attempts to restore lost energy
- The body attempts to repair damage
- Arousal levels are higher than usual but gradually reduce to normal
- Adrenal glands become enlarged

Stage 3: Exhaustion stage

Eventually the physiological systems in the previous stages become ineffective, and the initial ANS symptoms of arousal reappear (increased heart rate, sweating, etc.). In extreme cases, attempts to return to a normal state fail, and the final stage occurs:
- Body resources are diminished due to failure of the parasympathetic system's control of metabolism and energy storage
- Person becomes depressed, irritable, and unable to concentrate
- Immune system collapses, and stress-related diseases are more likely
- The person or animal may die

EVALUATION

STRENGTHS

- Selye correctly focused on the pituitary–adrenal system (HPA) and the importance of glucosteroids.
- He alerted medicine to the importance of stress and the effect it could have on physical health.

WEAKNESSES

- Selye did not pay much attention to the sympatho-medullary pathway (SAM) and he did not fully understand the relationship between HPA and SAM.
- He claimed that stress always produced the same physiological pattern but this is not so. Mason (1975) showed that stressors that produce different amounts of fear, anger, and uncertainty produce different patterns of adrenaline, noradrenaline, and cortisol secretions.
- Most (though not all) of Selye's work is based on rats, so it may not apply to all animals, including humans.
- Selye assumed people respond passively to stressors but Mason (1975) pointed out that people actively make a psychological appraisal when confronted with a stressor.

STRESS AND PHYSICAL ILLNESS

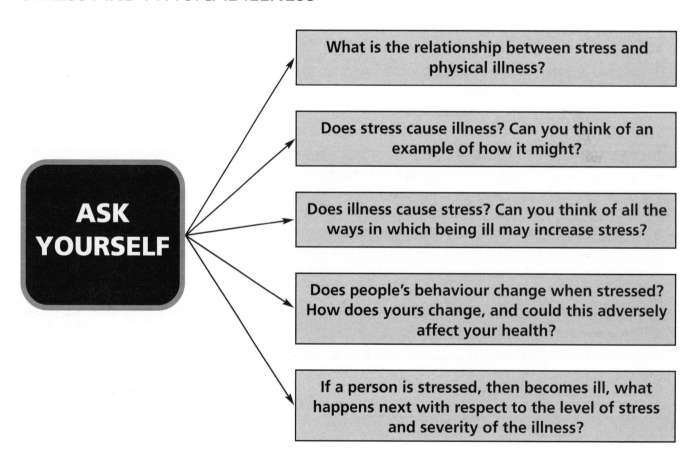

ASK YOURSELF

- What is the relationship between stress and physical illness?
- Does stress cause illness? Can you think of an example of how it might?
- Does illness cause stress? Can you think of all the ways in which being ill may increase stress?
- Does people's behaviour change when stressed? How does yours change, and could this adversely affect your health?
- If a person is stressed, then becomes ill, what happens next with respect to the level of stress and severity of the illness?

These questions may make you realise that the relationship between stress and health is complex. There are several ways in which stress may be related to illness:

- **Direct effect** Stress may cause a person to become unwell. A study by Cohen et al. (1991; see ASP4 p.225) showed that participants who experienced high levels of stress were more likely to develop colds when infected with cold viruses than were those with lower levels of stress. There is evidence that stress has a direct effect on the likelihood of illness by impairing the workings of the immune system, which is responsible for preventing and fighting illness. Obviously if the immune system cannot work effectively, people are more likely to succumb to illness.
- **Vulnerability** Stress may cause people who are already predisposed to illness to become unwell, as it causes them to be physically vulnerable. The study by Kiecolt-Glaser et al. (1995; see ASP4 p.228) demonstrates how stress can reduce the efficiency of the immune system.
- **Behavioural effects** Stress can cause people to behave in ways that may lead to deterioration in health. These can include poor eating habits, smoking, drinking too much alcohol, and experiencing a lack of sleep.
- **Downward spiral of ill health and stress** Being ill leads to stress, and the further decline in health leads to more stress and more illness. Therefore, a downward spiral is established.

Stress and Cardiovascular Disorders

Cardiovascular diseases consist of all disorders of the heart or blood vessels and include heart attacks and hypertension (very high blood pressure).

The heart specialists Friedman and Rosenman (1959; see ASP4 p.242) noted that many of their patients with coronary heart disease possessed a particular personality type called Type A personality.

There is evidence of a link between cardiovascular diseases and stress.

Research findings

- Cobb and Rose (1973; see ASP4 pp.221–222) found a link between stress and hypertension in air traffic controllers and airmen. Air traffic controllers working in airports with greater traffic density had higher levels of hypertension.
- Scuitemaker et al. (2004; see ASP4 p.222) Danish individuals suffering from burnout had three times the rate of heart attacks than the average.
- Melamed et al. (2006; see ASP4 p.222) Burnout is associated with increased activity of the sympathetic NS and impairment in the functioning of the immune system.
- Kuper et al. (2002; see ASP4 p.222) examined a relationship between work-related stress and coronary heart disease.

EVALUATION

- The major problems with the studies cited above is that participants are not randomly assigned to low and high stress groups so there may be important differences between them apart from the stress levels.
- Nevertheless, Kario et al. (2003; see ASP4 p.223) reported higher rates of heart attack in people living very near to the site of a major earthquake (i.e. experiencing high stress) than those living further away (i.e. experiencing low stress). There was no reason to believe that these two groups of people were different initially.

The reasons for this link

The mechanisms by which stress might cause cardiovascular diseases are not fully understood. It is possible that stressors produce increased blood pressure and heart rate. Over time this weakens the cardiovascular system leading to increased blood pressure and eventually cardiovascular disorder.

- Lucini et al. (2005; see ASP4 p.223) Chronically stressed individuals had higher blood pressure (systolic arterial pressure and diastolic arterial pressure) than controls.

EVALUATION

- As mentioned above, in most studies participants are not randomly assigned to high and low stress groups. It is possible, therefore, that other factors are responsible for the link. For example, an individual's personality may lead them into high stress jobs, so personality not just (or even) stress causes the health problems.
- It is not clear which stressors have a larger or smaller effect on developing cardiovascular disorders.
- Neither is it clear which cardiovascular disorders are most or least associated with chronic stress.
- A lot of the research has used short-term stressors in the lab, so we cannot be sure that the effects of chronic (long lasting) stressors in everyday life would have the same effect.

Stress and Other Forms of Physical Illness

Stress has been linked with many other physical illnesses including infectious diseases (e.g. influenza), diabetes, ulcers, asthma, headaches.

Research findings

- **Colds**
  - Cohen et al. (1991; see ASP4 p.225) Participants were asked to complete a questionnaire on how many stressful life events they had experienced; they were also given nasal drops containing cold viruses. Those with the highest levels of stress were twice as likely to develop colds as those with the lowest levels.
- **Stomach ulcers**
  - Brady (1958; see ASP4 p.225) Pairs of monkeys were given shocks every 20 seconds unless one particular one (called the executive monkey) pressed a lever to prevent it. Many executive monkeys died of perforated ulcers resulting from increased levels of gastrointestinal hormone caused by stress. The presence of control monkeys who experienced the same shocks but did not have the responsibility of turning them off demonstrated that ulcers were caused by stress, not the shocks.
  - Weiner et al. (1957; see ASP4 pp.225–226) classified army recruits as "oversecretors" or "undersecretors" of digestive enzymes. After 4 months of stressful training, 14% of the oversecretors and no undersecretors had developed ulcers. This indicates a link between stress and ulcers in humans.

EVALUATION

- Again, participants were not randomly assigned and there could be important differences between them other than the high or low stress. In the Brady study the monkeys who were responsible for turning off the shocks were not randomly assigned to that condition—they were the quickest to learn to turn off the shocks, so they may have been more anxious to start with. In the Cohen et al. and Weiner studies there could have been differences in the general health and/or physiological functioning of the two groups.
- In the Weiner et al. study, a large percentage of oversecretors did not develop ulcers, so there must be significant individual differences between them.
- It is not clear which stressors are most strongly associated with any given physical illness.

Effects of Stress on the Immune System

The immune system acts like an army, identifying and killing intruders to the body. There are two types of immune system cells:

- Cells involved in natural immunity (e.g. natural killer cells) that attack foreign bodies such as viruses and bacteria fairly quickly.
- Cells involved in specific immunity (e.g. T-helper cells) that are specific in their effects and take longer to work.

A convenient analogy for describing the actions of these two sets of cells is that when the body is invaded the natural immunity cells move in quickly to try to disable them. In the meantime, the more specialised cells (each group specific to a particular disorder) gather to make a second more concerted attack on the invaders.

Psychoneuroimmunology (PNI) is the field of research that looks at the links between stress and the immune system.

Research findings

- Riley (1981; see ASP4 p.227) found a marked decrease in the lymphocytes of mice who had been exposed to a 5-hour period of intense stress by being rotated rapidly on a turntable. In later research, Riley implanted cancer cells in mice and studied the effects of high stress (again using the rotating disc) with no stress. Tumour growth in the low stress group stopped whereas the tumours grew quite large in the high stress group. This was presumably because there were higher levels of lymphocytes in the mice who experienced no stress.
- Schliefer et al. (1983; see ASP4 p.227) The immune systems of a group of men whose wives had died functioned less well after they had been widowed.
- Segerstrom and Miller (2004; see ASP4 p.227) found similar results in six studies—death of a spouse led to a significant reduction in the effectiveness of natural killer cells.
- Kiecolt-Glaser and colleagues (see ASP4 pp.227–228) did a huge amount of research on stress and the immune system, including the way in which stress has its effects. Some important research findings are:
  - Natural killer cells decreased in medical students in the month before important examinations were taken.
  - Those students most affected were those who were lonely, had recently suffered stressful life events, or who were depressed or anxious.

- Compared with matched controls, women caring for a relative suffering from Alzheimer's disease took much longer to recover from a small wound. However, more of the caregivers were on medication, which could have affected their immune system. There were only 13 in each group so it is difficult to generalise from such a small sample.
- A wound in dental students took 40% longer to heal when it was made 3 days before an exam as compared with during a holiday. Obviously this study, being repeated measures design, controls for individual differences. Note that the stress of examinations is much less than the stress of long-term caring, but even this level of stress seems to impair healing.

A more detailed look at the relationship between stressors and the immune system

Segerstrom and Miller (2004; see ASP4 pp.228–229) point out that it would make no sense in adaptive terms if short-term stress impaired the immune system—after all, it is precisely these conditions that you would expect to result in increased help from the immune system. Segerstrom and Miller (2004) carried out a meta-analysis to clarify the effect of different stressors on both parts of the immune system. The important findings were:

- Short-term stressors increased natural immunity (increased levels of natural killer cells) and have no effect on specific immunity.
- Stressful event sequences involving death of a spouse result in a reduction in natural immunity.
- Stressful event sequences involving disasters lead to small increases in natural and specific immunity.
- Stressful life events in those over 55 years lead to significant reductions in natural and specific immunity.
- Stressful life events in those under 55 years are not associated with any change in natural or specific immunity.

To summarise Segerstrom and Miller (2004): *the precise effects of stressors on the immune system depend much more than is generally thought on the specific nature and duration of the stressor.*

EVALUATION

STRENGTHS

- There is good evidence for a relationship between stress and the immune system. The precise effects of stress on the immune system depend on several factors, including:
  - Whether the stressor is short or long term
  - The age of the stressed individual
  - The type of immunity (natural or short lived).
- There are important practical applications of the research, including sufficient knowledge to anticipate possible problems and provide appropriate interventions.

WEAKNESSES

- The functioning of the immune system in many stressed individuals is within the normal range, so it's unlikely that that could significantly increase the chances of such a person developing a serious condition such as coronary heart disease.

- We still don't know the precise relationship between stress and susceptibility to illness. It is possible that the relationship is not a simple one of stress directly leading to increased likelihood of ill health. It is possible, for example, that stressed individuals have less healthy lifestyles (e.g. are more likely to smoke and drink considerable amounts of alcohol).
- The immune system is so complex that it is too simplistic to say that stress reduces its effectiveness. Some researchers (e.g. Robles et al., 2005) believe that chronic stress enhances some aspects of immune system functioning.

STRESS IN EVERYDAY LIFE

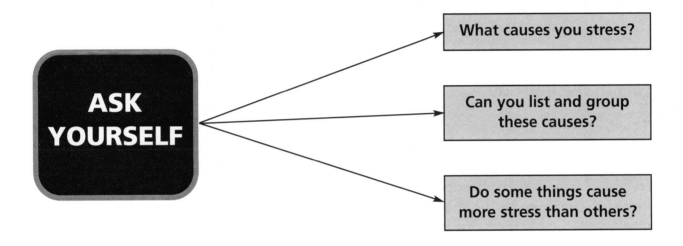

This shows that there are many sources of stress; we will look at four areas:

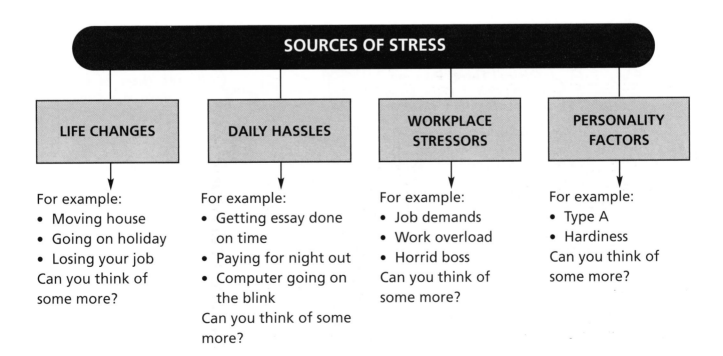

LIFE CHANGES

Holmes and Rahe (1967) constructed the *Social Readjustment Rating Scale* (SRRS; see ASP4 p.233) on which each life event was given a score and assessed as a "life change unit" (LCU).

For example:

- Death of a spouse   100
- Jail term   63
- Fired at work   47
- Vacation   13

The scale consists of 43 events, each with a score as shown above. An individual would calculate their score by adding the number of points for each event they had experienced in the last year.

The scale has been revised and used in over a thousand studies. These studies consistently showed a positive correlation between LCU and illness. People with a score over 300 LCUs in a year were found to be more at risk of a wide range of physical and mental disorders than low scorers.

The Role of the Individual

- Cox (1978) An individual's level of stress is caused by an interaction between the event and the individual. After all, some people are very "uptight" and take events very seriously whilst others are more "laid back" and don't let things get to them. This inevitably affects the stress they experience when something happens to them.
- Kendler et al. (2004; see ASP4 p.235) found a positive correlation between LCU and major depression but, of the high scorers, the people who were most susceptible to major depression were those who were rated high on neuroticism (the tendency to experience anxiety, tension, and other negative emotions).

Therefore it is not just the life events but the personality of the individual that is related to the risk of illness.

An individual's level of stress is caused by an interaction between the event and the individual.

EVALUATION

STRENGTHS

- The research has provided empirical support for the idea that life events can influence our physical and psychological well-being.
- An application of the research is the development of techniques to minimise the effects of life events, for example, by providing support for those who have suffered a bereavement or have been robbed. Another application is to try to control life events that can be controlled, such as seeking help for marital discord.

WEAKNESSES

- The link between LCUs and illness is correlational, but correlation does not mean causation.
- Life changes may lead to behaviour that damages health, which is an indirect link.
- Some life changes on the scale are positive, e.g. being promoted at work, or having a busy Christmas with your family. Where the stress response leads to feelings of happiness it is referred to as *eustress*. There is no evidence of a link between eustress and ill health, but the absence of positive life changes might increase stress.
- Personality and the amount of social support can influence the effect of life changes.
- The amount of stress for each life event (e.g. pregnancy) is not the same for everyone. You have to take account of circumstances, and individual differences in coping.

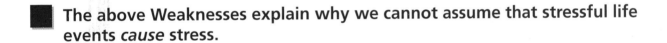 **The above Weaknesses explain why we cannot assume that stressful life events *cause* stress.**

DAILY HASSLES

DeLongis et al. (1982; see ASP4 pp.236–237) devised a *hassles scale* to measure the effect of problems encountered as part of the routine of life (e.g. getting essays in on time, doing the washing). They argued that whereas life events are fairly rare, hassles occur several times a day so they might have a greater effect on health. Their research confirmed this. They found the hassles scale to be a better predictor of ill health than the SRRS, as both the frequency and intensity of hassles were significantly correlated with overall health status and bodily symptoms. They also measured uplifts (e.g. good weather, recreation), but these seemed to have little effect on health. However, it should be noted that the sample of participants in this study consisted only of people over 45, so the findings cannot be generalised to younger people. Khan and Patel (1996) found that older people tended to have less severe and fewer hassles than younger people.

EVALUATION

STRENGTHS

- The research has useful applications. It can provide information to people on the potential danger to health of hassles so they are forewarned.
- It can also help in providing advice on coping with hassles in ways that minimise stress.

WEAKNESSES

- As with life events, it is necessary to take account of other factors before concluding that hassles cause illness. People who experience many hassles may make changes to their lifestyle. They may, for example, smoke more and take more physical exercise (Twisk et al., 1999).
- The research is correlational, so we cannot be sure that hassles cause illness.
- There are important individual differences in coping with hassles and the same hassle may vary in stressfulness depending on the situation. One person may get really irritated and impatient if they have to wait in a supermarket queue whilst another may simply read a magazine or send a text to a friend. Waiting in the queue is less likely to cause stress if you not in a hurry but can be very stressful if you need to get to an important appointment.
- There may also be an interaction between life events and hassles. Johnson et al. (1997) found that the number of psychiatric symptoms (anxiety, depression, etc.) was greater in students experiencing major life events if they were also had substantial numbers of daily hassles. We therefore need to take account of life changes and hassles.
- It is difficult to distinguish between hassles and chronic (long-lasting) stressors such as noisy neighbours, a damp house, lack of recreation facilities, money worries. It's not always possible to determine whether it's hassles or chronic stressors that affect health.
- Most research does not tell us how or why daily hassles have an adverse effect on health.

WORKPLACE STRESSORS

Both pressure of work and the work environment itself are sources of stress.

A study demonstrating the effect of workplace stress was conducted by Johansson et al. (1978). They compared high stress workers (those who did repetitive work with a machine regulating the pace and that they had to attend to continuously) with low stress workers in a highly mechanised factory. They found that the high stress group produced more adrenaline and noradrenaline, both hormones associated with stress. This group had higher levels of absenteeism and more psychosomatic illnesses than the low stress group.

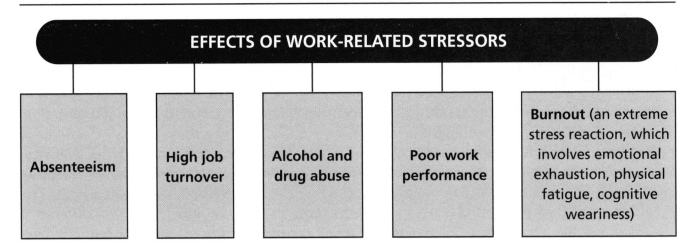

EFFECTS OF WORK-RELATED STRESSORS

| Absenteeism | High job turnover | Alcohol and drug abuse | Poor work performance | Burnout (an extreme stress reaction, which involves emotional exhaustion, physical fatigue, cognitive weariness) |

Major Sources of Stress at Work

The following are not the only sources of stress at work but they have been found to be the most important ones.

Job control

Low levels of job control are associated with frustration, anxiety, headaches, stomach upsets, visits to the doctor (Spector et al. 1988).

- Marmot et al. (1997) In a study of over 10,000 civil servants by using self-report questionnaires and independent assessments to measure job control, they found that workers with low job control were not only more likely to suffer from stress-related illnesses in general, they were four times more likely to die of a heart attack than those with high job control. In other words, there is a negative correlation between job control and illness—the *lower* the job control, the *higher* the risk of illness.

How many sources of workplace stress can you locate in this cartoon?

However, there are a number of problems with the above study:

- **Investigator effects** During observations the investigators may have been influenced by their own expectations.
- **Participant reactivity** The participants may have been influenced by the presence of the observers.
- **Bias on questionnaire responses** Some participants may have exaggerated lack of job control on the questionnaires if they suffered a lot of illness.
- **Correlation does not mean causation** We cannot conclude that low job control causes illness because other factors (such as the type of worker in a low/high control role) may have had an influence.
- **Factors other than job control** The jobs done by those in high and low job control differed in ways other than job control. Compared with low job control positions, on the whole the high job control roles were more interesting, were better paid, and provided more opportunities for mixing with other people.

Effort–reward imbalance

Effort–reward imbalance exists if a person's effort at work is not matched by the rewards they gain, such as salary, career opportunities, social approval.

- Smith et al. (2005; see ASP4 p.241) People with high effort–reward imbalance were more prone to cardio-vascular diseases.
- Kuper et al. (2002; see ASP4 p.241) With 10,000 civil servants, over an 11-year period effort–reward imbalance was associated with high levels of stress: heart attacks, poor mental and physical functioning.

Again, although there is a correlation between effort–reward imbalance and stress, we cannot be certain that effort–reward imbalance causes stress and consequent ill health because the data is correlational and other factors could be influential.

PERSONALITY FACTORS

Type A Personality

Friedman and Rosenman (1959; see ASP4 pp.242–245) distinguished two important personality types:

Type A	Type B
Competitive, ambitious, impatient, hostile, restless, and pressured.	Lack the characteristics of Type A and are more relaxed and carefree.

Friedman and Rosenman (1974) used a self-selected (volunteer) sample of healthy men, followed them up over 8½ years and found that Type As were almost twice as likely to suffer coronary heart disease than Type Bs. Type As had higher levels of adrenaline, noradrenaline, and cholesterol.

Type B personality types are more relaxed and carefree.

Conclusions were that personality has an effect on coronary heart disease. Type A personality is potentially very harmful to health. Type As are stressed individuals who, due to stress, have an inhibited digestive system, which leads to high levels of cholesterol, therefore increasing the risk of heart disease.

EVALUATION

STRENGTHS

- This study provided the first scientific evidence of the link between personality and coronary heart disease.
- It laid the foundations for much further research into the relationship between stress and illness, including the effects of stress on the immune system.
- It provided the medical profession with evidence on which to provide people with advice on how to change their lifestyles in order to reduce their risk of heart attack. It has probably saved many lives and enriched others.

WEAKNESSES

- The typologies of personality used was rather crude.
- Type A behaviour consists of several behaviour patterns (e.g. competitiveness, hostility, ambition). It was not clear from this study which aspects of this personality made an individual vulnerable to heart disease. The study lacked internal validity because it was measuring what was intended.
- It was a correlational study so we cannot be sure that Type A behaviour causes a vulnerability to heart disease.
- The findings have been difficult to replicate.

Further research

- Matthews et al. (1977; see ASP4 p.244) It is the hostility aspect of the Type A personality that is most strongly correlated with coronary heart disease.
- Ganster et al. (1991; see ASP4 p.244) They agree. They demonstrated that high levels of hostility produce increased activity within the sympathetic nervous system and this plays a role in the development of coronary heart disease.
- Myrtek's (2001; see ASP4 p.244) meta-analyses indicated that the correlation between the variables is smaller than it used to be. This may be because people are becoming more aware of the dangers of Type A behaviour and have adopted more healthy life styles.

EVALUATION

STRENGTHS

- The research has led researchers to take seriously the relationship between personality and coronary heart disease.
- It has led to a broader interest in the relationship between illness and stress.
- It has changed lifestyles for the better.

WEAKNESSES

- Not many people are Type A personality, so the findings only apply to a minority.
- Type A consists of a lot of personality components—hostility may be the most important one but this is not certain.
- Since the research is correlational, it cannot establish cause and effect.

Hardiness

Kobasa (1979; see ASP4 pp.245–247) describes a personality type, called hardiness, that is resistant to stress. The characteristics of a hardy person are (the 3 Cs):

- **Commitment** Finding meaning in work and life.
- **Challenge** Seeing potentially stressful situations as a challenge.
- **Control** Feeling you can influence events.

Kobasa claims that hardiness is directly related to a decreased vulnerability to ill health because:

- When coping with stress, hardy people use more approach-coping strategies (e.g. planning) and fewer avoidance strategies (e.g. alcohol, denial).
- Because of their coping strategies, hardy people experience less stress than non-hardy individuals.

Research evidence

- Kobasa (1979) and Kobasa et al. (1985; see ASP4 p.246) Highly stressed male business executives were studied—the hardy ones were less prone to illness.
- Crowley et al. (2003; see ASP4 p.246) Hardy individuals cope better than non-hardy ones with a predictable life event (the youngest child leaving home) and an unpredictable one (losing their job).
- Klag and Bradley (2004; see ASP4 pp.246–247) Hardiness was negatively correlated with illness in both men and women (a direct effect). However, when neuroticism was controlled for, there was no relationship. Stressful events were less likely to be associated with ill health in hardy than in non hardy men even when neuroticism was controlled for. This is a buffering effect. This did not apply to women who had no such buffering effect. Finally, they found that the beneficial effects of hardiness on physical health did not depend on the use of more approach than avoidance strategies.

An application of the work on hardiness has been *Harditraining.* There is evidence that this increases job satisfaction, improves health, and decreases blood pressure.

EVALUATION

STRENGTHS

- There is evidence for both the direct effect of hardiness and the buffering effects (Klag and Bradley, 2004).
- The success of Harditraining suggests that hardiness does promote good psychological and physical health.

WEAKNESSES

- The challenge component of hardiness may be irrelevant (Klag and Bradley, 2004).
- Most of the research is based on men. Studies that include women indicate that the findings may not be true of them.
- It's possible that the adverse effects of not being hardy are due to neuroticism not hardiness. When neuroticism is controlled for, some correlations are no longer significant.
- The positive correlation between hardiness and good health does not necessarily mean that hardiness causes good health. It is possible that unhealthy individuals become less hardy, so the relationship is the reverse.

STRESS MANAGEMENT

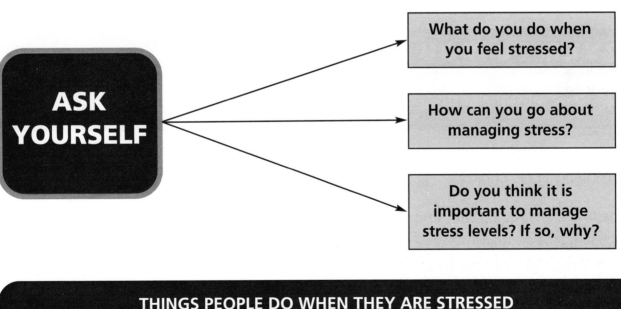

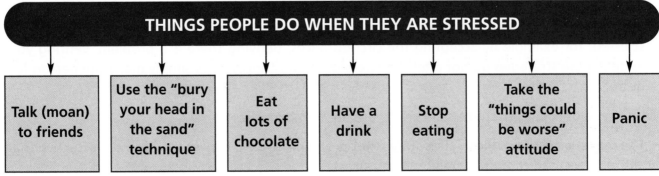

There are many ways of managing stress. Their effectiveness depends on the type of stressor, the particular individual, and the circumstances.

One way of classifying the ways of managing stress is to divide it into physiological and psychological methods:

Physiological Methods

The following drugs reduce the physiological effects of anxiety, usually by reducing heart rate and peripheral blood pressure:

- Beta blockers.
- Anti-anxiety drugs.

Most physiological methods are emotion focused (see later) because they deal with reducing the associated anxiety.

Psychological Methods

Cognitive Behavioural Therapies (CBTs) offer an especially appropriate psychological method of dealing with stress. The assumptions behind the cognitive approach are that it is not the problem that is the core issue, but whether the way you think about the problem is *maladaptive* or not, and if you can be trained to restructure your thinking and self-beliefs, the problem may simply disappear.

Some, but not all, psychological methods are problem-focused (see next sub-section).

The CBT we will consider later is stress inoculation training.

OVER TO YOU

Look at the list of Things People Do When They are Stressed (on the previous page). Are these problem-focused, emotion-focused, or neither?

COPING WITH STRESS

Two major ways of coping with stress can be classified as problem focused and emotion focused.

- **Problem-focused coping** Involves engaging in purposeful activity to improve the situation and reduce stress, for example, by obtaining relevant information, deciding priorities, dealing with the situation.
- **Emotion-focused coping** Involves efforts to reduce the negative emotions caused by being stressed, for example by accepting the circumstances, denying there is a problem, venting your anger. These strategies do not alter the stressful circumstances; they simply make the person feel better.

Which type of coping strategy is better? There are two hypotheses:

- **The mains-effect hypothesis** This states that problem-focused coping (pfc) is more effective than emotion-focused coping (efc) in reducing stress.

- **The goodness-of-fit hypothesis** This states that is best to use pfc when the stress is perceived as controllable and efc when the stress is perceived as uncontrollable. This implies that if you use pfc for uncontrollable stressors or efc for controllable stressors, then the strategy will not reduce stress because you do not have a "good fit".

Research evidence

- Folkman et al. (1986; see ASP4 p.249) Pfc was more effective than efc in reducing stress.
- Wu et al. (1993; see ASP4 p.249) Pfc produces both negative and positive outcomes. They found that doctors who accepted responsibility for their mistakes and changed their work habits for the better (a positive outcome) also felt more distress (a negative outcome).
- Folkman and Lazarus (1985; see ASP4 pp.249–250) Students changed their coping strategies to suit the situation. Before exams they used pfc (by, for example, revising) but while waiting for exam results they used efc (by, for example, putting the results to the back of their mind).
- Penley et al. (2002; see ASP4 p.250) support the main-effects hypothesis. In a meta-analysis, they found that several types of efc (e.g. avoidance, wishful thinking) were negatively correlated with healthy outcomes, while pfc strategies were positively correlated with healthy outcomes.
- Collins et al. (1983; see ASP4 p.250) in contrast, found that often efc is better than pfc especially when the stress is uncontrollable and there is nothing the individual can do to change the situation.
- Zakowski et al. (2001; see ASP4 p.250) provide partial support for the goodness-of-fit hypothesis. They found that, as predicted, efc was more successful with uncontrollable situations. However, pfc was no more successful with controllable stressors than with uncontrollable ones.

EVALUATION

STRENGTHS

- The two approaches together are sufficiently broad to provide effective strategies for most stressful situations.
- The goodness-of-fit hypothesis is supported by many studies which show that pfc works with controllable stressors and efc with uncontrollable ones.

WEAKNESSES

- There are other means of coping beside pfc and efc. Skinner et al. (2003; see ASP4 p.251) listed nine.
- The two types of coping are not distinct, they often overlap. For example, making a plan is pfc but also calms emotions.
- Different individuals use different coping strategies. It could be the individuals rather than the strategies that account for any differences.
- Coping strategies are often assessed by questionnaire. There are two main problems with this. Sometimes the coping strategies described are so general that they do not allow us to know what specific strategies an individual uses. Also, the strategies people say they use may not be those that are actually used in real life.

PSYCHOLOGICAL AND PHYSIOLOGICAL METHODS OF STRESS MANAGEMENT

Cognitive Behavioural Therapy

Stress inoculation training

This is a method to prevent stress responses occurring in the first place in order to inoculate the individual against stress.

Meichenbaum (1977, 1985; see ASP4 pp.252–253) developed a programme with three main phases:

1. **Assessment** Asking the question "What's the problem?"
2. **Stress-reduction techniques** Relaxation techniques, and self-instruction (e.g. "If I keep calm, I can cope" and "Stop worrying, it's pointless").
3. **Application and follow through** Imagining and role-playing the stress reduction techniques and then applying them to real-life situations.

- Meichenbaum (1977; see ASP4 pp.252–253) Stress inoculation training (SIT) generalises to several situations, so if people are trained in one situation (e.g. to cope with rat phobia) this generalises to another (e.g. a snake phobia). Therefore, it is more useful than specific treatments.
- Antoni et al. (2000) SIT reduced cortisol output and reduced distress symptoms in HIV positive gay men.
- Cruess et al. (1999) Lower levels of cortisol were found in breast cancer patients who had received SIT after surgery than in those who hadn't.
- Gaab et al. (2003; see ASP4 pp.253–254) One group of two matched groups of participants (the experimental group) was given SIT followed by a stress inducing short-term situation. The other group (the control group) experienced the same stress but without the training. Compared to the control group, the experimental group had significantly lower cortisol levels, considered the situation less stressful, and showed more competence in dealing with it.
- Foa et al. (1999; see ASP4 p.254) In a comparison of the effect of SIT with another CBT, of prolonged exposure, in which the traumatic event is relived in imagination, their participants were suffering PTSD following an assault, either sexual or non-sexual. The results showed that SIT was less effective than prolonged exposure in reducing anxiety and improving social adjustment (getting back to work, socialising with friends, and so on). There was no difference in the two techniques with respect to reducing PTSD and depression.
- Lee et al. (2002; see ASP4 p.254) The effect in reducing PTSD of SIT and another technique used for PTSD, that of eye-movement desensitisation and reprocessing, were compared. They found that the two treatments were equally effective in reducing PTSD at the end of the therapy sessions but that SIT was slightly better when the results were followed up later.

EVALUATION

STRENGTHS

- SIT has been shown to be effective with both chronic (long-term) and acute (short-term but intense) stressors.

- The training has been used effectively to treat a wide range of stresses, including from very serious to mild. It has even been effective in treating symptoms of those suffering PTSD.
- It has been shown to reduce stress significantly regardless of whether the stress is measured by self-report or by cortisol levels.
- It has the potential to provide effective stress relief before the stress reaches a level that precipitates a mental disorder.

WEAKNESSES

- SIT, like all CBTs, consists of many components and it is difficult to ascertain whether the behavioural or the cognitive changes are more important in managing stress.
- When SIT has been compared with other CBTs, it is often less successful than them. See Foa et al. (1999) and Lee et al. (2002) cited above.
- Stevens et al. (2000) provide evidence that factors common to all therapies (such as therapist warmth, the relationship between client and therapist) often play a considerable role in any beneficial effects; therefore we cannot be sure whether there are any special or distinctive elements in SIT that help reduce stress.

Drugs

Beta blockers

Beta blockers affect the body not the brain. Compared with anti-anxiety drugs, they have less effect on brain functions such as mental alertness. They decrease heart rate and lower peripheral blood pressure. They also reduce palpitations and hypertension.

EVALUATION

STRENGTHS

- They are useful in treating those with high blood pressure and those with heart disease (Lau et al., 1992; see ASP4 p.255). Metra et al. (2000; see ASP4 p.255) found reduction in heart attacks and mortality in 10,000 patients with heart failure.
- Also useful in treating performance anxiety. Lockwood (1989; see ASP4 pp.255–256) and Kenny (2006) report that beta blockers are used to control music performance anxiety. Brantigan et al. (1982; see ASP4 p.256) found that beta blockers improve musical performance but other studies (e.g. Gates et al., 1985; see ASP4 p.256) showed no such improvement.

WEAKNESSES

- Beta blockers have little effect on reducing anxiety in individuals with social phobias. This may be because social phobias involve problems of self-esteem as well as, or rather than, bodily symptoms.
- Problems include difficulties with drug withdrawal and unwanted side-effects, including sleep disturbance, muscle fatigue, and digestive problems.

Anti-Anxiety Drugs

Benzodiazepines

Benzodiazepines (e.g. Valium and Librium) increase the activity of GABA, the neurotransmitter produced when the body wants to relieve anxiety. GABA reduces serotonin activity, which in turn reduces arousal.

EVALUATION

STRENGTHS

- They work very quickly so high anxiety can be reduced rapidly.
- They are effective with most people and are generally well tolerated.
- If used for a short period, they rarely produce serious side-effects.

WEAKNESSES

- There are side-effects such as drowsiness and memory impairment, which may result in accidents.
- Long-term use may result in dependency and a return to high anxiety levels if discontinued.
- People may become drug-tolerant and need increasing doses in order for them to work effectively.
- It's possible that long-term use can result in impairment of some cognitive functions (such as visuo-spatial ability) (Stewart, 2005; see ASP4 p.257).

Buspirone

This helps the work of serotonin.

EVALUATION

STRENGTHS

- It does not have the sedative effects that benzodiazepines have.
- There are no withdrawal symptoms.
- There are adverse affects on cognitive functioning (Chamberlain et al., 2007; see ASP4 p.257).
- Davidson et al. (1999; see ASP4 p.257) found that, compared to a control group on no drugs, it reduced anxiety in those suffering from generalised anxiety disorder.

WEAKNESSES

- Davidson et al. (1999) also found that it was not as effective as an anti-depressant in treating generalised anxiety disorder.
- It has side effects of headaches and depression (Goa & Ward, 1986; see ASP4 p.257).

These drugs are effective at reducing intense feelings of stress and panic, but they do not address the actual causes of stress (but it is not always possible to do this anyway). They are therefore emotion-focused.

Because of side effects and withdrawal symptoms, Ashton (1997; see ASP4 pp.256–257) recommended that benzodiazepines should be limited to short-term use of no more than 4 weeks, that all drugs should only be used to treat intense stress and anxiety, only minimum effective doses should be prescribed, and for those already dependent, withdrawal should be gradual.

RESEARCH METHODS AND STRESS

There are several problems that psychologists encounter when trying to research stress.

- **The use of correlations** Much of the research into stress looks for a correlation between two variables. For example, Holmes and Rahe (see earlier) investigated whether there was a relationship between life change units and physical illness. The main problem with any correlation (regardless of what the investigators are looking at) is that *it cannot show cause and effect*. In other words, if researchers find a significant positive correlation between life change units and illnesses, they cannot conclude that the stress has *caused* the illness. Whenever there is a correlation between two variables, it necessary to think about whether one could cause the other (in either direction) or if a third factors is causing both of the other two. So in this instance there is, of course, the possibility that stress causes illness but there are also two other possibilities. It may be that it is the other way round, that illness is causing stress (people who are ill can't look after their family well, they may not be able to work, this may cause financial problems and therefore stress, and so on). Alternatively, people may live in a very unsavoury environment, which causes them to be stressed and also causes illness. So there are at least two other explanations for the correlation.
- **The groups are not matched** Often two groups are compared but they are not necessarily matched and may be different from one another in terms of factors other than stress. For example, some studies show that people in high stress jobs are more likely than in low stress ones to suffer health problems. However, as mentioned earlier, an individual's personality may lead them into a high stress job, so personality not just (or even) stress causes the health problems. Likewise, Marmot et al. (1997; see earlier) found that low job control was associated with more stress than high job control. However, there were several other differences between the jobs—the low control jobs were less interesting, worse paid, and provided fewer opportunities for socialising. Ideally, you need to compare people whose jobs differ only in the amount of control but this is very difficult. It does, however, mean that factors other than the independent variable (in this case job control) can have an effect.
- **Some research is done on animals** As just discussed, it would be unethical to cause great stress to humans, so some stress research is done on non-human animals. The use of animals not only causes ethical problems, it causes practical ones as well. As we've already said, non-human animals experience very different stress from humans and they do not experience the same range of emotions associated with stress. They are also likely to have different physical reactions to stress since these are, to some extent, *species specific* (different in every species). Therefore it is not possible to generalise the result of research on non-human animals to humans.

The Ethics of Research into Stress

As you have seen, much research on stress is carried out on non-human animals and involves them being subjected to extremely stressful, painful conditions sometimes resulting in death. This applies to the work of Selye (mainly on rats; see ASP4 p.219) and Brady (on monkeys; see ASP4 p.225).

Some people may consider it ethically very dubious to literally stress animals to death. They may also argue that it is particularly unethical because there is little evidence that, in practical terms, humans can greatly benefit from this research, given that non-human animals experience very different stress and do not experience the same range of emotions associated with stress. However, others would argue that because the work has provided the basis for useful research into the causes of serious illness in humans, it is justified to sacrifice animals to do this.

In terms of costs and benefits then, the costs are the cruel, painful treatment to which the animals are subjected and the fact that many die after a prolonged period of extreme discomfort and/or considerable pain as a result. The positives are that the research can be used to benefit humans in order to reduce the effects of stress in them.

SAMPLE QUESTIONS

? Outline the role of personality factors in the experience of stress. **5 MARKS**

? In a study of stress, scores for life changes were calculated using the Holmes–Rahe *Social Readjustment Rating Scale* for 15 people in full-time employment. These were correlated with the number of days the individuals had taken off sick and the data was plotted on the graph below.

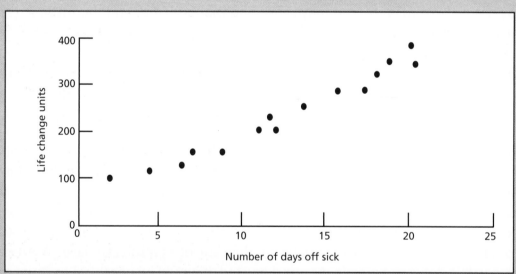

a. What type of graph is used to show a correlation?

b. What type of correlation is there between life change units and days off sick?

c. Explain difficulties in concluding that the stress of life changes may result in people taking time off work. What other possible reasons could there be for the data displayed in the graph?

1 MARK + 1 MARK + 4 MARKS

? Selye conducted studies in which rats were stressed until they died. Some people have criticised this research as being unethical. Discuss ethical issues raised by this type of research. **4 MARKS**

SOCIAL PSYCHOLOGY
Social Influence

6

What's it about?

Social psychology focuses on our interaction with each other and argues that humans are social creatures who are born into families and cultures. It is our interaction with others that influences the way we perceive and understand our world.

Particular areas of interest for social psychologists include studies on conformity and obedience, as well as looking at how a minority group can persuade the majority to change their minds or behaviour. This area of psychology also explores group behaviour, interpersonal attraction, leadership, and explanations of aggression and altruism. Underlying much of social psychology is the view that humans construct their social worlds and that situational variables have a key role in explaining why people do what they do.

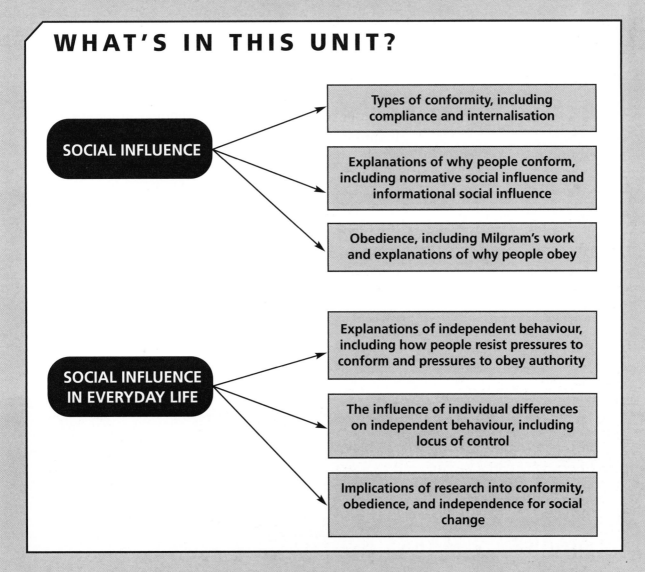

WHAT'S IN THIS UNIT?

SOCIAL INFLUENCE

- Types of conformity, including compliance and internalisation
- Explanations of why people conform, including normative social influence and informational social influence
- Obedience, including Milgram's work and explanations of why people obey

SOCIAL INFLUENCE IN EVERYDAY LIFE

- Explanations of independent behaviour, including how people resist pressures to conform and pressures to obey authority
- The influence of individual differences on independent behaviour, including locus of control
- Implications of research into conformity, obedience, and independence for social change

IMPORTANT TERMS AND CONCEPTS

As part of the AS exam:

- You may be asked to describe, explain, outline, or contrast different explanations of conformity and obedience.
- You could also be asked to discuss their strengths and weaknesses.
- You will be expected to know what factors contribute to people resisting the pressures to obey and to conform.
- You will need to be able to distinguish between situational factors and individual differences (such as the locus of control) when exploring social influence.
- The examiner may ask you to apply your knowledge to real-life situations and explore how research into social influence might be undertaken.
- Finally you will need to be able to discuss the implications of social influence research for our society.

The following terms are important for understanding this module so, although you will not be directly examined on their definitions, it will help you in the exam if you understand what they refer to. Make a list of definitions of the following terms and if you get stuck there is a glossary at the end of this book to help you.

Agentic state	**External validity**	**Minority influence**
Buffers	**Identification**	**Mundane realism**
Compliance	**Independent behaviour**	**Normative social influence**
Conformity	**Informational social**	**Obedience to authority**
Conversion	**influence**	**Protection of participants**
Debriefing	**Informed consent**	**from psychological harm**
Deception	**Internal validity**	**Right to withdraw**
Demand characteristics	**Internalisation**	**Situational explanation**
Dispositional explanation	**Locus of control**	
Ethical guidelines	**Majority influence**	

OVER TO YOU

Mary is with a group of friends who all agree that a television programme that Mary dislikes is the best thing they have seen on television for a long time. Using your knowledge of social influence outline two reasons why Mary might agree with her friends.

2 MARKS + 2 MARKS

SOCIAL INFLUENCE

If you have ever laughed at a joke that you didn't understand, or been persuaded by one or two people to change your views or behaviour, then you will be aware that other people have an influence on us.

Social influence can be defined as "the process whereby attitudes and behaviour are influenced by the real or implied presence of others" (Hogg & Vaughan, 2005). The AS exam explores two forms of social influence: *obedience* and *conformity*.

- **Obedience** This occurs when we behave as instructed. It usually takes place in hierarchical settings where the person giving the orders is of a higher status. This often results in people feeling that they cannot disobey the authority figure.
- **Conformity** This has been defined as "the degree to which people change their behaviour, views and attitudes to fit the views of others" and can result from:

MAJORITY INFLUENCE OR MINORITY INFLUENCE

MAJORITY INFLUENCE	**MINORITY INFLUENCE**
Occurs when people adopt the behaviour, attitudes, or values of the majority (dominant or largest) group after being exposed to their values or behaviour.	Occurs when the majority are influenced and accept the beliefs or behaviour of a minority.
Majority influence often leads to COMPLIANCE in that whilst the person may publicly change their views or behaviour in line with the majority, their private opinion remains as it was.	Minority influence often results in internalisation where people change their private view in line with minority. This is often referred to as CONVERSION.

Psychological research into Social Influence has provided psychology with some well known studies including Milgram's research into obedience, Asch's research into conformity, and Zimbardo's famous Stanford Prison Study (see ASP4 pp.275–277).

CONFORMITY

Types of Conformity

Although we may not be aware of it, most days we are influenced by others and conform to group norms and social expectations. Indeed if people didn't conform, their lives could be quite difficult. For example if someone decided they didn't want to wear clothes to work, others would probably be embarrassed or outraged, and the person, as well as being ridiculed, could well be arrested for indecent exposure!

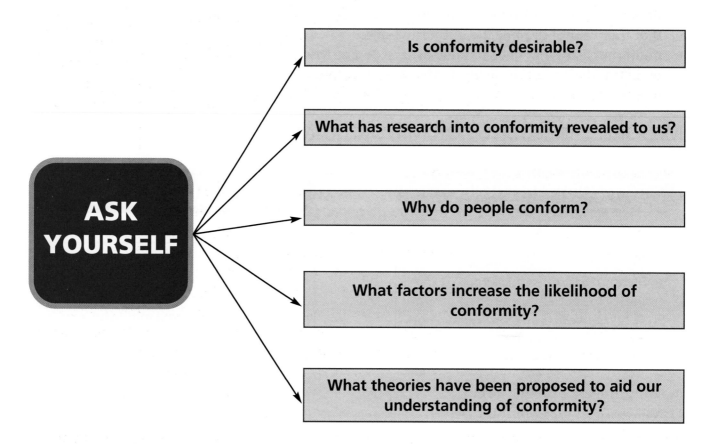

ASK YOURSELF

- Is conformity desirable?
- What has research into conformity revealed to us?
- Why do people conform?
- What factors increase the likelihood of conformity?
- What theories have been proposed to aid our understanding of conformity?

Explanations of Conformity

Kelman (1958; see ASP4 pp.271–272) was interested in how social influence affects us in everyday life. He thought it was important to distinguish between situations where we might publicly agree with others, while privately maintaining our own view, and situations where we change our private opinions too. He distinguished between three different types of conformity:

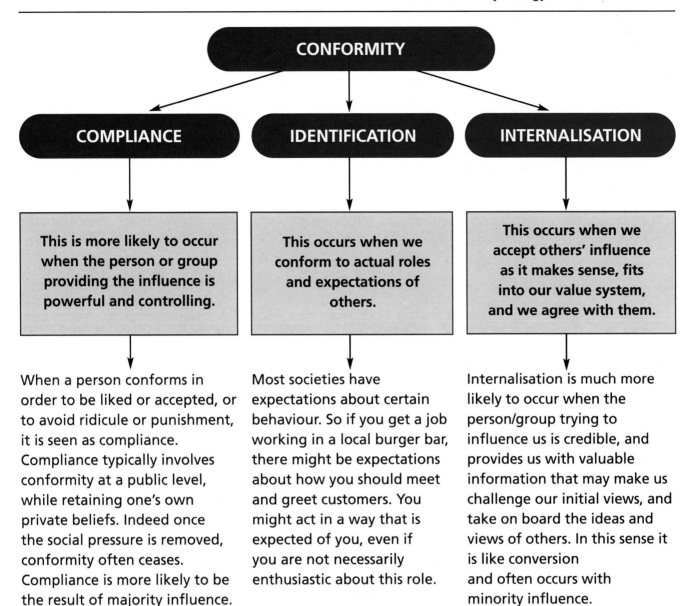

CONFORMITY

COMPLIANCE

This is more likely to occur when the person or group providing the influence is powerful and controlling.

When a person conforms in order to be liked or accepted, or to avoid ridicule or punishment, it is seen as compliance. Compliance typically involves conformity at a public level, while retaining one's own private beliefs. Indeed once the social pressure is removed, conformity often ceases. Compliance is more likely to be the result of majority influence.

IDENTIFICATION

This occurs when we conform to actual roles and expectations of others.

Most societies have expectations about certain behaviour. So if you get a job working in a local burger bar, there might be expectations about how you should meet and greet customers. You might act in a way that is expected of you, even if you are not necessarily enthusiastic about this role.

INTERNALISATION

This occurs when we accept others' influence as it makes sense, fits into our value system, and we agree with them.

Internalisation is much more likely to occur when the person/group trying to influence us is credible, and provides us with valuable information that may make us challenge our initial views, and take on board the ideas and views of others. In this sense it is like conversion and often occurs with minority influence.

Alongside Kelman's insights, three main theories of conformity have been proposed. It is important to stress that they do not necessarily operate independently.

- Normative social influence (= Kelman's *compliance*).
- Conforming to social roles and expectations (= Kelman's *identification*).
- Informational social influence (= Kelman's *internalisation*).

These theories have arisen out of research studies on both minority and majority influence, and can be linked to Kelman's three types of conformity.

MAJORITY INFLUENCE

Normative Social Influence

This occurs when we want to be liked by a group or want to avoid embarrassment and hence go along with the consensus even though we might not change our private opinions.

Normative social influence is reduced when people give their opinions privately, when they know that they can throw their information away, or when support is given by another social dissenter.

- Asch (1951; see ASP4 pp.265–267) Participants were asked to state which line was the same as a target line. The naive participant was placed in a group with six others, who were confederates of the experimenter. On critical trials, the confederates gave the wrong answer. On these trials, participants conformed and gave the wrong answer on 37% of trials. Variables manipulated included:
  - seating position
  - size of group
  - unanimity.

Post-experimental interviews revealed that the participants said that they felt self-conscious and feared disapproval. Interestingly, when participants were allowed to write their answers down, rather than saying them out loud, conformity rates dropped to 12.5%.

EVALUATION

STRENGTHS

- The study was very influential in showing the power of group pressure.
- The study provided a paradigm for future studies on conformity.

WEAKNESSES

- The task was trivial and not important to participants' belief systems (i.e. it lacked mundane realism).
- The study lacks experimental validity in that the findings may be the result of a particular historical time (see Perrin & Spencer, 1980; see ASP4 p.268) and may reflect a gender bias.
- The study raises ethical concerns in that the participants were deceived and thus did not give informed consent, and the study did cause some participants stress.

Conforming to Social Roles and Expectations

This theory suggests that we often conform and behave in a way that is expected of us. Thus on becoming a nurse or a teacher we act appropriately. In this sense we identify with the role and act according to expectations.

- Zimbardo (1973; see ASP4 pp.275–277) In the Stanford Prison Study participants agreed to take part in a study that involved them being assigned to either the role of prisoner or guard. After a short while the prisoners became subdued, submissive, slouched, and looked at the ground. The guards seemed to enjoy the power given and some became aggressive. The study was stopped early.

EVALUATION

STRENGTHS

- It was an interesting study revealing the power that roles play in influencing our behaviour.
- Zimbardo did get consent from the participants, although there is some debate about how informed the consent was.

WEAKNESSES

- There is some concern that the participants may have been play-acting, although the study clearly caused stress to the participants.
- In 2006, Reicher and Haslam carried out a similar study, some of which was broadcast by the BBC. In their study there were 5 guards and 10 prisoners. Interestingly in their study the guards failed to identify with the role of guards and in this sense challenged the view that people necessarily assume roles given to them (although knowing their behaviour was going to be broadcast may have influenced their behaviour).

Informational Social Influence

This often occurs when there is no correct or obvious answer to a question posed. In these circumstances we often turn to others for information, since we don't know what else to do.

For these reasons informational social influence tends to occur when the situation is ambiguous and when the participant doubts his/her ability. This may result in a change of private opinion.

- Sherif's autokinetic effect (1935; see ASP4 pp.264–265) Participants estimating the distance a non-moving light had moved, changed their personal estimates when placed in a group so that a group norm emerged.

EVALUATION

STRENGTH

- The study clearly shows that group norms emerge when people are in an ambiguous situation and are uncertain about their response.

WEAKNESSES

- The study lacks mundane realism.
- Sherif used a situation in which there was no obvious answer.
- The participants were deceived.

GENERAL EVALUATION

STRENGTHS

- Explanations of conformity are clearly supported by empirical research.
- The theories have broadened research into social influence, e.g. looking at the difference between expressing one's opinion privately and publicly and how this affects conformity or looking at whether the other members of the group are friends or strangers and how this influences our behaviour.

WEAKNESSES

- It is difficult to separate the influence of normative social influence from informational social influence.
- The theories need to explore how our relationship to other group members influences our level of conformity. Research suggests that group belongingness is an important variable.
- The theories tend to neglect individual differences and personal characteristics, focusing largely on situational factors.
- It is not quite clear how all the theories relate to minority research, although it is assumed that informational social influence is more likely to occur with minority influence.

MINORITY INFLUENCE

Minorities can and do influence majorities as social and scientific innovations clearly demonstrate. Research has explored how the behaviour of the minority can influence the majority. However, the experimental research rarely takes the historical or cultural context into consideration and yet for a minority to gain influence, the conditions for social change need to be there. In addition one major difference between majority influence and minority influence is that minorities often have less power and lower status in a society.

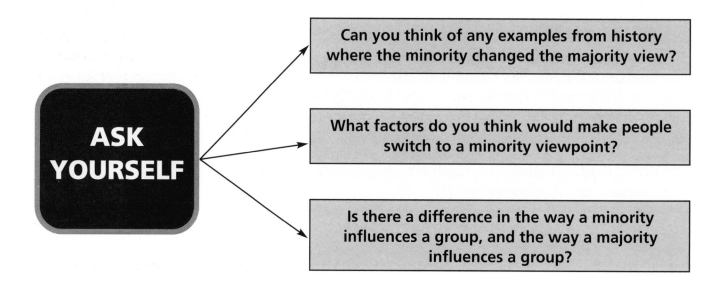

ASK YOURSELF

Can you think of any examples from history where the minority changed the majority view?

What factors do you think would make people switch to a minority viewpoint?

Is there a difference in the way a minority influences a group, and the way a majority influences a group?

Moscovici et al.'s (1969; see ASP4 pp.267–268) study of the influence of a consistent minority on the responses of a majority in a colour perception task aimed to demonstrate that a minority can influence the majority view.

Groups of six participants were presented with blue slides that varied in intensity. Participants were asked to name aloud the colour of the slide. There were two confederates of the experimenter in the group, who were instructed to say that the slides were green either on every trial or on two-thirds of the trials.

When the confederates said green on every trial the percentage of green responses from the other participants was 8.4%, and 32% yielded to minority influence at least once. When the confederates said green for two-thirds of the trials, the participants said the slide was green in only 1% of the trials.

The study demonstrated that when members of a minority are consistent in their opinions, they can on some occasions influence the majority.

EVALUATION

STRENGTH

- The study did direct our attention to how minorities may persuade a majority.

WEAKNESSES

- The experimental set-up was not very believable (lacked experimental realism) and participants may have answered as they thought the experimenter wanted them to (demand characteristics).
- Discussing the colour of slides is not usually of major importance to people's belief systems and so the study lacked mundane realism as it had little relevance to everyday life.

Explanations of Minority Influence

Given that people tend to like to think that they have reached their own decisions, they are unlikely to describe their own behaviour as resulting from conformity. Often when people take up a minority group's viewpoint or behaviour they will dissociate the ideas from the originators, especially if the initiators of the ideas are disliked. So whilst many people support "green issues" now, they tend not to see them as linked to earlier movements such as tree hugging (*dissociation model of minority influence*).

Both conformity to the majority and the minority are more likely if the behaviour or ideas are seen as originating from an "in group". David and Turner (1996) put forward a self-categorisation theory which suggested that ideas that come from an "out group" (people who have different values and beliefs from us) are less likely to be taken up than ideas that come from groups with whom we share our values and ideas (*self-categorisation theory*).

There is some debate as to whether minority and majority influence are the result of different types of influence.

- Latané and Wolf's (1981) *social impact theory* All social influence (whether minority or majority) is dependent on three factors.
- Moscovici's (1980, 1985; see ASP4 pp.272–273) *dual process theory* Minority and majority influence work in different ways.

Latané and Wolf's (1981) social impact theory

This theory suggests the following three factors play a key role in both majority and minority influence.

- **Strength** This describes the number of people present and the consistency with which the message is expressed.
- **Status and knowledge** The higher the person's status and expertise the greater the influence.
- **Immediacy** The closer the person is both physically and emotionally, the greater will be their effect.

Dual process theory

Moscovici (1980, 1985) suggested that majority and minority influence work in different ways. Majority influence arises from compliance, with the emphasis being placed on social factors: the person wants to belong to the group to be accepted and liked or to avoid punishment or ridicule. Minority influence is thought to cause conversion in that the emphasis is focused on cognitive factors and changing private opinions. This is largely because minority viewpoints often challenge us initially and therefore we have to process these ideas more thoroughly. In this sense minority influence is similar to Kelman's (1958) internalisation.

Research by Maas and Clark (1983; see ASP4 p.273) supports Moscovici's dual process theory. They undertook research into attitudes towards gay rights and found that publicly expressed attitudes tended to conform to the majority viewpoint suggesting that compliance had taken place, whilst privately expressed attitudes tended to agree with the minority viewpoint suggesting that conversion had taken place.

Moscovici argued that conversion is most likely to occur when the minority viewpoint is in line with social trends (social relevance).

In addition, research has suggested that the behaviour of the minority can influence the likelihood of others taking up their viewpoints.

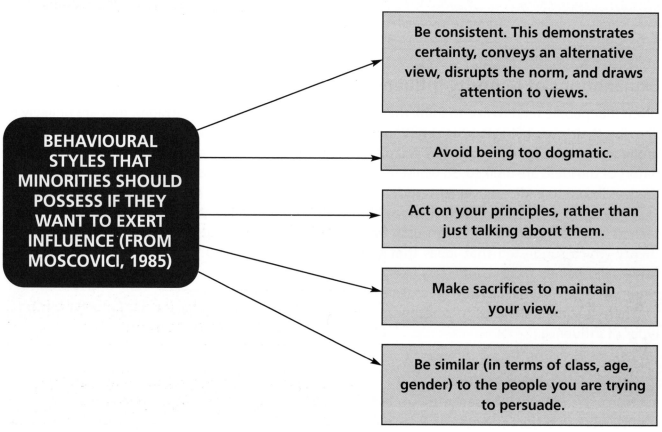

BEHAVIOURAL STYLES THAT MINORITIES SHOULD POSSESS IF THEY WANT TO EXERT INFLUENCE (FROM MOSCOVICI, 1985)

- Be consistent. This demonstrates certainty, conveys an alternative view, disrupts the norm, and draws attention to views.
- Avoid being too dogmatic.
- Act on your principles, rather than just talking about them.
- Make sacrifices to maintain your view.
- Be similar (in terms of class, age, gender) to the people you are trying to persuade.

EVALUATION

STRENGTHS

- Moscovici did direct our attention to how minorities can persuade majorities.
- The role of minorities in changing the way we think is relevant to shifts in our society such as the rise of the suffragettes and the growth of green issues.

WEAKNESS

- It may have overstated the distinction between minority and majority groups in that majority groups' influence can also lead to conversion and internalisation of the majority view.

OVER TO YOU

Using your knowledge of the factors affecting conformity, explain one reason why someone may conform to their group's insistence that they have another alcoholic drink, even if they don't want one.

3 MARKS

Outline and explain one factor that could enable the person to resist the group pressure.

3 MARKS

OBEDIENCE TO AUTHORITY

Milgram's Research and Explanations of Obedience

Obedience is the performance of an action in response to a direct order; usually the order comes from a person of higher status or authority (Franzoi, 1996).

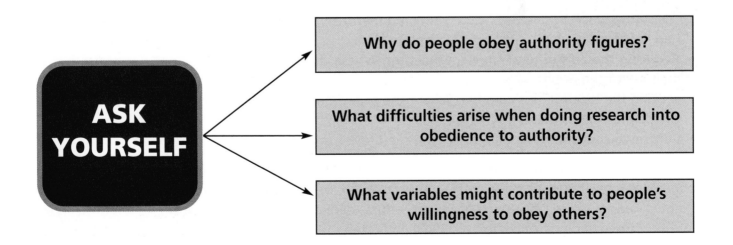

ASK YOURSELF

- Why do people obey authority figures?
- What difficulties arise when doing research into obedience to authority?
- What variables might contribute to people's willingness to obey others?

DIFFERENCES BETWEEN OBEDIENCE TO AUTHORITY AND CONFORMITY	
Obedience	Conformity
Occurs within a hierarchy	Can occur between people of equal status as well as within a hierarchy
The emphasis is on power	The emphasis is on acceptance
The behaviour adopted differs from the behaviour of the authority figure	The behaviour adopted is similar to that of the group
The prescription for action is explicit	The requirement to yield to group pressure is often, though not always, implicit
Participants embrace obedience to explain behaviour	Participants deny conformity

Studies of Obedience to Authority

Electric shocks and learning

Milgram (1963; see ASP4 pp.282–284) conducted a study that was designed to see whether participants would obey an experimenter when instructed to give another person potentially dangerous electric shocks. They were instructed to give the learner an electric shock (ranging from 15 to 450 volts) every time they made a mistake. No shocks were actually given and the learner was a confederate of the experimenter.

Obedience rates showed that 65% of the participants gave a potentially lethal shock to the learner. Milgram (1974; see ASP4 p.285) carried out several variations on his basic experiment, to increase the obviousness of the learner's plight, or to reduce the authority or influence of the experimenter (the obedience rates for these different conditions are shown in brackets):

- **Increasing the distance between experimenter and participant** The orders were given by telephone rather than face-to-face (20.5%).
- **Remote feedback** Where the victim was not seen or heard (66%).
- **Voice feedback** Where the victim could be heard but not seen (62%).
- **Proximity** Where the victim was only 1 metre away from the participant (40%).
- **Touch proximity** Where the victim was only 1 metre away from the participant and the participant had to force their hand onto the shock plate (30%).
- **Reducing the authority of the experimenter** Where the experimenter was not a scientist, but a member of the public (20%).
- **Making the location less credible** Where the experiment was conducted in a seedy office rather than a prestigious university (48%).
- **Refusal to conform** Where another confederate refused to give shocks (10%).

Cross-cultural research by Smith and Bond (1993; see ASP4 pp.268–269) in Europe yielded a total obedience rate of 80% or more in Italy, Austria, Spain, Germany, and Holland. However, there were slight variations in the key aspects of the procedure used in each of these countries, so it is difficult to interpret these findings. Ancona et al. (1968) replicated the study in Italy, to find a total obedience rate of 80%, and Schurz (1985) studied Austrians and found the obedience rate to be 85%. Kilham and Mann (1974) found that Australian males only conformed by 40% and Australian females only conformed by 16%. In this last study, the person being shocked was a student and this raises questions about whether similarity between the victim and the participant influences obedience rates.

EVALUATION

STRENGTHS

- Helped people review their value systems and become aware of destructive obedience.
- 74% said they had learned something of personal importance.
- It "made visible the invisible, and showed how social forces direct and control us".
- A creative and inventive way of studying obedience.
- Participants did believe they were giving actual shocks.
- Exposed the power relationship between experimenter and participant.

WEAKNESSES

- Involved psychological stress, deception, and embarrassment.
- There was no informed consent and pressure was placed on participants who wanted to withdraw.
- Debriefing may have lowered participants' self-esteem.
- Biased sample since all were volunteers.
- Orne and Holland suggested that the study lacked both experimental realism and mundane realism.
- The study did not reveal why some participants did NOT obey.
- Possibly lacks ecological validity.
- Differs markedly from the Holocaust, where the dominant ideology led to dehumanising people and the "relationship" between the guards and victims was markedly different from Milgram's study.

Milgram's Research and the Question of Experimental Validity

Research into social influence raises questions about experimental validity. Psychologists distinguish between *internal validity* (what goes on within the experiment) and *external validity* (how much the findings can be applied outside the study). You need to know the differences between these two types of validity, so let us consider each in turn.

Internal validity

This validity explores whether the experiment measured what it set out to measure: that is, did the experimental design actually do the job it set out to do?

If the experimental set-up was not believable then the participants probably would not behave as they normally do in such situations. For example, did the participants in Milgram's research really believe that they were giving the "learner" electric shocks, or was the situation such that the participants were not behaving how they would usually behave?

Orne and Holland (1968; see ASP4 p.284) argued that the study lacked experimental realism because the participants didn't really believe that they were giving the person an electric shock. However, replications of Milgram's research have shown that 70% of the participants reported that they had believed the whole set-up. In addition, Orne and Holland argued that the obedience of the participants was more due to demand characteristics and the participants doing what was expected of them rather than real obedience. This too has been challenged since the lab environment is a real-life social setting where power relationships still occur. Finally, Orne and Holland pointed out that by paying the participants, Milgram may have made them feel obliged to continue because they had entered a social contract. Again, Milgram replied that this is a reflection of real-life situations where people feel obliged to do as others tell them because they have agreed to do what is required of them.

External validity

This describes the extent to which the findings can be generalised to other settings (ecological validity), to other populations (population validity), and other periods of time (temporal validity).

Milgram argued that his study had clear applications to other settings.

Other Research into Obedience

Milgram's findings have been supported by other research such as that of Hofling et al. (1966; see ASP4 pp.287–288) and Bickman (1974; see ASP4 p.287).

Nurses obeying doctors

Hofling et al. (1966; see ASP4 pp.287–288) conducted a study in which nurses were instructed by a "Dr Smith" to give a patient 20mg of the drug Astroten. This instruction broke several rules as it was above the maximum dose (10mg), no written authority was given, and the nurses did not know if Dr Smith was a genuine doctor. 21 of the 22 nurses in the study obeyed Dr Smith and were willing to give the 20mg dose of Astroten.

EVALUATION

STRENGTHS

- Raises important questions about hospital practices.
- Has external validity.

WEAKNESSES

- Does not follow ethical guidelines: nurses were deceived, there was no informed consent, nurses did not have the right to withdraw.
- Attempts to replicate Hofling's research have failed (e.g. Rank & Jacobsen, 1977), although Lesar et al. (1977) did find that nurses did obey doctors' orders, even when they had good reason to doubt them.

Cross-cultural support for obedience research

Meeus and Raaijmakers (1995; see ASP4 pp.288–289) asked Dutch participants to interview job applicants and give them negative feedback about their performance in the form of "stress remarks" that ranged from mild to severe. The interviewees were confederates of the experimenter, and as the interviewer's statements became more humiliating, the applicants pleaded with the interviewer to stop interrupting and then refused to answer any more questions. 22 out of the 24 participants delivered all 15 stress remarks to the interviewee.

EVALUATION

STRENGTHS

- Interesting variation on Milgram's work, dealing with psychological rather than physical stress.
- Is thought to have greater ecological validity and mundane realism than Milgram's work.
- Provides an insight into obedience in Holland.

WEAKNESSES

- Participants were deceived.
- There was no informed consent.
- Some participants may not have minded giving negative comments, yet the experimental design assumed that they would.

The effect of uniforms

Bickman (1974; see ASP4 p.287) explored the role of uniforms when participants were either asked for a dime for a parking meter, asked to pick up a bag, or told to stand on the other side of a bus stop. Obedience rates differed with different uniforms, so participants were more likely to obey if the experimenter was dressed as a guard rather than a milkman or civilian.

Obedience can be related to the amount of perceived authority.

EVALUATION

STRENGTH

- Has mundane realism.

WEAKNESSES

- Participants were deceived.
- There was no informed consent.

Explanations for Obedience to Authority

Psychologists have used studies of obedience to try to establish why people obey others. Their explanations can be divided between *situational* and *dispositional* explanations. Situational explanations can be summed up by Milgram's comment that it is "not so much the kind of person a man is as the kind of situation he finds himself in that determines how he will act". Dispositional explanations look at the person's personality.

Situational explanations

The following are features of the situation that are conducive to obedience.

- **Legitimate authority** We assume that the people in authority have some knowledge or expertise, and therefore think they know more than us. For this reason we have a tendency to defer responsibility for our actions to their authority.
  FOR EXAMPLE: In Milgram's study the assumption was that the experimenter knew what he was doing—after all, he was a psychologist!
- **Graduated commitment** This is sometimes called the foot-in-the-door technique. It works because once we agree to a fairly reasonable small request we then tend to feel obliged to agree to greater requests, even if they are unreasonable.
  FOR EXAMPLE: In Milgram's study, having agreed to give 15-volt shocks, it was difficult to then refuse to give 45 volts.
- **The agentic state** People argue that they are not responsible for their own actions, and are merely carrying out the orders of the authority figure. The alternative to the agentic state is the autonomous state, in which we are aware of the consequences of our actions and therefore voluntarily direct our behaviour.
  FOR EXAMPLE: In Milgram's study the participants argued that the university had sanctioned the study.
- **Buffers** A buffer is anything that prevents the person seeing the consequences of their actions.
  FOR EXAMPLE: In Milgram's study this occurred when the participants could not see the victim.

EVALUATION

STRENGTHS

- It has been convincingly demonstrated that the factors identified by Milgram do play a part in producing obedience. Milgram (1974) demonstrated that obedience was reduced:
  - if the victim's plight was obvious (they were in the same room as the participant)
  - if the researcher was not wearing a white coat
  - if the researcher gave orders by telephone
  - if another confederate refused to obey orders.

WEAKNESSES

- Despite suggesting that we obey because we enter an agentic state and aren't really thinking for ourselves, participants in Milgram's studies clearly were still thinking, in that they experienced a conflict between what they were asked to do, and their conscience. Indeed they became anxious and tense.
- The explanations given don't help explain why some people are more likely to obey than others.
- Experimental research like Milgram's does not take ideological factors into account in that his study does not explain the horrors of Nazi Germany. There are marked differences between the two experiences. The most obvious include the difference between the victims and the perpetrators. In Milgram's study the victim appeared to volunteer for the study. The way the study was set up it could just have easily been the participant. This was clearly not the case with the Holocaust. The Nazis could not perceive their victims as volunteers. Whereas Milgram's participants showed tension and conflict in obeying orders, the Nazis believed that what they were doing was right and saw their victims as less than human.

Blass and Scmitt (2001; see ASP4 pp.291–292) suggest that we need to distinguish between different types of social power:

- Harsh external influences often seen as hierarchical and legitimate.
- Soft influences such as the expertise and credibility of the authority figure.

Both harsh and soft influences play a key role in obedience to authority and it might be that some people are more responsive to soft authority than harsh external authority.

Dispositional explanations

Adorno et al. (1950; see ASP4 pp.292–293) felt that there are certain dispositional factors that contribute to whether or not a person will obey orders.

- **Personality** Adorno suggested that childhood experiences played a key role in the development of personality. Children who are treated harshly as children may develop hostility towards their parents. This hostility remains but gets displaced onto minority groups in the form of prejudice. He called this personality type an authoritarian personality and developed an *F scale* to measure their attitudes. Authoritarian personalities believe in conventional values, are hostile to out groups, are intolerant of ambiguity, and have a submissive attitude to authority figures. Milgram found that participants with high scores on the F scale gave stronger shocks than low scorers.

- **Passivity** Some people dislike confrontation so much that they will do anything to avoid it. Thus, rather than challenge authority, they will prefer to do what they are told to avoid a scene or embarrassment.
- **Moral development** Kohlberg suggested that different people reach different levels of moral development, and that very few reach stage six where universal ethical principles govern the person's behaviour. Some people remain at stage one or stage two where the fear of punishment or the promise of reward dominates their decisions.

OVER TO YOU

Milgram carried out an experiment investigating obedience. One criticism of his study was that it lacked experimental validity. To what extent do you think this is a fair criticism of his research?

6 MARKS

SOCIAL INFLUENCE IN EVERYDAY LIFE

One of the key questions raised by research into social influence is: Why are some people more able to be independent than others when it comes to group pressures and authority demands?

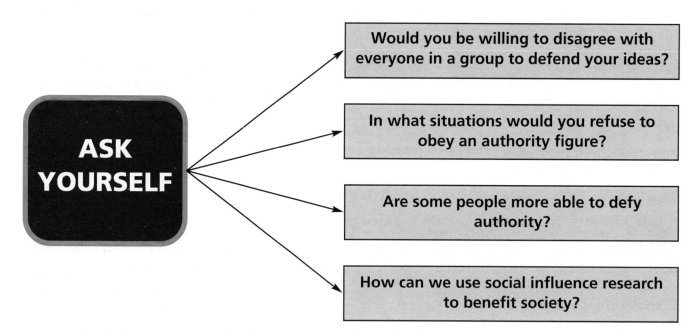

ASK YOURSELF

Would you be willing to disagree with everyone in a group to defend your ideas?

In what situations would you refuse to obey an authority figure?

Are some people more able to defy authority?

How can we use social influence research to benefit society?

HOW CAN YOU RESIST PRESSURES TO CONFORM?

- Perceive the group members who are putting pressure on you as members of an out group, rather than members of an in group.
- Look for support from someone else who is also independent.
- Increase your self-esteem.
- Increase your confidence in the task being undertaken.

There are a number of factors that influence whether or not a person will conform, and you can use the mnemonic **CHIGGUT** to help you remember them:

Cultural factors. Smith and Bond (1993; see ASP4 pp.268–269) suggested that there might be a difference between individualist cultures and collectivist cultures. After analysing numerous Asch-type studies in several countries, it was found that there was less conformity in individualist cultures (e.g. Europe and Northern America—25.3%) than in collectivist cultures (e.g. Asia and Africa—37.1%).

Historical factors. These may influence conformity in that it has been argued that America in the 1950s was more conformist than in the 1960s and 1970s. Replications of Asch's study in later decades have found lower levels of conformity (Perrin & Spencer, 1980; see ASP4 p.268).

Individual differences. These may play a part in whether people are more likely to remain independent. It has been found that people with a high need for social approval and low self-esteem are more likely to conform, whereas people who are highly knowledgeable and intelligent are less likely to be affected by informational social influence.

Gender differences. There is some controversy as to whether there are gender differences in the likelihood of conforming to a group. Eagly (1978; see ASP4 p.270) has suggested that any differences may be explained by women being more oriented towards interpersonal goals. However when Maslach et al. (1987) used more gender relevant tasks, no gender difference was found.

Group size. Asch (1951; see ASP4 pp.265–266) found that conformity increased as the number of confederates rose from 1 to 3, but after this the group size didn't make much difference except if the answer was obviously wrong and a very large number of people gave the wrong answer. In these cases the participants became suspicious.

Unanimity. This is a key variable in determining the likelihood of conformity. Asch (1956; see ASP4 pp.266–267) found that if the naive participant had one supporter they were less likely to conform.

Type of task. If the task is difficult or the participant isn't quite sure what to do, then conformity is more likely. However if the task is familiar, conformity is less likely, as was demonstrated in Perrin and Spencer's (1980; see ASP4 pp.268) study where engineers did not conform so readily as participants did in the Asch study. Lucas found that when students were asked to give answers to easy and hard problems in mathematics, there was more conformity to the incorrect answers of others, when the problems were hard. This was particularly true of participants who doubted their mathematical ability.

HOW CAN YOU RESIST PRESSURES TO OBEY?

It has been suggested that by understanding obedience, people will be more able to resist obeying others when their instructions are a cause of concern.

Situational Factors that Lead to Independent Behaviour

- Provide role models who refuse to obey in that if we see someone else stand up to authority, it shows us that there are alternative ways of responding.
- Get people to think about the consequences of their actions, by making the results of their actions clear. When participants actually had to hold the victim's hand onto the shock plate in Milgram's study, obedience fell to 30%.
- Remind people that they are responsible for their own actions.
- Reduce the status of the authority figure (e.g. when Milgram's study took place in a rundown building the obedience rate fell to 48%).
- Question the motives of authority figures when you think they are giving unreasonable orders.
- Educate people about the problems of "blind obedience".

In terms of **dispositional factors**, there is a greater likelihood of resisting obedience if the person:

- Wants to maintain control.
- Is confident enough to be independent.
- Has a high level of moral development.
- Has a need to maintain their individuality.
- Can voice their protest early.

THE INFLUENCE OF INDIVIDUAL DIFFERENCES ON INDEPENDENT BEHAVIOUR

Attribution Theory

Underlying attribution theory is the notion that we are naive scientists who are trying to find ways of explaining our own and others' behaviour. Sometimes we attribute the causes of our own actions to internal factors and sometimes we attribute the causes to external factors.

So if we trip up the stairs we might argue that someone left a shoe on the staircase (*external factor*) or if someone else trips up the stairs we might argue that they are clumsy (*internal factor*).

How we explain our own behaviour is thought to influence our self-esteem, health, and confidence. For example if the reasons you give for splitting up with a partner are external (e.g. we lived too far apart, we had different interests) you are more likely to feel better than if you attribute the split to internal causes (I'm boring, dull, and uninteresting).

Attribution theory and independent behaviour

Attribution theory is thought to aid our understanding of independent behaviour, in that humans have a tendency to underestimate the degree to which their behaviour is situationally or externally controlled. This is known as the *fundamental attribution error* and can explain why people were surprised at Milgram's results. Although the participants were actually influenced by external factors (the institution, the experimenter, the need to advance science), people assumed that internal factors would dominate (their conscience).

Similarly in Asch's research the participants were influenced by external factors (other people giving the wrong answer) rather than internal factors (what they actually believed). Indeed the participants who were more likely to conform seemed to reason that it was preferable to appear competent at a task, rather than appear weak in going along with a patently wrong answer.

Locus of Control

Rotter (1966; see ASP4 pp.300–303) believed that individuals differ in their *locus of control*, a personality dimension in which people differ in how they explain what happens to them.

For example, people with an *internal locus of control* might explain doing well in their exams by using internal factors, such as "I worked really hard and I am good at that subject". People with an *external locus of control* might use external factors to explain their exam result, such as "it was luck", or "it was an easy paper".

It has been suggested that people with an internal locus of control are more likely to show independent behaviour and be less influenced by others.

EVALUATION

STRENGTHS

- The fundamental attribution error helps us understand why people were so surprised with Milgram's research in that they underestimated the role of situational variables preferring to think that behaviour is largely the result of internal factors.
- The locus of control theory has been supported by empirical research, in that Shute (1975; see ASP4 p.300) found that participants with an internal locus of control were less likely to conform to peer pressure on attitudes to drugs, than participants with an external locus of control.
- Using a meta-analysis of studies on the the effects of locus of control on social influence, Avtgis (1998) found that people with an internal locus of control were less prone to social influence that those with an external locus of control.
- De Man, Morrison, and Drumheller (1993; see ASP4 p.301) found that people with low scores in authoritarianism tended to be more likely to have an internal locus of control. This links to Milgram's finding that lower scores in authoritarianism were associated with

more independent behaviour. A similar correlation has been found between participants having an internal locus of control and scoring more highly on measures of self-esteem.

WEAKNESSES

- Some research hasn't supported the link between independent behaviour and an internal locus of control. Williams and Warchal (1981) identified individuals having high and low scores for majority influence on Asch-type tasks. The two groups didn't differ in locus of control.
- Rotter's measure of internal locus of control is a somewhat general measure, and so it is difficult to use to make predictions about specific situations. In addition it might be that we explain some aspects of our behaviour using an internal locus of control (doing well in sport) while other aspects of our behaviour may be explained using an external locus of control (lucky that exam question came up).
- Some people may appear independent in obedience studies, even if they do have an internal locus of control. For example psychopaths may be driven by internal factors (e.g. enjoyment of hurting others) and could see Milgram's study as the ideal opportunity to put these desires into practice.
- The independence of the participant could be a combination of both internal and external factors and indeed the notion that they are entirely separate is problematic. Thus in Milgram's research a participant might refuse to obey because they can't stand hearing someone in pain (external) and because they always empathise with others (internal).

THE IMPLICATIONS OF SOCIAL INFLUENCE RESEARCH AND ITS ROLE IN SOCIAL CHANGE

Overview

The research you have looked at in this section of the course may leave you with a somewhat negative view of humanity. Asch clearly demonstrated that people will go along with a group's views even if the views are patently incorrect. Milgram frighteningly demonstrated "the extreme willingness of adults to go to almost any lengths on the command of authority".

Both research into conformity and obedience has shown us that we can't simply explain some of the evils of our society by suggesting that some people are just evil. As Hannah Arendt (1963) suggested, the Nazi regime highlighted the banality of evil in that the Nazis were "terrifyingly normal".

In addition it would seem that people with low self-esteem, authoritarian personalities, and an external locus of control are more vulnerable to social influence.

Yet despite this somewhat pessimistic view there are grounds for optimism, in that it is clear that educational programmes can be used to broaden people's awareness of these issues.

Grounds for Optimism

Research into conformity

- We need to remember that only 5% of Asch's participants conformed on every trial and on two-thirds of the trials participants did not conform.

- Asch's research used the length of lines as a task and this may not be particularly important to people who might be much more willing to be independent in dicussions on prejudice, animal research, or recycling.
- In real life we often ask others and chat about concerns we have when we disagree with group norms. Indeed it is often easier to disagree with close friends as we know they like us for ourselves and not our opinions.
- The research suggests that people may change their public opinion, but actually keep their own views and in this sense are trying to avoid embarrassment or ridicule. However, their views haven't actually changed at all.
- In a sense the research that suggests that conformity is higher with friendship groups could be used to suggest that people are supportive of one another.
- Research by Smith and Bond (1993) has shown that conformity is decreasing.

Research into obedience

- It needs to be pointed out that some people did refuse to obey the experimenter in Milgram's study and this can be used for further research to see what factors contributed to their independence.
- The people in Milgram's study did show signs of tension and unease, which suggests that they hadn't become automatons just obeying orders. They were stressed and exceptionally relieved when they found out that the learner hadn't been shocked. This suggests that they weren't in a totally agentic state, thinking others would take responsibility for their actions.
- Although Milgram thought the study showed similarities between the Nazi regime and his participants, there are clear differences. First, Milgram's participants often reduced the shocks if the experimenter left the room, if the participants showed signs of distress, and if they thought the victim was like them—a volunteer dedicated to advancing science. This was not true of the Nazi regime who often committed atrocities without the authority figure watching over them, and who felt no remorse for their behaviour since they thought the victims were less than human.
- Milgram's research isolated the participants from family, friends, and colleagues, yet in real life these are often the people we turn to to dicuss our decisions. In a replication of Hofling et al.'s (1966) research, Rank and Jacobsen (1997) found that only 11% of nurses were willing to obey a doctor's instruction to give too high a dose of a medicine to patients if they had the chance to chat to their colleagues beforehand.

HOW CAN WE PROMOTE SOCIAL CHANGE?

The research has highlighted some factors that can prevent "blind obedience" and conforming to undesirable group norms.

- Getting social support can aid us in being less pressured to obey or conform. Mutual support has often enabled minorities to stand together in the face of others.
- Getting people to think about the consequences of their actions can reduce obedience. Sherman (1980; see ASP4 p.306) asked a colleague to phone people and discuss what they would do if faced with acting in a morally or socially undesirable way. Interestingly when the same people were asked much later by an authority figure to carry out the act, two out of three refused.
- Getting people to think more positively about themselves and their opinions can aid independent behaviour. Arndt (2002) asked participants to focus on some aspect of themselves that was

unchanging and made them feel good about themselves. These participants were more independent than the controls when they rated a painting having been given other people's ratings of the painting.

- Getting people to see each other as equal members of the human race rather than as superiors and inferiors would lessen obedience to authority. Studies have shown that conformity increases when the participant perceives the other members as higher in status. This was also the case in studies on obedience.

 But remember, it is not always the case that obedience and conformity are negative actions. Obeying authority figures because they are experts makes sense, as does conforming to many of society's norms.

RESEARCH METHODS AND SOCIAL INFLUENCE

Perhaps more than any other area in psychology, research into social influence has become public knowledge, with both Milgram's research into obedience and Zimbardo's Stanford Prison Study arising from real-life concerns.

Milgram's research was influenced by the case study of what happened during the Vietnam War at Mai Lai. Soldiers killed the inhabitants of the village, saying they were "just obeying orders".

His initial research into obedience was more like an observation of what people would do in the situation he had set up, but as he explored obedience further he began to manipulate a range of variables to see their influence on the degree of obedience shown by the participants.

He found that changing the environment where the study occurred, making the distance from the victim closer or having someone other than the participant disobey the experimenter influenced the participants' obedience levels.

Whereas Milgram's research took place in a lab, Hofling's study of nurses is an example of a field study in that it took place in the natural environment of a hospital.

Studies of conformity also allow the experimenter to manipulate variables, such as where the naive participant is sitting, whether there is another supporter in the group, and whether the group is made up of friends or strangers. These studies often make use of questionnaires and interviews to obtain more in-depth information about the participants' responses after the study took place.

Social influence research also uses meta-analysis, which involves numerous research studies being compared and analysed to extract key themes and differences. This has been particularly useful in cross-cultural research, as demonstrated by Smith and Bond (1993) looking at the differences between individualist and collectivist cultures.

The Ethics of Research into Social Influence

Research into social influence has raised some of the most heated debates about the treatment of participants, most notably in Milgram's and Zimbardo's studies. Given the ethical guidelines, it is clear that these studies raise ethical issues.

However you also need to consider what would have happened if Milgram's participants hadn't been deceived, or if Asch's participants were told that the study was on conformity rather than the judgement of line lengths. How would Milgram's participants react after being debriefed? Were the participants given the opportunity to withdraw from the study? Did Zimbardo's study cause participants undue stress?

One major critic of Milgram was Baumrind (1964), and a summary of the key issues in the Milgram–Baumrind debate follows.

PARTICIPANTS SHOULD NOT BE DECEIVED

Baumrind's concerns
Participants were deceived on two counts. First, they were told that the study was about the effects of punishment, and then they believed that they were giving someone real electric shocks and that the confederate was another participant.

Milgram's reply
Without the deception the study couldn't have taken place, and it did reveal truly surprising results. Participants were debriefed and 74% said they had learned something of personal importance.

PARTICIPANTS SHOULD GIVE INFORMED CONSENT

Baumrind's concerns
Participants hadn't given their consent to take part in a study on obedience.

Milgram's reply
Although this was the case, other writers such as Rosnow argued that the study helped people review their value systems and made them aware of the destructiveness of obedience.

PARTICIPANTS SHOULD BE PROTECTED FROM PSYCHOLOGICAL HARM

Baumrind's concerns
Participants experienced a loss of self-esteem, dignity, and trust in authority, and it was a stressful experience for some.

Milgram's reply
Milgram argued that the participants were fully debriefed, and psychiatric examination one year after the study revealed no sign of psychological damage. In addition, stress was not anticipated.

PARTICIPANTS SHOULD BE ALLOWED TO WITHDRAW FROM THE STUDY

Baumrind's concerns
Participants who wanted to withdraw were informed that they had no choice but to go on.

Milgram's reply
By persuading participants to remain, Milgram was demonstrating the power of the scientific establishment and authority figures, and he argued that they were not physically detained.

In addition to Baumrind's points, there was some concern over confidentiality in that the names of the participants were published in the press and they were also interviewed.

OVER TO YOU

In what ways could it be argued that Asch, Hofling et al., Zimbardo, and Meeus and Raaijmakers did not consider ethical issues to the extent they should have done?

Do the ends justify the means?

Social psychologists face a dilemma when investigating social influence. On the one hand they want to use their research skills to advance our knowledge and understanding of humanity, but on the other hand they have a responsibility to the people who are willing to take part in their research. The participants are not objects of study, but human beings.

One major concern revolves around whether deception should take place. Without deception, it is argued that participants' behaviour in a research situation would not be an accurate portrayal of how they would behave in a real-life scenario. Attempts to get round this difficulty by using role play exercises have led psychologists to argue that role plays simply result in participants guessing how they should behave, rather than behaving how they would normally. Preventing psychologists from undertaking any research that might involve stress or conflict would necessarily result in a somewhat "lopsided" view of psychology. However, if psychologists do undertake such research they can be accused of abusing their power and being disrespectful towards fellow human beings.

It has been suggested that psychologists should do a *cost–benefit analysis* of the research, with the benefits focusing on the gains for both psychology and in some cases the participants, whilst the costs focus on the perceived harm to the participants or the profession. Diener and Crandall (1978; see ASP4 p.184) suggested the following drawbacks to the cost–benefit approach:

- It is almost impossible to predict both costs and benefits prior to conducting a study.
- Even after the study, it is hard to quantify costs and benefits, partly because it can depend on who is making the judgements. For example, a participant may judge the costs differently from the researcher, and benefits may be judged differently in years to come.
- It tends to ignore the substantive rights of individuals in favour of practical, utilitarian considerations.

Baumrind felt very strongly that Milgram's study should not be judged on a cost–benefit analysis, since this directed emphasis away from human suffering. Milgram argued that his study had revealed important findings, summarised in the following quotes:

"It is not so much the kind of person a man is as the kind of situation he finds himself in that determines how he will act."

"Participants who refused to obey showed a powerful affirmation of human ideals."

"My body of work makes visible the invisible to show us the subtle and not so subtle forces at play around us, how they direct us and even control us. We are so immersed in these networks of power and rituals of communication that we no longer see them . . . just as the fish is the last to notice it is surrounded by water."

Cost–benefit analysis

Ethics are determined by a balance between benefit and cost, or a cost–benefit analysis. Some things may be less acceptable than others, but if the ultimate end is for the good of humankind then psychological researchers may feel that an undesirable behaviour, such as causing stress to an animal or deceiving participants as to the nature of the study, is acceptable.

COST–BENEFIT ANALYSIS	
Costs	Benefits
• Participants may be distressed at finding out something about themselves that they would have preferred not to know. • Participants may feel that they have been "tricked" or lied to. • Participants may have lowered self-esteem as a result of taking part in the study. • Participants are not given the opportunity to give informed consent. • Participants may say that they are pleased that they took part in the study because they feel obliged to, rather than because they did (*demand characteristics*). • It may bring the psychological profession into disrepute as an "institutionalised candid camera".	• The results may make us more aware of our own and others' behaviour and raise consciousness about important issues. • Milgram's study may result in people taking more responsibility for their own actions and not blindly obeying others. • Asch's research may make us challenge group norms and stand up for our own beliefs, and the rights of others. • Zimbardo's research may help us understand why some of the atrocities that take place in prisons occur, and how being given power can change people in a negative way. • Hofling et al.'s research may encourage people working in institutional settings like hospitals to check whether the orders given are in the best interest of the patient. • Such obedience research can also benefit the participants by giving them insight into their own behaviour.

OVER TO YOU

What do you think about Milgram's viewpoint? Is he justified in his research? Go through the above lists of costs and benefits and add any more "cost" and "benefit" points that you can think of.

Informed Consent

It is considered the right of participants to provide *voluntary informed consent*. This means several things:

• Being informed about the purpose of the research.
• Being informed about what will be required.

- Being informed about your rights as a participant, e.g. the right to confidentiality, and the right to withdraw.
- Giving your full consent to take part in the study.

However, there are many situations where this is just not possible to obtain prior to the study commencing. In an attempt to resolve the difficulty of obtaining informed consent when participants are being deceived, other methods of obtaining consent have been proposed, and we will now consider each one in turn.

Presumptive consent
This involves asking members of the population, who are similar to the participants, whether they would consider the research to be acceptable.

Prior general consent
This involves asking people who volunteer to take part in research general questions before they are chosen.

- **FOR EXAMPLE:** "Would you mind taking part in a study that involved your being misinformed about its true nature?"
    "Would you mind being involved in a study that might cause you stress?"

Participants who agree may later be chosen, since it is assumed that they have agreed in principle to take part. This consent is sometimes referred to as *partially informed consent* for obvious reasons.

Retrospective consent
Some psychologists suggest that by fully debriefing the participants and giving them the opportunity to withdraw their data, the participants have provided retrospective consent. The assumption is that giving them the right to withdraw their data gives them the same power as if they had refused to take part in the first place.

However consent is obtained you need to remember that people sometimes agree to take part in a study without really thinking through exactly what it involves. In other cases, the consent is given by another person, such as a parent or other authority figure.

SAMPLE QUESTIONS

? Using your knowledge of obedience explain two ways the situation would have to change to increase resistance to obedience. **3 MARKS + 3 MARKS**

? Explain why the validity of social influence research has been questioned. **5 MARKS**

? Outline two ethical issues that arose in one study into obedience. **3 MARKS + 3 MARKS**

INDIVIDUAL DIFFERENCES
Psychopathology (Abnormality)

7

What's it about?

Research into individual differences looks at why people differ along certain dimensions such as intelligence, personality, and mental health. This involves examining the role that both genetics and the environment play in shaping us into the people that we become. Studies of individual differences embrace a range of perspectives. The biological approach explores our differences in terms of our genetics, biochemistry, and neuroanatomy. The psychodynamic approach focuses on our early childhood experiences and unresolved conflicts. The cognitive perspective suggests that differences between us stem from different ways of thinking about the world. The behaviourists explain our differences by looking at different reinforcement histories and conditioning. In addition to these perspectives, psychologists also devise classification systems and methods of measuring individual differences, and treatments when differences are considered abnormal.

WHAT'S IN THIS UNIT?

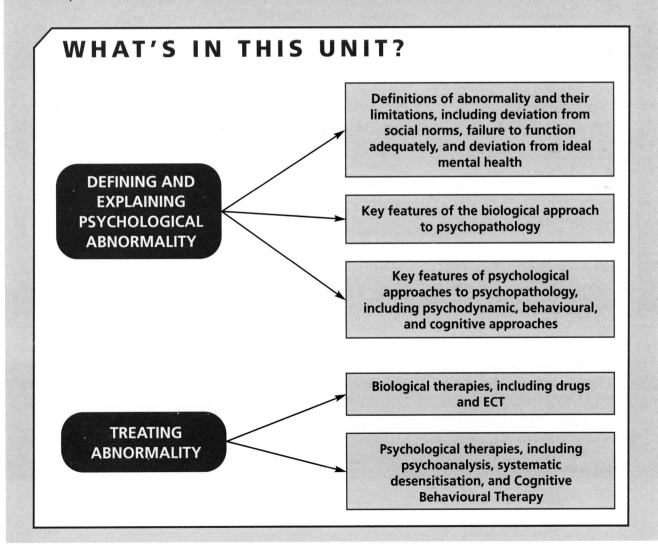

DEFINING AND EXPLAINING PSYCHOLOGICAL ABNORMALITY

- Definitions of abnormality and their limitations, including deviation from social norms, failure to function adequately, and deviation from ideal mental health
- Key features of the biological approach to psychopathology
- Key features of psychological approaches to psychopathology, including psychodynamic, behavioural, and cognitive approaches

TREATING ABNORMALITY

- Biological therapies, including drugs and ECT
- Psychological therapies, including psychoanalysis, systematic desensitisation, and Cognitive Behavioural Therapy

IMPORTANT TERMS AND CONCEPTS

As part of the AS exam:

- You may be asked to describe, explain, outline, or contrast different definitions, explanations of and treatments of abnormal behaviour.
- You could also be asked to discuss their strengths and weaknesses.
- You might be asked to identify which approach is being used to explain the behaviour and link the approach with relevant treatment.
- In addition the examiner may ask you to apply your knowledge to real-life situations or explore how research into abnormality might be undertaken.

The following terms are important for understanding this module so it will help you in the exam if you understand what they refer to. Make a list of definitions of the following terms, and if you get stuck, go to the glossary at the end of this book.

Abnormality	Defence mechanisms	Modelling
Anxiety	Deviation from social	Oedipus complex
Behaviour therapy	norms	Operant conditioning
Behavioural model of	Diathesis–stress model	Pleasure principle
abnormality	Ego	Projection
Benzodiazepines	Electroconvulsive therapy	Psychoanalysis
Biological (medical) model	(ECT)	Psychodynamic model
Bipolar disorder	Exposure therapy	Psychosexual development
Buspirone	Extinction	Reciprocal inhibition
Classical conditioning	Failure to function	Regression
Cognitive Behavioural	adequately	Repression
Therapy	Fixation	Safety-seeking behaviour
Cognitive model of	Id	Schizophrenia
abnormality	Ideal mental health	Serotonin
Cultural relativism	Insight	Superego
Culture-bound syndromes	Major depressive disorder	Systematic de-sensitisation

OVER TO YOU

Outline key features of the psychodynamic approach to psychopathology.

6 MARKS

DEFINING AND EXPLAINING PSYCHOLOGICAL ABNORMALITY

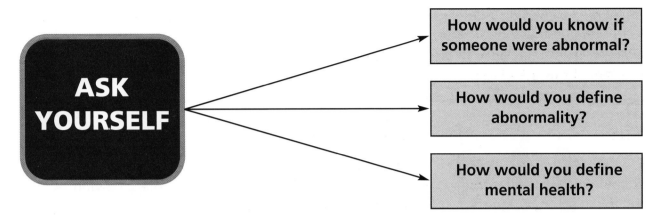

Several theories have been proposed to aid our understanding of abnormality. The starting point of all these theories is an attempt to define abnormality, but this is harder than most people think.

After reading *AS Level Psychology, Fourth Edition* you should be familiar with the following ideas:

- Deviation from social norms.
- Failure to function adequately.
- Deviation from ideal mental health.

This unit also requires an understanding of different theoretical perspectives including:

- The biological (medical) model.
- The psychodynamic model.
- The behavioural model.
- The cognitive model.

For each, you will need to be able to:

- Describe the model.
- Give examples of how the model is used to explain abnormality.
- Evaluate the model.

We can now consider each of these approaches to defining psychological abnormality in turn.

DEFINITIONS OF ABNORMALITY

Deviation from Social Norms

To define people's mental health in terms of deviation from social norms (see ASP4 pp.313–316) suggests that those who behave in a socially deviant or incomprehensible way should be regarded as abnormal because they break with conventions and do not do what is normally expected. This approach has obvious limitations:

- Norms change over time so that what might have been seen as socially deviant 50 years ago may be the norm today, such as living together before getting married.

- Whether behaviour is perceived as deviant is dependent on context. Taking off one's clothes to get in a bath is the norm; however, taking them off in a lesson is not!
- At times, breaking with the dominant culture is something to be applauded rather than criticised as being abnormal. For example, freedom fighters who opposed apartheid in South Africa were not abnormal, but people who believed in racial equality.
- Norms differ between cultures, e.g. the Mormons believe it is acceptable for a man to have several wives.

We all want to be mentally healthy, but should we all want to be totally "normal"?

Failure to Function Adequately

Underlying this definition (see ASP4 pp.317–318) is the notion that people who cannot cope with the demands of everyday life, such as getting up, getting dressed, and being able to look after themselves, may in some ways be perceived as abnormal. Rosenhan and Seligman (1989; see ASP4 pp.317–318) expanded this approach to cover a list of seven abnormal characteristics: suffering, maladaptiveness, vividness and unconventionality of behaviour, unpredictability and loss of control, irrationality and incomprehensibility, observer discomfort, and violation of moral and ideal standards.

The limitations of this approach are as follows:

- It involves making value judgements about others as to what constitutes failure to function adequately, and such judgements will always be open to error and misinterpretation.
- The person themselves may not think they have a problem even though others think they do. It might not worry them that they don't get up or get dressed, so using failure to function adequately as a criterion for abnormality may not be appropriate.
- Suffering is part of human life and it is difficult to decide when suffering is maladaptive after serious life events have occurred.

Deviation from Ideal Mental Health

This definition (see ASP4 pp.319–321) looks at the problem of defining abnormality by focusing on what we understand by normal/mentally healthy, and working backwards from that. Jahoda (1958; see ASP4 pp.319–320) suggested that normal mental health includes:

- **Self-attitudes** Having high self-esteem and a strong sense of identity.
- **Personal growth** The extent to which an individual grows, develops, and becomes self-actualised affects their mental health.
- **Integration** How the above two concepts are integrated, which can be assessed by how an individual will cope with a stressful situation.
- **Autonomy** The degree to which a person is independent of social influences and able to regulate himself or herself.

- **Perception of reality** Being free from the need to distort one's own perception of reality, and demonstrating empathy and social sensitivity.
- **Environmental mastery** The extent to which an individual is successful and well adapted.

Abnormality would therefore be an absence of these qualities. On the positive side, this approach considers how people's lives can be improved, but there are also important limitations:

Can psychological problems be treated in the same way as physical problems?

- There is some concern that measuring mental health differs markedly from measuring physical health (e.g. how do we know that someone has a strong sense of identity?).
- After looking at the criteria it might be suggested that few people are in fact mentally healthy.
- The list of attributes has been criticised for being ethnocentric in that it describes individualist cultures (e.g. the United States) rather than collectivist ones (e.g. China).

Cultural Relativism

Given that cultures differ in their beliefs, values, and norms, it has been argued that we cannot make absolute statements about what is normal and what is abnormal in human behaviour. For example, in the Trobriand Islands it is normal for a son to clean his dead father's bones and give them to relatives to wear, and it would be seen as abnormal if the widow did not wear the bones of her deceased husband. In British culture, such behaviour would be a cause of concern. The concept of *cultural relativism* means that value judgements are relative to individual cultural contexts and we cannot make absolute statements about what is normal or abnormal in human behaviour.

OVER TO YOU
Outline and evaluate any one definition of abnormality.

4 MARKS

BIOLOGICAL AND PSYCHOLOGICAL MODELS OF ABNORMALITY

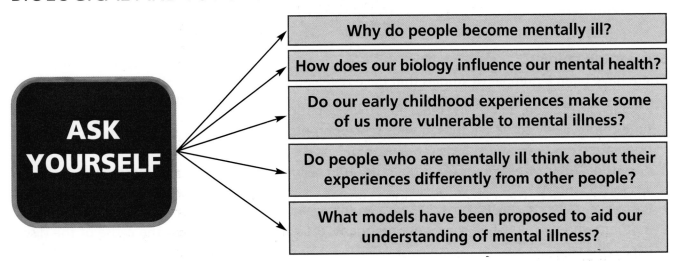

ASK YOURSELF

Why do people become mentally ill?

How does our biology influence our mental health?

Do our early childhood experiences make some of us more vulnerable to mental illness?

Do people who are mentally ill think about their experiences differently from other people?

What models have been proposed to aid our understanding of mental illness?

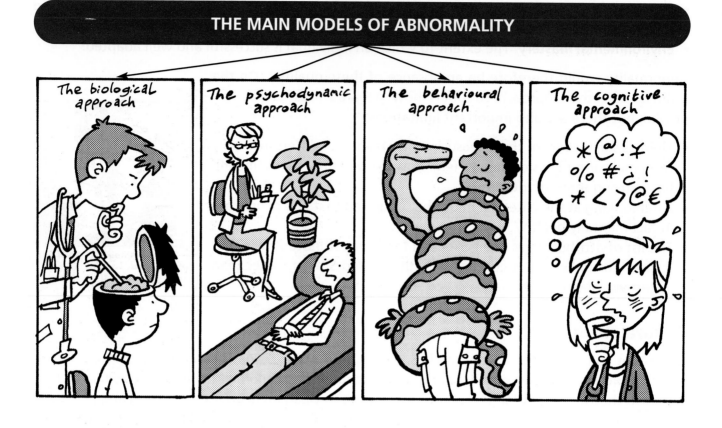

Biological (Medical) Model

Assumptions

The biological (medical) model (see ASP4 p.323) assumes that abnormal behaviours result from physical problems and should be treated medically. Key areas of interest focus on genetics, biochemistry, infections, and neuroanatomy. The implication of this model for treatment is that it is possible to cure the patient by changing their biological processes, and the following treatments are seen to be suitable:

- Electroconvulsive therapy (ECT).
- Drugs.
- Psychosurgery.

Supporting studies

There have been a number of studies that have revealed a link between biology and mental illness:

- Kendler, Masterson, and Davis (1985) Relatives of patients diagnosed with schizophrenia were 18 times more likely to be diagnosed with schizophrenia than randomly selected members of the population.
- Berrettini (2000; see ASP4 p.324) Bipolar disorder is linked to genes on chromosomes 4, 6, 11, 12, 13, 15, 18, and 22.
- Barr et al. (1990; see ASP4 pp.323–324) An increased incidence of schizophrenia was found in mothers who had flu when they were pregnant, thereby suggesting that the cause of the disorder might be a disease.

- The condition phenylketonuria (PKU; see ASP4 pp.325–326) This is a form of mental retardation caused by an inability to process the amino acid phenylalanine—it can be simply and effectively treated by physical means.

EVALUATION

STRENGTHS

- The biological (medical) model does explain some disorders, e.g. PKU.
- The model is based on well-established sciences.
- It does help provide some treatments for some disorders, e.g. depression, but treatments do not help all sufferers, e.g. some schizophrenics.
- A positive ethical issue is that it removes the "blame" culture from the patient.

WEAKNESSES

- It raises the question of whether mental illness is the same as physical illness. Szasz (1960) argued that mental illness is not an illness or a disease but rather a problem with living.
- There is rarely a 100% concordance rate for identical twins developing schizophrenia, which suggests that genetic factors do not tell the whole story.
- Research is often correlational and hence it is difficult to establish whether biological factors are the cause or the result of the disorder.
- By focusing on the symptoms, less attention is given to the patients' feelings, experiences, and life events as possible causes.
- A negative ethical issue is that genetic explanations of mental illness may result in relatives becoming anxious, and such explanations also raise questions and concerns about the use of sterilisation to prevent the continuation of such disorders.
- The biological model is somewhat narrow and it ignores social, cultural, and psychological factors.

Psychodynamic Model

Assumptions

The psychodynamic model (see ASP4 pp.328–330) contrasts sharply with the biological (medical) model by suggesting that mental illness "arises out of unresolved unconscious conflicts in early childhood". The model is based on the Freudian understanding that much of our behaviour is driven by unconscious motives and that childhood is a critical period of development. Key areas of interest focus on:

- The mind—the conflicts between the id, ego, and superego.
- The stages of psychosexual development.
- Defence mechanisms.

Conflicts occur most often between the id's desire for immediate gratification and the superego's desire to maintain moral standards and ideals. One major conflict experienced by the child is their love for the opposite sex parent and their jealousy of the same sex parent who they perceive as a rival (the Oedipus Conflict).

When considering Freud's stages of psychosexual development (oral, anal, phallic, latency, and genital), the psychodynamic viewpoint states that at times of great personal stress a person may regress to an earlier stage of development (*fixation*). Conflicts cause anxiety, and the ego defends itself against anxiety by using defence mechanisms such as *repression, regression, projection*, and *displacement*. The implication of this model for treatment is to attempt to bring the repressed material into consciousness to gain insight. This is achieved by psychoanalysis, including *dream analysis* and *free association*.

Supporting studies

Psychodynamic theories tend to gain support from case studies rather than experimental data:

- Freud (1895; see ASP4 p.351) and his colleague Breuer In a case study of Anna O, Anna's inability to drink, despite her tormenting thirst, was traced back to her witnessing her governess' dog drinking from her glass. Also, Anna's disturbed eye movements were traced back to caring for her sick father and needing to hide her anxiety and tears.
- Kendler (1996) Parental loss in childhood is related to an above average tendency to suffer from depression and alcoholism in adult life.
- Caspi et al. (1996; see ASP4 p.352) Children who were undercontrolled at three were more likely to have developed anti-personality social disorder by the time they reached 21.

EVALUATION

STRENGTHS

- The model changed people's perspectives about mental illness by looking at psychological factors.
- It identifies traumatic childhood experiences as having a role in adult disorders.
- A positive ethical point is that the person is not responsible for their disorder or behaviour, since it is hidden from them in their unconscious.

WEAKNESSES

- There is an overemphasis on the patient's past, rather than their current problems.
- There is an overemphasis on sexual experiences, rather than exploring other interpersonal and social factors.
- Freud has been accused of sexism since the theory stresses that biology is destiny, rather than seeing inequality in terms of social or cultural factors.
- The model is non-scientific since it cannot be falsified (it is not possible to disprove these theories).

- The model may be less applicable to some disorders, e.g. schizophrenia.
- Some of the key concepts of Freudian theory (e.g. id, ego, and superego) have been criticised for being imprecise.
- In terms of ethics, the emphasis on early childhood may result in parental blame.
- There are also problems surrounding false memory syndrome, as it has been found that patients undergoing psychoanalysis have made untrue allegations about childhood abuse that have no basis in fact.

Behavioural Model

Assumptions
The behavioural model (see ASP4 pp.330–332) suggests that most human behaviour is learned and that mental disorders arise from maladaptive learning. Key areas of interest focus on:

- Classical conditioning.
- Operant conditioning.
- Observational learning or modelling.

The implication of this model for treatment is that if the abnormal behaviour is the result of maladaptive learning, then the behaviour can be "unlearned" using one of the following techniques:

- Aversion therapy and systematic desensitisation (based on classical conditioning).
- Token economy (based on operant conditioning).
- Modelling (based on observational learning).

Supporting studies
The nature of the behaviourist approach means that it lends itself well to research:

- Watson and Rayner (1920; see ASP4 p.331) In a well-known study of Little Albert, they demonstrated classical conditioning of the fear response by frightening him with a loud noise every time he saw a white furry object. Eventually any neutral white fluffy stimulus produced the same fear response as the frightening stimulus.
- Bandura and Rosenthal (1966; see ASP4 p.333) By studying the use of modelling to treat phobias, where the patient models the response of the therapist to the feared object, they found that using live examples (such as real snakes) worked better than using symbolic representations of the feared object (such as models of snakes).

EVALUATION

STRENGTHS

- It is successful in treating specific phobias.
- Some psychologists suggest that the behaviourist model is sensitive to environmental cues and social or cultural factors. However, others argue that the model supports the dominant culture by getting patients to conform to what is expected by society.
- A positive ethical point is that this model gives the patient the power to change, since they can unlearn what has been learned.

- The patient is not seen as a victim of an illness.
- Concepts underlying this model are sensitive to experimental research.

WEAKNESSES

- The focus is on the symptoms rather than the cause of the symptoms and this, according to the psychoanalysts, will lead to symptom substitution (the idea that another disorder will develop since the cause of the initial disorder has not been dealt with).
- By exaggerating the importance of the environment it minimises the role of biological factors such as genetics.
- It is over simplistic. We rarely know the details of the learning experiences of patients such as their reinforcement histories and so it becomes difficult to test in real life.
- The treatments used have been criticised for being unethical, e.g. aversion therapy and token economies.
- The emphasis on behaviour tends to devalue the person's feelings and experiences.
- The behavioural model often uses animal research and it may be that conditioning is less important for human behaviour since we use language and cognitive processes to inhabit our world.
- There is some concern that the treatments are for the benefit of society rather than to benefit the patient.

Cognitive Model

Assumptions

The cognitive model (see ASP4 pp.335–338) states that maladaptive behaviour is caused by faulty and irrational cognitive processes. Key areas of interest focus on:

- Making incorrect inferences.
- Being dominated by the "shoulds", "oughts", and "musts" of life.
- The cognitive triad, involving negative thoughts about oneself, the world, and the future (Beck, 1976).

The implication of this model for treatment is that if the problem is caused by distorted thinking then the therapist has to help the patient replace the irrational and distorted thoughts with ones that are rational. This is achieved by the process of *cognitive restructuring*, which intends to make the patient's thoughts and beliefs more positive and rational.

Supporting studies

Research has tended to explore links between disorders and the way people think, as well as seeing if changing patients' thought patterns improves their condition:

- Beck and Clark (1988; see ASP4 p.337) Distorted and irrational beliefs are common among patients with mental disorders, most notably anxiety disorders and depression. However, the link has not been shown for most other disorders.
- Lewinsohn et al. (2001; see ASP4 p.337) Distorted beliefs may play a part in the development of depression.

EVALUATION

STRENGTHS

- This model focuses on people's experiences, feelings, and interpretations.
- It gives people power to change and increases their self-belief.
- A positive ethical point is that it allows the person to take responsibility for changing their undesirable behaviour.

WEAKNESSES

- The model is limited in its application in that it works better with anxiety disorders than schizophrenia.
- It tends to ignore other possible causes such as genetics or faulty biochemistry.
- It is unclear whether the negative thinking is the cause of the depression or actually the result of the depression.
- By focusing on thinking, the model pays less attention to the social and interpersonal factors that influence humans.
- It raises the ethical question of whether people have the right to say that someone's belief system is faulty, especially if that person's life experiences support their negative world view.
- It could be argued that this model implies that the person is responsible for their unhappiness.

The Multi-dimensional Approach

Which model is the best?

Asking the question "Which model is the best?" is not particularly helpful, as it takes the wrong approach. Rather, it is more sensible to ask how the models can be used to explain a range of disorders or offer treatments at different levels or stages of the disorder. Some models are more useful to explain schizophrenia (e.g. biological model), whereas other models are more useful at explaining phobias (e.g. behavioural model). Most psychologists adopt a multi-dimensional approach to abnormality. One way to express this is in terms of the *diathesis–stress model*.

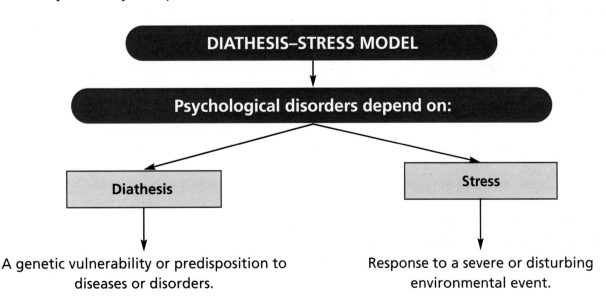

The key notion in the diathesis–stress model is that both diatheses *and* stress are necessary for a psychological disorder to occur. This approach explains the following:

- When one identical twin develops a disorder, their twin does not always go on to develop the disorder—because an environmental trigger is required.
- When an individual has a disorder but their sibling who has had similar childhood experiences does not develop the disorder—because they are genetically different, so only one sibling had the genetic vulnerability in the first place.

OVER TO YOU

Outline key features of the psychodynamic approach to psychopathology.

6 MARKS

Explain one way in which this approach differs from the cognitive approach.

3 MARKS

TREATING ABNORMALITY

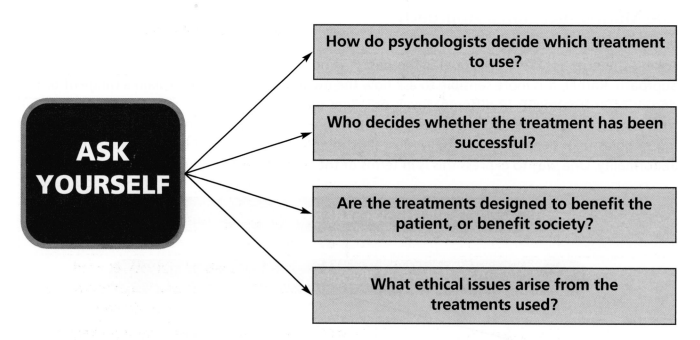

ASK YOURSELF

- How do psychologists decide which treatment to use?
- Who decides whether the treatment has been successful?
- Are the treatments designed to benefit the patient, or benefit society?
- What ethical issues arise from the treatments used?

The therapies used to treat abnormality derive from the approaches used to explain abnormality. However, caution is needed before we conclude that just because a treatment is successful, it can actually explain the cause of the illness. This is known as the *treatment aetiology fallacy* and would occur if you were to argue that a lack of electrical stimulation was the cause of depression, since ECT (which involves passing an electric current through the brain) can, in some cases, treat depression successfully.

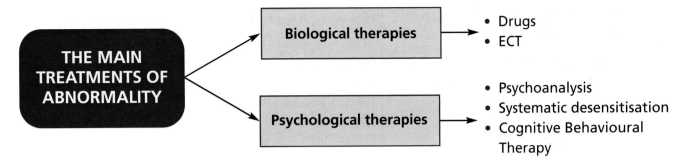

BIOLOGICAL THERAPIES

These include some of the most popular therapies for treating mental illness, such as drugs. In 2003, 13 million prescriptions for benzodiazepines were written in the UK. Other biological therapies include the use of ECT and lobotomies, although the latter are rarely used.

Underlying these therapies is the idea that something has gone wrong with the biological make-up of the patient, which the treatment is designed to rectify.

Drugs

Typically drugs have been designed to:

- Increase the levels of neurotransmitters serotonin and noradrenaline in the treatment of depression.
- Enhance the ability of GABA to inhibit bodily arousal and anxiety in the treatment of anxiety disorders.
- Block the activity of the neurotransmitter dopamine in treating schizophrenia.

DRUG TREATMENTS OF DEPRESSION			
Disorder	*Drug/group of drugs*	*How they work*	*Side-effects*
Depression (major)	Monoamine oxidase inhibitors	Inhibit oxidation of monoamine neuro-transmitters (including dopamine, serotonin, and noradrenaline), so that levels increase	Can cause high blood pressure. Patients need to avoid foods containing tyramine
	Trycyclic anti-depressant drugs	As MAOIs, increase levels of neurotransmitters	Dizziness, blurred vision, dry mouth, may impair driving
	SSRIs (e.g. Prozac)	As MAOIs, but mainly affect levels of serotonin	Patients less likely to suffer from dry mouth and constipation, but in some cases may lead to a preoccupation with suicide and violence

Depression (bipolar)	Lithium carbonate	One notion is that this drug alters potassium and sodium ion activity in the neurons and hence transmission of nerve impulses. Anti-mania, but mechanism is imperfectly understood	Side effects on CNS, cardio-vascular and digestive systems. Overdose can be fatal
Anxiety disorders	Barbiturates	Treats symptoms of anxiety; palpitations, shortness of breath, accelerated heart rate, feelings of choking, nausea, dizziness	Problems of concentration, lack of co-ordination, slurred speech. Addictive. Withdrawal symptoms include delirium and irritability
	Benzodiazepines (e.g. Valium, Librium)	Bind to receptor sites in the brain that receive the neurotransmitter GABA. The drugs increase the ability of GABA to bind to these sites, thus enhancing the ability of GABA to inhibit bodily arousal and anxiety	Poor concentration, sedative effects (sleepiness), memory loss, physical dependence
	Buspirone	Stimulates serotonin receptors in the brain	Can lead to headaches and depression, but doesn't appear to have a sedative effect
Schizophrenia	Neuroleptic drugs (e.g. Thorazine, Prolixin, Haldol). More effective on positive symptoms of schizophrenia—delusions and hallucinations	Block neurotransmitter dopamine within 48 hours. Reduces delusions and hallucinations	Some patients report grogginess, sedation, difficulty in concentrating, dry mouth, blurred vision. Can develop symptoms similar to those of Parkinson's disease, e.g. tremors, muscle rigidity, foot shuffling
	Atypical anti-psychotic drugs (e.g. Clozaril, Risperal, Zyprexa). More effective with negative symptoms of schizophrenia—lack of motivation, lack of emotion, social withdrawal	As neuroleptics	Expensive. May produce fatal blood disease in 1–2% of patients

EVALUATION

STRENGTHS

- Drug therapy can prevent suicide.
- It can be beneficial for treating depression, anxiety, and schizophrenia.
- Prien and Potter (1993; see ASP4 p.344) found Lithium had a beneficial effect on about 80% of patients, especially in reducing the symptoms associated with manic disorders.
- Mitte (2005) undertook meta-analyses of 65 studies of drug-based approaches to the treatment of generalised anxiety disorder and found that it was mostly effective.

WEAKNESSES

- Relapse is common after drug therapy.
- The drop-out rate is fairly high (i.e. people stop taking the drugs).
- Some drugs produce psychological or physical dependency or both.
- There can be serious side-effects, some of which can even be life-threatening.

ECT (Electroconvulsive Therapy)

This treatment involves passing an electric current through the patient's head in order to produce a convulsion. A strong muscle relaxant is given to prevent participants from breaking any bones during the convulsion and also to prevent their experiencing any terror. A recent development in the use of ECT is to pass the current only through the non-dominant hemisphere. Although this technique is thought to reduce memory loss, it is also thought to be less effective than passing the current through both hemispheres of the brain.

EVALUATION

STRENGTHS

- Petrides et al. (2001) reported between 65% and 85% of patients with depression had a favourable response to ECT.
- Some patients report finding this treatment more beneficial than others. Vreede, Burger, and van Vliet (2005; see ASP4 p.349) identified four patient factors that predicted a good response to ECT:
  - aged over 65
  - absence of a psychotic depression
  - absence of a personality disorder
  - responding well to anti-depressants.
- There is some support for its use in treating schizophrenia. Tharayan and Adams (2005; see ASP4 p.349) suggested it had beneficial effects in the short term, but smaller than those obtained with drugs.

WEAKNESSES

- There is still no detailed understanding of why ECT is effective.
- There are side-effects including memory loss and cognitive impairments, although these may be short term.

- Long-term effects, especially when used to treat schizophrenia, are less clear.
- Subjective reports suggesting that the person feels better may reflect their not wanting to have any more ECT treatment, rather than its beneficial effect.

PSYCHOLOGICAL THERAPIES

Psychoanalysis

Psychoanalysis has tended to be used predominantly to treat people suffering from neuroses such as anxiety disorders or from depression. The treatments derive from psychoanalytical theory, which focuses on conflicts between the ego, id, and superego and the use of defence mechanisms such as repression and regression.

Freud believed that the best way to cure neuroses was to allow the patient to gain access to his or her repressed ideas and conflicts and face up to whatever emerges from the unconscious. For the patient to appreciate the full significance of the repressed material they need to engage with it emotionally. This enables them to gain *insight* into what produced the emotional conflict or deficits in their psychological development.

Psychoanalysts use several techniques to bring the repressed material to the surface.

Hypnosis	In the early days of psychoanalysis, hypnosis was used to get to the repressed material. However Freud found that many clients were difficult to hypnotise and in addition hypnosis made some patients too suggestible. For these reasons he developed other methods.
Free association	This involves the therapist telling the patient to respond with the first thing that comes into his/her mind when presented with certain words or ideas. If a patient finds it difficult to come up with an association it is often seen as evidence that they are getting close to an important repressed idea.
Dream analysis	This was described by Freud as the "royal road to the unconscious", since our censor is less vigilant when we are asleep. However, our dreams may still distort or disguise our repressed ideas because of their unacceptable nature.

Progress in therapy depends partly on *transference*, which involves the patient transferring the powerful emotional reactions previously directed to their parents or significant others, onto the therapist. These emotions may be positive or negative. This transference often provides a link to childhood and to dramatic conflicts experienced by the patient as a child, and thus helps bring repressed material to the surface.

EVALUATION

STRENGTHS

- First systematic form of psychological treatment for mental disorders and has strongly influenced subsequent forms of therapy.
- Kivlighan et al. (2000; see ASP4 p.353) studied 12 clients who received 20 sessions of psychoanalytic counselling and found there were steady decreases in symptoms across sessions along with progressive increases in insight.
- Matt and Navarro (1997; see ASP4 pp.353–354) found evidence that suggested it proved moderately effective.
- The distinction between different levels of consciousness/awareness has been supported.

WEAKNESSES

- There is some concern that clients may be saying what they think the therapist wants to hear, rather than what they are really thinking.
- Some of the concepts underlying the theory are vague.
- Høglend (2004; see ASP4 p.353) failed to find any evidence for the role of transference in facilitating recovery.
- By focusing on early childhood conflicts, less attention is given to the individual's current problems and the difficulties they might be experiencing at the social and interpersonal level.
- It could be argued that, rather than insight leading to recovery, it is the recovery that leads to insight.

Behaviour Therapy

Behaviour therapy aims to change the behaviour of the patient since the underlying idea of this therapy is that abnormality is due to maladaptive learning.

Behaviour therapy makes use of:

- **Operant conditioning** Operant conditioning has contributed to the development of token economy where patients are given a reinforcement (a token) for behaving appropriately.
- **Modelling** Modelling has been used with patients who suffer from phobias and who learn by observing someone else behave appropriately around their phobic object, such as a snake or a mouse.
- **Classical conditioning** Classical conditioning has contributed to the development of:
  - aversion therapy
  - systematic desensitisation
  - exposure therapy.

Based on Pavlov's research with dogs, classical conditioning involves transferring a reflex response from an unconditioned stimulus (e.g. salivation to food) to a conditioned stimulus (e.g. salivating to the sound of a bell).

Aversion therapy

Pavlov's initial research formed the basis of aversion therapy where maladaptive behaviour such as alcoholism/gambling might be paired with a noxious stimulus to reduce or remove the behaviour.

Thus patients might be given the drug Antabuse, which causes them to vomit. Pairing this drug with alcohol or gambling behaviour would result in the patient feeling sick when drinking alcohol or starting to gamble. Although this may work for a short time, once the pairing stops the maladaptive behaviour may re-occur.

Systematic de-sensitisation

This treatment is based on the assumption that phobias are developed through classical conditioning as was shown by Watson and Rayner's (1920) study on Little Albert. However, attempts to replicate this study have not always been successful.

Two main techniques are thought to contribute to systematic de-sensitisation.

- **Reciprocal inhibition** Wolpe (1958; see ASP4 p.356) suggested that any treatment of phobias would need to break the initial link or association between the feared object (e.g. spiders, mice, dogs) and anxiety and fear. To do this, he suggested substituting a competing response to inhibit the anxiety experienced by the patient. He therefore developed a series of relaxation techniques that could be practised by the patient.
- **Building anxiety hierarchies** Underlying the use of anxiety hierarchies are Pavlov's findings on stimulus generalisation. Pavlov realised that dogs would not only respond to the original stimulus of a bell, but also respond to similar sounds. He found that the response would lessen the further the sound was from the original stimulus. Using this finding, therapists help patients devise anxiety hierarchies. The therapist can start with a stimulus that causes the patient very little anxiety (e.g. a picture of a cartoon spider in a book) and then gradually build up to the most fear provoking situation or stimulus (e.g. a spider running across the patient's hand).

Systematic de-sensitisation works as follows:

- Patients are given relaxation training involving deep muscle relaxation.
- Patients, with the help of the therapist, construct an anxiety/fear hierarchy ranging from least feared (fluffy toy mouse) to most feared (mouse running across hand). The therapist also tries to identify the cause of the anxiety.
- Patients use their relaxation techniques whilst they imagine or interact with the objects or situations they fear. Real-life de-sensitisation is called vivo de-sensitisation.
- As the patient begins to feel more in control they move up the hierarchy, so that they can eventually deal with the object/situation that they feared initially.

So how important are the relaxation techniques? Wolpe suggested that systematic de-sensitisation works by substituting the anxious response with the competing response of relaxation. However, Wilson and Davison (1971; see ASP4 p.356) suggested that the factor contributing to the success of systematic de-sensitisation is not the relaxation techniques but *extinction*. They suggest that the strength of the anxiety response is reduced because there are no adverse effects after repeated exposure of the noxious stimulus and if this is the case, then the relaxation exercises are somewhat redundant.

Levin and Gross (1985; see ASP4 p.357) reviewed the literature and compared systematic de-sensitisation with and without relaxation and found inconsistent findings. 10 studies showed that systematic de-sensitisation was as effective without relaxation as with, while 15 studies found relaxation did contribute to the success rates.

However, the anomaly can be explained by the fact that extinction takes time to reduce the response and if there were only a few treatment sessions then relaxation techniques would be beneficial.

Another method used to see whether relaxation plays a crucial role in the treatment is the development of *exposure therapy* (or *flooding*). This therapy involves exposing patients to the object or situation they fear for lengthy periods of time until their anxiety is diminished. This exposure may take place in real-life settings (e.g. crowded lifts) or in virtual reality and demonstrates to the patients that the adverse consequences they fear don't actually happen to them.

Exposure therapy has been found to be very effective and more effective than systematic de-sensitisation. However, the dropout rate can be high as patients do not want to be exposed to what they fear for long periods of time.

EVALUATION

STRENGTHS

- Choy et al. (2007; see ASP4 p.357) found that decreased anxiety and decreased avoidance were maintained in a six-month follow up.
- Denholz et al. (1978; see ASP4 p.357) found that 60% of patients treated for flying phobias continued to fly during the three and a half year follow up.
- Systematic de-sensitisation is based on theoretical research into conditioning and can be studied using experimental methods.
- It has contributed to the development of other treatments, e.g. exposure therapy.

WEAKNESSES

- Systematic de-sensitisation is designed for use with anxiety disorders, so it is not useful for other disorders. Even with some of these conditions, such as generalised anxiety disorder, it is not very useful because it is difficult to define the specific stimuli that cause the generalised anxiety.
- Some patients find it difficult to imagine the feared object or situation so it is not helpful for them.
- A lot of evidence (e.g. Choy et al., 2007; see ASP4 p.357) indicates that systematic de-sensitisation is less effective than exposure therapy in the treatment of phobias.
- It is not clear why systematic de-sensitisation is effective. There is an argument that muscle relaxation is not important in the therapy since exposure therapy works without it.

Cognitive Behavioural Therapy

Underlying this therapy is the idea that the maladaptive behaviour is caused by faulty or irrational thinking. The patients often don't test their faulty theories out, as they have developed safety-seeking behaviour to reduce their anxiety. They believe that if they did not use these strategies, then what they fear most could happen. Thus people with a social phobia may avoid eye contact, not talk about themselves, and not join in conversations, to avoid being judged or being seen as stupid and inadequate.

The treatment therefore attempts to change the person's thinking and their behaviour arguing that the two are inextricably linked.

Cognitive Behavioural Therapy stresses that:

- Patients' interpretations of events are often biased and they perceive things negatively (interpretative bias).

- The patient's thoughts, behaviour, and feelings are interrelated.
- Patients need to change the way they think about themselves and about the world.
- Both cognitive processes and behaviour need to change.

To demonstrate patients' faulty or negative thinking Beck (1976; see ASP4 p.359) would give them homework to do, which would involve their testing their (faulty) hypotheses. He theorised that this would make them realise that their fears or anxieties were groundless and that the strategies they were using to protect themselves from their fears (safety-seeking behaviours) were irrelevant.

EVALUATION

STRENGTHS

- Salkovskis et al. (1999; see ASP4 p.361) treated patients suffering from panic disorder with agoraphobia. Patients who were told to avoid safety-seeking behaviours showed a greater reduction in catastrophic beliefs and anxiety.
- Roth and Fonagy (2005; see ASP4 p.361) found it to be effective in the treatment of major depression, generalised anxiety disorder, panic disorder with agoraphobia, and post-traumatic stress disorder.
- It is a broad and effective therapy since it focuses on both thought and behaviour.
- It is based on experimental research.
- It is beginning to be used beneficially with patients suffering from schizophrenia.
- It is relatively cheap in comparison with long-term psychotherapy, or the cost of some medication.

WEAKNESSES

- Who decides whether the thoughts of someone else are irrational? Some anxious and depressed patients may have extremely difficult lives and their thoughts might not be distortions of reality.
- Little attention is paid to underlying biological factors or early childhood traumas.
- How can we ascertain if people have actually changed their thinking, in that their verbal reports may reflect what the therapists wants to hear, rather than what the patient actually thinks?
- People may be aware that their thoughts are irrational, but find it hard to change them and their behaviour.

RESEARCH METHODS AND ABNORMALITY

A wide range of research methods are used to help us try to understand abnormal behaviour.

- **Psychodynamic approach** This method makes use of case studies, where detailed information is obtained about one person to identify the key factors that could have contributed to their behaviour and feelings. Breuer and Freud's case study of Anna O is a classic example.
- **Content analysis** This forms part of the work undertaken in dream analysis, where the psychoanalyst may identify themes and links from the patient's manifest dream. Dream analysis demonstrates

the richness of using qualitative data, but also highlights the problems involved in the interpretation of this material.

- **Correlational studies** In an attempt to understand the genetic contribution to disorders such as schizophrenia and bipolar disorder, correlational studies using twins and family members have been beneficial. These studies focus on whether there is a significant relationship between genetic similarity and the development of the disorder. Twin studies where monozygotic twins have been separated at birth are thought to be particularly important, as the role of the shared environment has been controlled for, since they have been raised in different families.

- **Control groups** One valuable experimental method for studying the efficacy of treatments is the use of control groups who are given a placebo. This method helps us find out whether it is the treatment that is aiding recovery, or whether it is the expectation that the treatment will aid recovery that helps the patient. This method has been used to explore the effectiveness of ECT but it does raise ethical concerns, for if the treatment works, one group has been denied a beneficial treatment.

- **Questionnaires and interviews** These often give us insight into the patients' understanding of their problems and their fears. They prove beneficial in systematic desensitisation when building an anxiety hierarchy with the patient. However, one major concern with interviews is that the patient may be saying what they think the therapist wants to hear, rather than want the patient actually thinks.

- **Natural experiments** In some cases, natural experiments have provided us with insight into the effects of brain damage. The case study of Phineas Gage showed how damage to the temporal lobe resulted in a change of personality. Animal research to explore this finding followed, and contributed to the development of frontal lobotomies, most notably by Moniz (1937).

However, given the nature of abnormal behaviour there is some concern that studies on animals may not be easily generalised to humans where social, cultural, and cognitive factors may contribute to the development of abnormal behaviour.

The Ethics of Research into Psychopathology

Research into psychopathology raises a range of ethical concerns:

- The use of placebos when trying to find out if a treatment is beneficial raises concerns for the patients receiving the placebo. If the treatment does actually work they have not received the beneficial treatment, and this might make their condition worse.

- Research into the benefits of drugs and how they affect neurotransmitters and the structures of the brain has involved animal research, which has raised ethical concerns as to whether such studies should be used to benefit humans.

- Concern has also been expressed about the use of drug treatment with humans. First, patients may be encouraged to take them, but might not be fully aware of the side-effects. Second, in some cases drugs that were designed to reduce depression have later been cited as reasons for the person committing suicide. Third, there is some concern that patients might be forced to take the drugs if they refuse to take them voluntarily.

- Other treatments have also raised ethical concerns, most notably the use of aversion therapy, especially in its use with people with different sexual orientations. In some cases, people were given the choice of going to prison or having aversion therapy, particularly when homosexuality was illegal.

- Discussions about treatments also raise the ethical concerns as to who the treatments are for. Is it to benefit the patient or is it to benefit society by changing the patient's unusual behaviour to fit into what is expected?
- The publication of research into psychopathology also has ethical implications, in that research suggesting the genetic basis of any abnormal behaviour raises concerns about the use of sterilisation programmes being suggested to remove the abnormality from society. The Nazis exterminated people with mental disorders and sterilisation programmes took place in the USA.

SAMPLE QUESTIONS

? Outline key features of the psychodynamic approach to psychopathology. **6 MARKS**

? Give strengths of the scientific approach used as part of the biological model of abnormality. **4 MARKS**

? Explain the ethical issues associated with the use of systematic de-sensitisation. **5 MARKS**

GLOSSARY

The following list is a glossary of important terms and concepts. They are for your information only, as you will not be specifically asked to define these in the exam—however it will be of immense help as part of your revision if you clearly understand to what the terms refer.

Abnormal or atypical psychology: the study of individuals who differ from the norm, such as those with mental disorders.

Abnormality: an undesirable state producing severe impairment in a person's social and personal functioning, often causing anguish. Abnormal behaviour deviates from statistical or social norms, causes distress to the individual or others, and is seen as a failure to function adequately.

Acoustic coding: encoding words in terms of their sound using information stored in long-term memory.

Adaptive: the extent to which a behaviour increases the reproductive potential of an individual and survival of its genes.

Adrenal glands: the endocrine glands that are located adjacent to, and covering, the upper part of the kidneys.

Adrenaline: one of the hormones (along with **noradrenaline**) produced by the adrenal glands, which increases arousal by activating the sympathetic nervous system and reducing activity in the parasympathetic system.

Adrenocorticotrophic hormone (ACTH): a hormone produced by the anterior pituitary gland, which stimulates the adrenal cortex.

Agentic state: a state of feeling controlled by an authority figure, and therefore lacking a sense of personal responsibility.

Aims: the purpose of a research study.

Alternative hypothesis: another term for the experimental hypothesis. The experimental hypothesis is the alternative to the null hypothesis.

Amae: a Japanese word referring to a positive form of attachment that involves emotional dependence, clinging, and attention-seeking behaviour. Such behaviour is regarded more negatively in Western countries.

Anaclitic depression: a severe form of depression in infants who experience prolonged separations from their mothers. The term "anaclitic" means "arising from emotional dependency on another".

Animal behaviour: the study of non-human animals in their own right.

Antigens: foreign substances such as bacteria or viruses that can cause disease and that trigger an immune response.

ANS (autonomic nervous system): that part of the nervous system that controls vital body functions, which is self-regulating and needs no conscious control (automatic).

Anxiety: a normal emotion similar to nervousness, worry, or apprehension, but if excessive it can interfere with everyday life and might then be judged an anxiety disorder.

Attachment: a strong, emotional bond between an infant and his or her caregiver(s) that is characterised by a desire to maintain proximity. Such bonds may be secure or insecure.

Authoritarian personality: identified by Adorno et al. as someone who is more likely to be obedient. These people tend to hold rigid beliefs, and to be hostile towards other groups and submissive to authority.

Autokinetic effect: a visual illusion where a small spot of light in a darkened room appears to be moving when in fact it is stationary.

Autonomic nervous system: see **ANS**.

Autonomous state: being aware of the consequences of our actions and therefore taking voluntary control of our behaviour.

Bar chart: like a histogram, a representation of frequency data, but the categories do not have to be continuous; used for nominal data.

Behavioural model of abnormality: a model of abnormality which considers that individuals who suffer from mental disorders possess maladaptive forms of behaviour, which have been learned.

Behaviour therapy: therapy based on the assumption that the best way to treat mental disorders is through techniques that allow the individual to learn new forms of behaviour more appropriate than their current behaviour. More specifically, **classical** and **operant conditioning** are used to replace unwanted patterns of behaviour.

Benzodiazepines: anti-anxiety drugs such as Valium and Librium. They work by reducing **serotonin** levels.

Beta blockers: drugs reducing stress by reducing activity in the sympathetic nervous system.

Bimodal: a distribution with two modes.

Biochemistry: the study of the chemical processes of living organisms.

Biological (medical) model: a model of abnormality that regards mental disorders as illnesses with a physical cause.

Biological therapies: forms of treatment that involve manipulations of the body, e.g. drugs or ECT.

Bipolar disorder: a mood disorder in which there are depressive and manic (elated) episodes.

Black box: the term used by behaviourists to refer to the mind. Their focus was on what goes in (a stimulus) and what comes out (a response).

Bond disruption: occurs when a child is deprived of their main attachment object, in the short or long term, and receives no substitute emotional care.

Bonding: the process of forming close ties with another.

Buffering effect: occurs when a personality characteristic (e.g. **hardiness**) helps to protect or buffer the individual from the adverse effects of stress.

Buffers: aspects of situations that protect people from having to confront the results of their actions.

Burnout: physical and/or emotional exhaustion produced especially by stress.

Buspirone: a more recent anti-anxiety drug, which increases the production of **serotonin** and has fewer side effects than **benzodiazepines**.

Cardiovascular disorders: disorders of the heart and circulatory system; for example atherosclerosis, where the arteries start to block up, and hypertension, or very high blood pressure.

Case study: detailed study of a single individual, event, or group.

Categorical clustering: the tendency for categorised word lists (even with the words presented in random order) to be recalled category by category.

Central executive: the key component of working memory. It is a modality-free system (i.e. not visual or auditory) of limited capacity and is similar to "paying attention" to something.

Central nervous system: see **CNS**.

Chunks: integrated units of information.

Chunking: the process of combining individual items (e.g. letters; numbers) into larger, meaningful units.

Classical conditioning: learning through association; a neutral stimulus becomes associated with a known stimulus–reflex response.

Client-centred therapy: a form of humanistic therapy introduced by Rogers and designed to increase the client's self-esteem and reduce incongruence between self and ideal self.

Clinician (or clinical psychologist): a person who works in clinical psychology, concerned with the diagnosis and treatment of abnormal behaviour.

CNS (central nervous system): part of the nervous system that consists of the brain and the spinal cord.

Cognitive Behavioural Therapy: a development of cognitive therapy in which attempts to change behaviour directly are added to thought and belief restructuring.

Cognitive interview: an interview technique that is based on our knowledge about the way human memory works; paying attention, for example, to the use of retrieval cues.

Cognitive therapy: a form of treatment that involves attempts to change or restructure the client's thoughts and beliefs.

Collectivistic cultures: cultures where individuals share tasks, belongings, and income. The people may live in large family groups and value interdependence.

Comparative psychology: the study of non-human animals, in which comparisons are made between animals of different species to find out more about human behaviour.

Compliance: conforming to the majority view in order to be liked, or to avoid ridicule or social exclusion. Compliance occurs more readily with public behaviour than private behaviour, and is based on power.

Concordance rate: in twin studies, the probability that if one twin has a given disorder the other twin also has the same disorder.

Conditioning: simple forms of learning in which certain responses become more or less likely to occur in a given situation.

Confidentiality: the requirement for ethical research that information provided by participants in research is not made available to other people.

Conformity: changes in behaviour and/or attitudes occurring in response to group pressure.

Confounding variables: variables that are mistakenly manipulated or allowed to vary along with the **independent variable** and therefore affect the **dependent variable**.

Content analysis: A qualitative research method involving the analysis of behaviours or the written or spoken word into pre-set categories, a process known as coding, to produce an overview of the research area.

Control group: the group of participants who receive no treatment and act as a comparison to the experimental group to study any effects of the treatment.

Controlled observations: observations in which the researcher exercises control over some aspects of the environment in which the observations are made.

Conversion: the influence of the minority on the majority. This is likely to affect private beliefs more than public behaviour.

Coping: efforts to deal with demanding and stressful situations by using strategies designed to master the situation, reduce the demands, or tolerate the situation; many coping strategies can be classified as problem-focused or emotion-focused.

Correlation: an association that is found between two variables.

Correlation coefficient: a number that expresses the extent to which two variables are related or vary together.

Correlational analysis: testing a hypothesis using an association that is found between two variables.

Cortisol: a **hormone** produced by the adrenal gland that elevates blood sugar and is important in digestion, especially at times of stress.

Cost–benefit analysis: a comparison between the costs of something and the related benefits, in order to decide on a course of action.

Counterbalancing: used with repeated measures design to overcome the problems of practice and order effects, and involves ensuring that each condition is equally likely to be used first and second by participants.

Co-variables: the variables involved in a correlational study that may vary together (co-vary).

Critical period: a biologically determined period of time during which an animal is exclusively receptive to certain changes.

Cultural relativism: the view that to understand and judge a culture it must be viewed from within that culture, and not from the perspective of the observer's own culture if that is a different one.

Culture-bound syndromes: patterns of abnormal behaviour that are only found in one or a small number of cultures.

Daily hassles: the minor challenges and problems experienced in our everyday lives.

Day care: care that is provided by people other than the parent or relatives of the infant, for example, nurseries, childminders, play groups, etc. A temporary alternative to the caregiver, day care is distinct from institutionalised care, which provides permanent substitute care.

Debriefing: attempts by the experimenter at the end of a study to provide detailed information for the participants about the study and to reduce any distress they might have felt.

Deception: in research ethics, deception refers to deliberately misleading participants, which was accepted in the past. Currently the view is that deception should be avoided wherever possible, as it could lead to psychological harm or a negative view of psychological research.

Declarative knowledge: knowledge related to "knowing that", including episodic and semantic memory.

Defence mechanisms: strategies used by the ego to defend itself against anxiety.

Deindividuation: losing one's sense of personal identity.

Demand characteristics: features of an experiment that help participants to work out what is expected of them, and lead them to behave in certain predictable ways.

Dependent variable (DV): an aspect of the participant's behaviour that is measured in the study.

Deprivation: to lose something, such as the care of an attachment figure, for a long period of time.

Deviation from social norms: behaviour that does not follow accepted social patterns, or unwritten social rules. Such violation is considered abnormal. These norms vary from culture to culture and from era to era.

Diathesis–stress model: the notion that psychological disorders occur when there is a genetically determined vulnerability (diathesis) and relevant stressful conditions.

Direct effect: occurs when there is a significant relationship or correlation between personality and some other measure (e.g. stress; physical health).

Directional (one-tailed) hypothesis: a prediction that there will be a difference or correlation between two variables and a statement of the direction of this difference.

Discourse analysis: a qualitative method involving the analysis of meanings expressed in various forms of language (e.g. speeches; writings). The emphasis is often on effects of social context on language use.

Displacement: one of the defence mechanisms identified by Freud in which impulses are unconsciously moved away from a very threatening object towards a non-threatening one.

Dispositional explanation: deciding that other people's actions are caused by their internal characteristics or dispositions.

Double blind: a procedure where neither the participant nor the experimenter knows the precise aims of the study. This reduces experimenter effects.

Dysexecutive syndrome: a condition caused by brain damage (typically in the frontal lobes) in which there is severe impairment of the functioning of the central executive component of working memory.

Effort–reward imbalance: a stressful situation in which workers are required to make considerable efforts at work but receive few rewards in terms of salary, career opportunities, and so on in return.

Ego: the conscious, rational part of the mind, which is guided by the reality principle.

Electroconvulsive therapy (ECT): a form of therapy used to treat depressed patients, in which brain seizures are created by passing an electric current through the head.

Emotion-focused coping: involves the use of thoughts or actions to act directly on the emotional state experienced when faced by a stressful situation. It can involve distraction, avoidance of the situation, seeking social support, emotional control, distancing (detaching oneself from the situation), positive reappraisal of the situation, and relaxation. Generally of most use when the situation probably cannot be changed for the better.

Encoding: involves the transfer of information into code, leading to the creation of a memory trace, which can be registered in the memory store.

Endocrine system: a system of a number of ductless glands located throughout the body that produce the body's chemical messengers, called **hormones**.

Ethical committees: committees of psychologists and lay individuals who consider all research proposals from the perspective of the rights and dignity of the participants.

Ethical guidelines: written codes of conduct and practice to guide and aid psychologists in planning and running research studies to an approved standard, and dealing with any issues that may arise.

Ethics: a set of moral principles used to guide human behaviour.

Ethologists: individuals who study animal behaviour in its natural environment, focusing on the importance of innate capacities and the functions of behaviours.

Evaluation apprehension: concern felt by research participants that their performance is being judged.

Event sampling: a technique for collecting data in an observational study. The observer focuses only on actions or events that are of particular interest to the study.

Experiment: a procedure undertaken to make a discovery about causal relationships. The experimenter manipulates one variable to see its effect on another variable.

Experimental group: the group receiving the experimental treatment.

Experimental hypothesis: the hypothesis written prior to conducting an experiment, which usually specifies the independent and dependent variables.

Experimental realism: the use of an artificial situation in which participants become so involved that they are fooled into thinking the set-up is real rather than artificial.

Experimental treatment: the alteration of the independent variable.

Experimenter bias: the effect that the experimenter's expectations have on the participants and therefore the results of the study.

Experimenter expectancy: the systematic effects that an experimenter's expectations have on the performance of the participants.

Exposure therapy: a form of therapy in which patients are exposed to the object or situation they fear for lengthy periods of time until their anxiety level is substantially reduced.

Externalising problems: various types of behaviour problems such as aggression, assertiveness, and disobedience.

External validity: the validity of an experiment outside the research situation itself; the extent to which the findings of a research study are applicable to other situations, especially "everyday" situations.

Extinction: elimination of a conditioned response when the conditioned stimulus is not followed by the unconditioned stimulus or a response is not followed by a reward.

Eyewitness testimony: an account or evidence provided by people who witnessed an event such as a crime, reporting from their memory. Research suggests that this evidence may not be factually accurate.

F (Fascism) Scale: a test of tendencies towards fascism. High scorers are prejudiced and racist.

Failure to function adequately: a model of abnormality based on an inability to cope with day-to-day life caused by psychological distress or discomfort.

False memory syndrome: a condition where an adult "recovers" apparently repressed memories. In fact the memories are for events that did not happen, thus "false memory".

Fear hierarchy: a list of feared situations or objects, starting with those creating only small amounts of fear and moving on to those creating large amounts of fear; used in the treatment of **phobias**.

Field experiment: a study in which the experimental method is used in a more naturalistic situation.

Fixation: in Freudian terms, spending a long time at a given stage of development because of over- or under-gratification.

Free association: a technique used in psychoanalysis, in which the patient says the first thing that comes into his/her mind.

Fundamental attribution error: the tendency to explain the causes of another person's behaviour in terms of dispositional rather than situational factors.

Gene: a unit of inheritance that forms part of a chromosome. Some characteristics are determined by one gene whereas for others many genes are involved.

Gene mapping: determining the effect of a particular gene on physical or psychological characteristics.

General Adaptation Syndrome (GAS): the body's non-specific response to stress that consists of three stages:

the alarm reaction, when the body responds with the heightened physiological reactivity of the "fight or flight" response to meet the demands of the stressor; resistance, when the body tries to cope with the stressor and outwardly appears to have returned to normal but inwardly is releasing high levels of stress hormones; and exhaustion, where resources are depleted and the body's defence against disease and illness is decreased.

Generalisability: the extent to which the findings of a study can be applied to other settings, populations, times, and measures.

Generalisation: in classical conditioning, the tendency to transfer a response from one stimulus to another that is quite similar.

Glucose: a form of sugar that is one of the main sources of energy for the brain.

Hardiness: a cluster of traits possessed by those people best able to cope with stress.

Hindsight bias: the tendency to be wise after the event, using the benefit of hindsight.

Histogram: a graph in which the frequencies of scores in each category are represented by a vertical column; data on the y-axis must be continuous with a true zero.

Homeostasis: the process of maintaining a reasonably constant internal environment.

Hormones: chemical substances that are produced by one tissue before proceeding via the bloodstream to a second tissue.

Humanistic psychology: an approach to psychology that focuses on higher motivation, self-development, and on each individual as unique.

Hypertension: a condition associated with very high blood pressure.

Hypothalamus: the part of the brain that integrates the activity of the **autonomic nervous system**. Involved with emotion, stress, motivation, and hunger.

Hypothesis: a statement of what you believe to be true.

Id: in Freudian theory, that part of the mind motivated by the pleasure principle and sexual instincts.

Ideal mental health: a state of contentment that we all strive to achieve.

Identification: conforming to the demands of a given role because of a desire to be like a particular person in that role.

Immune system: a system of cells (white blood cells) within the body that is concerned with fighting disease. The white blood cells, called leucocytes, include T and B cells and natural killer cells. They help prevent illness by fighting invading **antigens** such as viruses and bacteria.

Imposed etic: the use of a technique developed in one culture to study another culture.

Imprinting: a restricted form of learning that takes place rapidly and has both short-term effects (e.g. a following response) and long-lasting effects (e.g. choice of reproductive partner).

Independent behaviour: resisting the pressures to conform or to obey authority.

Independent groups design: a research design in which each participant is in one condition only. Each separate group of participants experiences different levels of the IV. Sometimes referred to as an unrelated or between-subjects design.

Independent variable (IV): some aspect of the research situation that is manipulated by the researcher in order to observe whether a change occurs in another variable.

Individual differences: the characteristics that vary from one individual to another.

Individualistic cultures: cultures that emphasise individuality, individual needs, and independence. People in these cultures tend to live in small nuclear families.

Informational social influence: when someone conforms because others are thought to possess more knowledge.

Informed consent: relates to an ethical guideline which advises that participants should understand what they are agreeing to take part in. They should be aware of what the research involves, and their own part in this.

Innate: inborn, a product of genetic factors.

Insecure attachment: a weak emotional bond between child and caregiver(s) leading to an anxious and insecure relationship, which can have a negative effect on development.

Insight: in Freud's theory this involves recovering traumatic and other distressing memories from the unconscious and considering them in terms of their true emotional significance. Insight allows the client to recognise how these traumatic and other events have adversely affected their lives, which provides a basis for him/her to recover from mental illness.

Institutionalisation: the adverse effects on children of being placed in an institution; these effects can influence cognitive and social development.

Internal validity: the validity of an experiment in terms of the context in which it is carried out. Concerns events within the experiment as distinct from **external validity**.

Internal working model: a mental model of the world that enables individuals to predict, control, and manipulate their environment. The infant has many of them, some of which will be related to relationships.

Internalisation: conformity behaviour where the individual has completely accepted the views of the majority.

Interpretive bias: the tendency shown by most anxious and depressed patients to interpret ambiguous stimuli and situations in a negative or threatening way.

Interquartile range: the spread of the middle 50% of an ordered or ranked set of scores.

Interview: a verbal research method in which the participant answers a series of questions.

Interviewer bias: the effects of an interviewer's expectations on the responses made by an interviewee.

Introspection: the process by which a person considers their inner thoughts as a means of understanding how the mind works.

Investigator effects: the effects of an investigator's expectations on the response of a participant.

Sometimes referred to as experimenter expectancy effect.

IV: see **independent variable**.

Laboratory experiment: an experiment conducted in a laboratory setting or other contrived setting away from the participants' normal environments. The experimenter is able to manipulate the IV and accurately measure the DV, and considerable control can be exercised over confounding variables.

Learning: a relatively permanent change in behaviour, which is not due to maturation.

Learning theory: the explanation of behaviour using the principles of classical and operant conditioning; the view that all behaviour is learned.

Life changes: significant changes in the pattern of life, such as a divorce or a holiday, that require some kind of social readjustment. Each life change has a score and total scores over a year can predict psychological upset.

Life events: events that are common to many people, which involve change from a steady state.

Locus of control: a personality dimension concerned with perceptions about the factors controlling what happens to us.

Longitudinal: over an extended period of time, especially with reference to studies.

Long-term memory: a relatively permanent memory store with an unlimited capacity and duration, containing different components such as episodic (personal events), semantic (facts and information), and procedural (actions and skills) memory.

Major depressive disorder: a disorder characterised by symptoms such as sad depressed mood, tiredness, and loss of interest in various activities.

Majority influence: occurs when people adopt the behaviour, attitudes, or values of the majority (dominant or largest group) after being exposed to their values or behaviour.

Maladaptive: the extent to which a behaviour is not adaptive.

Matched pairs design: a research design that matches participants on a one-to-one basis rather than as a whole group.

Maternal deprivation hypothesis: Bowlby's view that separation from the primary caregiver leads to disruption and perhaps breaking of the attachment bond, with long-term adverse and possibly permanent effects on emotional development.

Maternal sensitivity hypothesis: the notion that individual differences in infant attachment are due mainly to the sensitivity (or otherwise) of the mother.

Mean: an average worked out by dividing the total of participants' scores by the number of participants.

Measures of central tendency: any means of representing the mid-point of a set of data, such as the mean, median, and mode.

Measures of dispersion: any means of expressing the spread of the data, such as range or standard deviation.

Median: the middle score out of all the participants' scores.

Memory: the mental processes involved in encoding, storage, and retrieval of information. Encoding depends on which sense provides the input; storage is the information being held in memory; retrieval involves accessing the stored information.

Memory span: an assessment of how much can be stored in short-term memory (STM) at any time.

Mental rotation: a type of task in which participants imagine rotating two- or three-dimensional objects in order to perform some task.

Meta-analysis: a form of analysis in which the data from several related studies are combined to obtain an overall estimate.

Metabolism: all the chemical processes within the living organism.

Method of loci: a **mnemonic technique** in which various items of information are remembered by associating them with successive locations (e.g. along a favourite walk).

Mind map: a complex diagram in which several ideas are organised via links around some central idea or theme.

Minority influence: a majority being influenced to accept the beliefs or behaviour of a minority.

Misleading information: incorrect information that may be given in good faith or deliberately (also known as misinformation).

Mnemonic techniques: artificial systems or methods that are used to enhance people's memory. The techniques all involve providing a structure so that even random material can be organised effectively at the time of learning, and they provide a retrieval structure (typically through the use of cues) that makes it easy to recall learned material.

Mode: the most frequently occurring score among participants' scores in a given condition.

Modelling: a form of learning or therapy based on observing a model and imitating that behaviour.

Monotropy hypothesis: the notion that infants have an innate tendency to form strong bonds with one caregiver, usually their mother.

Multi-store model: a model in which memory is divided into three stores; sensory, short-term, and long-term memory. This model is no longer favoured, as research has shown that memory is much more complex than this.

Mundane realism: the use of an artificial situation that closely resembles a natural situation.

Mutation: a genetic change that can then be inherited by any offspring.

Natural experiment: a type of experiment where use is made of some naturally occurring variable(s).

Natural selection: the process by which individuals are selected because they are best adapted to their environment.

Naturalistic observation: an unobtrusive observational study conducted in a natural setting.

Negative correlation: as one co-variable increases the other decreases. They still vary in a constant relationship.

Neuroanatomy: the anatomy of the nervous system, i.e. the study of its structure and function.

Neuroticism: a personality dimension proposed by H. J. Eysenck; high scorers experience more intense negative emotional states than low scorers.

Noradrenaline: one of the hormones (along with **adrenaline**) produced by the adrenal glands that increases arousal by activating the sympathetic nervous system and reducing activity in the parasympathetic system.

Normal distribution: a bell-shaped distribution in which most of the scores are close to the mean. This characteristic shape is produced when measuring many psychological and biological variables, such as IQ and height.

Normative social influence: when someone conforms in order to gain liking or respect from others.

Null hypothesis: a hypothesis which states that any findings are due to chance factors and do not reflect a true difference, effect, or relationship.

Obedience to authority: behaving as instructed, usually in response to individual rather than group pressure, often in a hierarchy where the instructor is of higher status so the individual feels unable to resist or refuse to obey, though their private opinion is unlikely to change.

Observational learning: learning through imitating or copying the behaviour of others.

Observational techniques: those research techniques that involve observing behaviour, covertly or openly or as a participant in the activity.

Oedipus complex: Freud's explanation of how a boy resolves his love for his mother and feelings of rivalry towards his father by identifying with his father.

Operant conditioning: learning through reinforcement; a behaviour becomes more likely because the outcome is reinforced. Learning that is contingent on the response.

Operationalisation: defining all variables in such a way that it is easy to measure them.

Opportunity sampling: participants are selected because they are available, not because they are representative of a population.

Parasympathetic branch: the part of the **autonomic nervous system** that monitors the relaxed state, conserving resources and promoting digestion and metabolism.

Participant observations: observations in natural situations where the observer interacts directly with the participants.

Participant reactivity: the situation in which an **independent variable** has an effect on participants merely because they know they are being observed.

Pegword method: a **mnemonic technique** in which each word on a to-be-learned list is associated with those from a previously memorised list; an interactive image is formed of each pair of words.

Peripheral nervous system: see **PNS**.

Phonological loop: a component of the working memory system concerned with speech perception and production.

Physiological: concerning the study of living organisms and their parts.

Physiological approaches to stress management: techniques that try to control the body's response to stress by reducing physiological reactivity; for example taking anti-anxiety drugs to decrease the "fight or flight" responses such as raised blood pressure.

Pilot study: a smaller, preliminary study that makes it possible to check out standardised procedures and general design before investing time and money in the major study.

Pituitary–adrenal system: the second part of the stress response, where the **hypothalamus** activates the pituitary gland, which in turn activates the adrenal cortex to release corticosteroid stress hormones.

Pituitary gland: an endocrine gland located in the brain. Called the "master gland" because it directs much of the activity of the endocrine system.

Placebo effect: positive responses to a drug or form of therapy based on the patient's beliefs that the drug or therapy will be effective, rather than on the actual make-up of the drug or therapy.

Planning fallacy: the false belief that a plan will succeed even though past experience suggests it won't.

Pleasure principle: the drive to do things that produce pleasure or gratification.

PNS (peripheral nervous system): part of the nervous system that excludes the brain and spinal cord, but consists of all other nerve cells in the body. The PNS is divided into the somatic nervous system and the autonomic nervous system.

Point sampling: a technique used in an observational study. One individual is observed in order to categorise their current behaviour, after which a second individual is observed.

Population: the total number of cases about which a specific statement can be made. This in itself may be unrepresentative.

Positive correlation: when two co-variables increase at the same time.

Positive reinforcement: a reward (e.g. food; money) that serves to increase the probability of any response produced shortly before it is presented.

Practice effect: an improvement in performance as a result of having done the task before.

Presumptive consent: a substitute for voluntary informed consent, it is presumed that if one set of people regard an experimental procedure as acceptable this applies to all people, including the experimental participants whose consent has not been obtained.

Primary reinforcer: something that provides positive reinforcement because it serves to satisfy some basic drive; for example, food and drink are primary reinforcers because they satisfy our hunger and thirst drives, respectively.

Prior general consent: obtaining apparent consent from research participants by arranging for them to agree in general to taking part in certain kinds of research before enlisting their involvement in an experiment.

Privation: an absence of attachments, as opposed to the loss of attachments, due to the lack of an appropriate attachment figure. Privation is likely to lead to permanent emotional damage.

Problem-focused coping: involves the use of thoughts or actions to act directly on a stressful situation. It can involve seeking information, purposeful or direct action, decision making, planning, and so on. Generally of most use when the situation can potentially be changed for the better.

Procedural knowledge: knowledge related to "knowing how", including motor skills.

Projection: attributing one's undesirable characteristics to others, as a means of coping with emotionally threatening information and protecting the ego.

Prospective study: a study designed to follow participants forward in time to observe certain events or outcomes (e.g. coronary heart disease) that may happen to them over time.

Protection of participants from psychological harm: an ethical guideline saying that participants should be protected from psychological harm, such as distress, ridicule, or loss of self-esteem. Any risks involved in the research should be no greater than those in the participants' own lives. Debriefing can be used to counter any concern over psychological harm.

Psychiatrist: a medically trained person who specialises in the diagnosis and treatment of mental disorders.

Psychoanalysis: the form of therapy derived from psychoanalytic theory.

Psychodynamic model: a model of abnormality that regards the origin of mental disorders as psychological rather than physical, and suggests that mental illness arises out of unresolved unconscious conflicts.

Psychodynamic theory: this is an approach to understanding human behaviour and development pioneered by Freud and then developed by others; it forms part of the basis for psychoanalysis and other forms of psychodynamic therapy.

Psychological approaches to stress management: techniques to control cognitive, social, and emotional responses to stress by attempting to address underlying causes of stress, such as faulty thinking, and inappropriate emotional responses, by changing the person's perceptions of the stressor or their own control.

Psychological therapies: forms of treatment that involve the use of various psychological techniques, e.g. psychoanalysis.

Psychoneuroimmunology (PNI): the study of the effects of both stress and other psychological factors on the immune system.

Psychosexual development: Freud's stages in personality development based on the child's changing focus on different parts of the body (e.g. the mouth and the anal region). "Sexual" is roughly equivalent to "physical pleasure".

Pygmalion effect: an effect in which individuals perform surprisingly well because others expect them to; it is a kind of self-fulfilling effect in which others' expectations turn into reality.

Qualitative data: data in the form of categories (e.g. has fun watching movies; has fun watching TV).

Quantitative data: data in the form of scores or numbers (e.g. on a scale running from 1 to 7).

Quasi-experiment: research that is similar to an experiment but certain key features are lacking, such as the direct manipulation of the independent variable by the experimenter and random allocation of participants to conditions.

Questionnaire: a survey requiring written answers.

Random allocation: placing participants in different experimental conditions using random methods to ensure no differences between the groups.

Random sampling: selecting participants on some random basis (e.g. picking numbers out of a hat). Every member of the population has an equal chance of being selected.

Randomisation: the allocation of participants to conditions on a random basis, i.e. totally unbiased distribution.

Range: the difference between the highest and lowest score in any condition.

Raw scores: the data before they have been summarised in some way.

Reading span: the largest number of sentences read for comprehension from which an individual can recall all the final words more than 50% of the time; it is used as a measure of working memory capacity.

Reality principle: the drive to accommodate to the demands of the environment.

Recency effect: better free recall of the last few items in a list, where higher performance is due to the information being in short-term store.

Reciprocal inhibition: the process of inhibiting anxiety by substituting a competing response.

Reductionist: an argument or theory that reduces complex factors to a set of simple principles.

Regression: in Freudian terms, returning to an earlier stage of development as a means of coping with anxiety.

Rehearsal: the verbal repetition of information (often words), which typically has the effect of increasing our long-term memory for the rehearsed information.

Reinforced: a behaviour is more likely to re-occur because the response was agreeable.

Reliability: the extent to which a method of measurement or test produces consistent findings.

Replication: the ability to repeat the methods used in a study and achieve the same findings.

Representative sample: the notion that the sample is representative of the whole population from which it is drawn.

Repression: a main ego defence mechanism suggested by Freud, where anxiety-causing memories are kept out of conscious memory to protect the individual. This is a type of motivated forgetting, and the repressed memories can sometimes be recalled during **psychoanalysis**.

Research: the process of gaining knowledge and understanding via either theory or empirical data collection.

Research hypothesis: a statement put forward at the beginning of a study stating what you expect to happen, generated by a theory.

Retrieval: the process of recovering information stored in long-term memory. If retrieval is successful, the individual remembers the information in question.

Right to privacy: the requirement for ethical research that no participants are observed in situations that would be considered private.

Right to withdraw: the basic right of participants in a research study to stop their involvement at any point, and to withdraw their results if they wish to do so.

Role-playing experiments: studies in which participants are asked to imagine how they would behave in certain situations.

Safety-seeking behaviours: actions taken by individuals with anxiety disorders to reduce their anxiety level and prevent feared consequences.

Sample: a part of a population selected such that it is considered to be representative of the population as a whole.

Sampling bias: some people have a greater or lesser chance of being selected than they should be, given their frequency in the population.

Scattergram/scattergraph: two-dimensional representation of all the participants' scores in a correlational study.

Schema: an "organised" packet of information about the world, events, or people that is stored in long-term memory. For example, most people have a schema containing information about the normal sequence of events when having a meal in a restaurant.

Schizophrenia: a very severe disorder characterised by hallucinations, delusions, lack of emotion, and very impaired social functioning.

Science: a branch of knowledge conducted on objective principles. It is both an activity and an organised body of knowledge.

Secondary reinforcer: a reinforcer that has no natural properties of reinforcement but, through association with a primary reinforcer, becomes a reinforcer, i.e. it is learned.

Secure attachment: the result of a strong positive bond between infant and caregiver, so that although the child shows distress at separation, he or she is easily comforted by the caregiver's return.

Selection bias: when different types of individuals are assigned to groups that are to be compared, differences in behaviour between the two groups may be due to this bias rather than to differences in the ways in which the groups are treated.

Self-actualisation: fulfilling one's potential in the broadest sense.

Self-esteem: the feelings that an individual has about himself or herself.

Self-report techniques: participants provide their own account of themselves, usually by means of questionnaires, surveys, or interviews.

Semantic coding: encoding or processing words in terms of their meaning based on information stored in long-term memory.

Sensitive: in the context of statistics, "sensitive" means more precise, able to reflect small differences or changes.

Separation: the absence of the caregiver (e.g. due to work commitments, divorce, or hospitalisation), which usually causes great distress but not necessarily permanent bond disruption. Separation has a number of effects, such as protest, despair, or detachment, and if prolonged it may result in **deprivation**.

Separation anxiety: the sense of concern felt by a child when separated from their attachment figure.

Separation protest: the infant's behaviour when separated—crying or holding out their arms. Some insecurely attached infants show no protest when left by their attachment figure, whereas securely attached children do.

Serotonin: a neurotransmitter that is associated with lower arousal, sleepiness, and reduced anxiety.

Short-term memory: a temporary place for storing information during which it receives limited processing (e.g. verbal rehearsal). Short-term memory has a very limited capacity and short duration, unless the information in it is maintained through rehearsal.

Single blind: a procedure in which the participants are not informed of the condition in which they have been placed.

Situational explanation: deciding that people's actions are caused by the situation in which they find themselves rather than by their personality.

Sociability: the tendency to seek and enjoy the company of others.

Social change: the process of changing social norms such as attitudes and beliefs.

Social development: the development of a child's social skills, such as the ability to relate to and empathise with others, which is the result of interaction between the child's genes and their environment.

Social influence: how we are influenced by others, either by a group (**majority influence**) or an individual (**minority influence** or **obedience**), to change our behaviour, thinking, and/or attitudes.

Social learning theory: the view that behaviour can be explained in terms of direct and indirect reinforcement, through imitation, identification, and modelling.

Social releasers: a social behaviour or characteristic that elicits a caregiving reaction. Bowlby suggested that these were innate and critical in the process of forming attachments.

Specific phobia: extreme fear and avoidance of specific kinds of stimuli (e.g. snakes, spiders).

Split-half technique: a technique used to establish reliability by assigning items from one test randomly to two sub-tests (split-halves). The same person does both sub-tests simultaneously and their scores are compared to see if they are similar, which would suggest that the test items are reliable.

SQ3R: five strategies for effective reading: Survey, Question, Read, Recite, Review.

S–R link: an abbreviation for stimulus–response link.

Standard deviation: a measure of the spread of the scores around the mean. It is the square root of the variance and takes account of every measurement.

Standardised tests: tests on which an individual's score can be evaluated against those of a large representative sample.

Statistical infrequency/deviation from statistical norms: behaviours that are statistically rare, or deviate from the average/statistical norm as illustrated by the normal distribution curve, are classed as abnormal.

Storage: storing a memory for a period of time so that it can be used later.

Story method: a **mnemonic technique** in which a list of words is learned by linking them together within the context of a story.

Strange Situation: an experimental procedure used to test the security of a child's attachment to a caregiver. The key features are what the child does when it is left by the caregiver, and the child's behaviour at reunion, as well as responses to a stranger.

Stranger anxiety: the distress experienced by a child when approached by a stranger.

Stress: a state of psychological and physical tension produced, according to the transactional model, when there is a mismatch between the perceived demands of a situation (the stressor[s]) and the individual's perceived ability to cope. The consequent state of tension can be adaptive (eustress) or maladaptive (distress).

Stress inoculation training: a technique to reduce stress through the use of stress-management techniques and self-statements that aim to restructure the way the client thinks.

Stress management: the attempt to cope with stress by reducing the stress response, either by psychological methods (e.g. **Cognitive Behavioural Therapy**) or physiological ones (e.g. drugs).

Stressor: any factor that can trigger the stress response. Stressors are examples of individual differences, as different people respond differently to different stressors, such as exam revision. Stressors may be major life changes or daily hassles, and may be environmental or in the workplace.

Stroop task: a task that involves naming the colours in which words are printed. Performance is slowed when the words are conflicting colour words (e.g. the word RED printed in green).

Subjective organisation: the tendency for people who are asked to learn a list of random words to impose their own organisational structure on the list.

Superego: in Freud's theory, the part of the mind that embodies one's conscience. It is formed through identification with the same-sex parent.

Sympathetic branch: the part of the autonomic nervous system that activates internal organs.

Sympatho-medullary pathway: the source of the immediate stress response, also known as fight or flight, where the hypothalamus activates the ANS, which in turn activates the adrenal medulla, producing the release of the stress hormones **adrenaline** and **noradrenaline**.

Systematic de-sensitisation: a form of behaviour therapy designed to treat **phobias**, in which relaxation training and a fear hierarchy are used.

Systematic sampling: a modified version of random sampling in which the participants are selected in a quasi-random way (e.g. every 100th name from a population list).

Tardive dyskinesia: some of the long-term effects of taking neuroleptic drugs, including involuntary sucking and chewing, jerky movements, and writhing movements of the mouth or face.

Temperament hypothesis: the view that a child's temperament is responsible for the quality of attachment between the child and its caregiver, as opposed to the view that experience is more important.

Test–retest: a technique used to establish reliability, by giving the same test to participants on two separate occasions to see if their scores remain relatively similar.

Theory: a general explanation of a set of findings. It is used to produce an experimental hypothesis.

Theory of evolution: an explanation for the diversity of living species. Darwin's theory was based on the principle of natural selection.

Time sampling: a technique used in observational studies. Observations are only made during specified time periods (e.g. the first 10 minutes of each hour).

Trait: a characteristic distinguishing a particular individual.

Transactional model: an explanation for behaviour, which focuses on the interaction between various factors. The transactional model of stress explains stress in terms of the interaction between the demands of the environment and the individual's ability to cope.

Transference: the transfer of the patient's strong feelings concerning one or both parents onto the therapist.

True experiment: research where an independent variable is manipulated to observe its effects on a dependent variable and so determine a cause-and-effect relationship.

Type A personality: in biopsychology, a personality type who is typically impatient, competitive, time pressured, and hostile.

Undisclosed observation: an observational study where the participants have not been informed that it is taking place.

Validity: the soundness of the measurement tool; the extent to which it is measuring something that is real or valid.

Variables: things that vary or change.

Variance: the extent of variation of the scores around the mean.

Vicarious conditioning: receiving reinforcement by observing someone else being rewarded.

Visuo-spatial sketch pad: a component within the working memory system designed for spatial and/or visual coding.

Volunteer bias: the systematic difference between volunteers and non-volunteers.

Volunteer sampling: choosing research participants who have volunteered, e.g. by replying to an advertisement. Volunteer samples may not be representative of the general population, which means the research may not be generalisable.

Weapon focus: the finding that eyewitnesses pay so much attention to a weapon that they ignore other details and so can't remember them.

Working memory model: the model of short-term memory proposed to replace the multi-store model. It consists of a central executive plus slave systems that deal with different sensory modalities.

Working memory system: the concept that short-term (or working) memory can be subdivided into other stores that handle different modalities (sound and visual data).